ETHICS AND THE
FOR

MW00606626

013

Modernity has challenged the ancient ideal of a universal quest for wisdom, and today's world of conflicting cultures and values has raised further doubts regarding the possibility of objective ethical standards. Robert Kane refocuses the debate on the philosophical quest for wisdom, and argues that ethical principles about right action and the good life can be seen to emerge from that very quest itself. His book contends that the search for wisdom involves a persistent striving to overcome narrowness of vision that comes from the inevitable limitations of finite points of view. When applied to questions of value and the good life, this striving has ethical implications about the way we should treat ourselves and others. This study argues for the merits of this central thesis against alternative theories in contemporary normative ethics, and discusses its practical applications for social ethics, political philosophy, law and moral education.

ROBERT KANE is University Distinguished Teaching Professor of Philosophy Emeritus and Professor of Law at the University of Texas at Austin. He is the author of seven books including *Through the Moral Maze* (1994), *The Significance of Free Will* (1996) and *A Contemporary Introduction to Free Will* (2005), as well as over sixty articles.

# ETHICS AND THE QUEST FOR WISDOM

### ROBERT KANE
*The University of Texas at Austin*

CAMBRIDGE
UNIVERSITY PRESS

CAMBRIDGE UNIVERSITY PRESS
Cambridge, New York, Melbourne, Madrid, Cape Town,
Singapore, São Paulo, Delhi, Mexico City

Cambridge University Press
The Edinburgh Building, Cambridge CB2 8RU, UK

Published in the United States of America by Cambridge University Press, New York

www.cambridge.org
Information on this title: www.cambridge.org/9781107621534

© Robert Kane 2010

First published 2010
First paperback edition 2013

*A catalogue record for this publication is available from the British Library*

*Library of Congress Cataloguing in Publication Data*
Kane, Robert, 1938–
Ethics and the quest for wisdom / Robert Kane.
p.   cm.
Includes bibliographical references and index.
ISBN 978-0-521-19993-3
1. Ethics, Modern.   2. Ethics.   3. Wisdom.   I. Title.
BJ1012.K273 2010
170–dc22          2010021898

ISBN 978-1-107-62153-4 Paperback

*To*
*CLAUDETTE DRENNAN KANE*
*Whose wisdom is reflected throughout this book*

# Contents

vii

# *Acknowledgements*

This book has been many years in the making and I have received feedback over these years from many quarters. I am indebted in some way to every author whose work is cited; and I am further indebted to many others for feedback at one time or another during its long genesis, including the following: Robert Audi, Amelie Benedikt, Michael Benedikt, Mark Bernstein, Stephen Bero, Reid Blackman, Daniel Bonevac, David Braybrooke, Sarah Broadie, Gillian Brock, Jay Budzizewski, Tom Christiano, David Copp, Howard Curzer, Jonathan Dancy, John Deigh, Richard Double, Ian Farrell, John Martin Fischer, James Fishkin, William Galston, George Graham, Ishtiyaque Haji, George Harris, Neal Judisch, James Justus, Brian Leiter, Noah Lemos, Noelle MacAfee, Lynne McFall, Michael McKenna, Al Mele, Tom Miles, John Moskop, Liam Murphy, Alastair Norcross, Gregory Pappas, Edmund Pincoffs, John Post, Frank Richardson, Kevin Rouintree, Thomas Seung, Russ Shafer-Landau, Neil Sinhababu, Michael Slote, Paul H. Smith, Robert Solomon, Richard Sorabji, David Sosa, David Spiller, Jack Tannous, Jeffrey Tlumak, T. C. Turner, Warren von Eschenbach, Gary Watson, Emrys Westacott, Michael White, Stephen White, Paul Woodruff, Michael Zimmerman.

# CHAPTER I

# Introduction: pluralism and uncertainty

## I. ANCIENT WISDOM, MODERN CHALLENGES

For most ancient and medieval thinkers of the Western tradition, theoretical and practical inquiry, fact and value, scientific explanation and purpose, merged in an overall quest for wisdom. Knowledge of facts about the natural world and human beings would tell us what was good and valuable. Theoretical inquiry into the nature of things (*theoria*) would answer practical questions about how to live (*praxis*); and explanations of why things behaved as they do, including humans, would tell us what ends or purposes they should pursue. We know how this worked for the great ancient thinkers. Aristotle held that among the *archai* or explaining causes of all things were final causes or ends that tell us what was worth striving for, for each thing. And for Plato, the intelligible world included not only mathematical forms that inform us about the structure of the natural world, but also ideal forms, such as Justice and Beauty, that tell us what to strive for. As a consequence, for these ancient thinkers, theory and practice, fact and value, explanation and purpose, were inextricably linked.

The modern age, by contrast, is characterized by what Hegel called "sunderings" (*Entzweiungen*) of these and many other contrasts. There has been a tendency in the modern era to pry apart considerations of (1) fact from value, (2) theoretical inquiry from practical inquiry (about the good) and (3) scientific explanation from purpose, with the consequence that the unified quest for wisdom of the ancient philosophers was threatened as well. A chief culprit in this process was the development of modern science. The story is by now familiar. As the modern era evolved, explanation of objective fact about the cosmos increasingly became the province of the new natural sciences of Galileo, Newton and their successors, which described a physical cosmos devoid of values, final causes and purposes.

The situation was somewhat different for the human sciences (behavioral and social) which came on the scene later in the modern era. Anthropologists, sociologists and other behavioral scientists did indeed have to talk about human values and purposes. But they embraced a kind of value neutrality of their own in the name of scientific objectivity. Social scientists might tell us what persons or societies or cultures *believed* was good or right or wrong, but they could not say what really *was* right or wrong. That would amount to injecting their own values and points of view into their research – an offense against the scientific ideal of objectivity.

So, while objectivity in the modern natural sciences seemed to imply an absence of value in the world described by them, in the human sciences it amounted to something quite different. Objectivity in the human sciences suggested a value *relativism – too much value*, too many cultures, forms of life, views of right and wrong, with no non-neutral way of deciding between them. As a consequence, two other conditions of modernity entered the picture, helping to render problematic the modern search for objectivity about values and ethics. These two further conditions – made more insistent by modern anthropology and other human sciences – were a greater recognition of (4) *pluralism* of conflicting cultures, forms of life and points of view about right and wrong, together with an (5) *uncertainty* about how to show definitively which of the competing points of view was the objectively right one.

It is ironic that ideals of scientific *objectivity* in both the natural and human sciences, which had inspired the ancient search for wisdom about the cosmos and human nature, should have promoted in modern times *subjectivist* and *relativist* views about values and ethics.[1] But that is an important part of the modern story.

### 2. PLAN OF THE BOOK

The question I want to address in this book may be stated in terms of these modern challenges to the ancient quest for wisdom: How, if at all, can that quest for wisdom about the objective good and right be pursued in the light of these intellectual challenges of the modern era? This is not a new question and there is no scarcity of attempted answers to it. But I want to suggest some new ways of looking at this question in the

---

[1] Subjectivist views are defined and discussed in Chapters 5–7; relativist views in Chapters 2, 7, 8 and responses to them made in Chapters 2–4 and 9–14.

following pages. The five conditions of modernity just mentioned – the alleged sunderings of (1) fact from value, (2) theoretical from practical inquiry, (3) explanation of fact from purpose, together with a greater recognition of (4) pluralism and (5) uncertainty in matters of value – block certain traditional paths of inquiry into the nature of the objective good. But I will argue that these modern conditions also suggest other paths of inquiry about the good that are as yet unexplored and worth exploring.

I begin here with a brief overview of the book and its aims.

In the second half of this introductory chapter, I take as a starting point two of these five conditions of modernity, pluralism and uncertainty. The chapter considers how these two conditions have conspired to raise doubts about the possibility of objective values and ethical standards in the minds of ordinary persons as well as in the human sciences and philosophy. The diversity of cultures and ways of life, and the conditions of human social life, suggest that our views about good and evil, right and wrong, are formed from particular perspectives, limited by culture and history. The question then naturally arises of how, if at all, we can climb out of our historically and culturally limited points of view to find an objective standpoint above all competing points of view from which to judge what is universally right or wrong?

Chapters 2 to 4 suggest an answer to this question. The argument of these chapters introduces the central theme of the book: Ethical principles about right action and the good life can be seen to emerge *from the philosophical quest for wisdom* itself, as the ancient philosophers believed, but not exactly in the way they believed. The search for wisdom about what is objectively true and good, I shall argue, involves a persistent striving to overcome, to the degree possible, narrowness of vision that comes from the inevitable limitations of finite points of view. When applied to questions of value and the good life, I further argue that this persistent striving to overcome narrowness of vision in the search for wisdom has ethical implications about the way we should treat ourselves and others.

Chapter 2 presents a preliminary statement of the argument for these conclusions and hence an initial statement of the central theme of the book. The argument presented in Chapter 2 raises many questions and is in need of refinement. But it serves thereafter as a template that is progressively refined in subsequent chapters in response to questions and objections.

In Chapter 3, the argument of Chapter 2 is further developed and certain objections to it addressed in terms of a thought experiment involving a "retreat" of peoples representing different cultures, religions, ideologies, points of view and ways of life, who are given the collective task of determining which of their competing views is the correct one. This retreat will remind readers of hypothetical scenarios characteristic of some contractarian and contractualist ethical theories. But it differs from all such scenarios in ways explained in Chapter 3. The goal of the "retreatants," as I call them – unlike the hypothetical contractors of the contractarian tradition – is not to reach agreement, actual or hypothetical (which in fact they fail to do), but to seek wisdom.

In Chapter 4, the argument of Chapters 2 and 3 is refined still further by comparing its conclusions to features of Kantian moral theory. The argument of Chapters 2 and 3, I argue, leads to a moral principle that is similar to one of Kant's formulations of his Categorical Imperative, namely, his Formula of Humanity: "Act so that you treat humanity, whether in your own person or in that of another, always at the same time as an end and never as a means only." But there are revealing differences. The principle at which the argument of Chapters 2 and 3 arrives, which I call the "Ends Principle" ("Treat all persons as ends in every situation and no one as means only") is not derived in the rationalist manner of Kantian theory, is differently interpreted, and allows in a natural way for exceptions to common moral rules ("Don't steal, lie, cheat," etc.). Nonetheless, the comparison with Kantian theory allows one to spell out in greater detail the implications of the ethical theory arrived at by the arguments of Chapters 2 and 3, which I refer to thereafter as a "moral sphere theory" (MST) of the right (or right action).

The argument for this theory in Chapters 2–4 is incomplete in a number of ways. Subsequent chapters attempt to fill in the gaps by situating the argument of Chapters 2–4 in a broader theory of value (Chapters 5–8) and in a theory about the nature of philosophical inquiry (Chapters 9–11, which spell out the idea of a "search for wisdom"). The first of these two tasks (undertaken in Chapters 5–8) is to situate the moral theory of the *right* (or right action) arrived at in Chapters 2–4 in a broader theory of the *good* (or value).

Taking cues from Aristotle's contention that "'good' is said in many ways," Chapters 5–8 argue that human value can be viewed in four dimensions. The first dimension, the subject of Chapter 5, is *experiential* value. Clues are taken here from Spinoza (who pointed out that our first encounter with good and evil is through experiences of certain characteristic kinds, such as joy (*laetitia*) and sadness (*tristitia*)) as well as from other philosophers, including Moore and Ross. Chapter 6 considers a second dimension of value, in which value expands outward from mere subjective experience to the realm of action and practical engagements with the world. Value in this second dimension is related to John Stuart Mill's seminal notion of "experiments in living," a notion discussed in Chapter 6 that plays a pivotal role in subsequent arguments of the book.

In a third dimension of value, considered in Chapter 7, activities and experiences are not merely viewed practically in terms of what we get from them, but more importantly, in terms of how they define what we *are*. In this dimension, the hunter in a primitive tribe does not merely hunt for food, but takes pride in his skill with the bow because of what it says about his standing as a human being. The activity signifies he is an *excellent* archer, a *good* provider for his family, a *loyal* member of his tribe. In general, the value of activities and experiences in this third dimension derives from their role in *social practices* and *forms of life* which give them meaning; and it involves the pursuit of various *virtues* or *excellences* recognized in, and necessary to the flourishing of, these practices and forms of life.

These first three dimensions of value are familiar to us. We live in them, so to speak, as we live in the three familiar dimensions of space. What I mean by a fourth dimension of value (the subject of Chapter 8) is more elusive, like a fourth dimension of space. Fourth-dimensional value, to put a name on it, is *non-relative* or universal *worth* – not merely what is good from the point of view of some individual or group or in some form of life, but rather what is worthy of being recognized as good by all persons, from every point of view. Relativists about value deny that such a fourth dimension of value exists. The challenge of value relativism is thus considered in Chapter 8. The kind of relativism that troubles most people, I argue, is the denial that we can rise above the particular historically and culturally limited points of view and forms of life of the first three dimensions of value to find an objective standpoint above them all from which to judge what is good period and should be recognized as good from every point of view.

This challenge, as it turns out, is the one faced by the retreatants in Chapter 3. I thus return in Chapter 9 to the retreat for some clues about how to meet it. The retreatants, I argue, are motivated by an "aspiration to wisdom in the ancient philosophical sense." This motivation, which is related to the nature of philosophy as the love (*philia*) of wisdom (*sophia*), is explored in the next three Chapters (9–11). Chapter 9 focuses on the idea of "aspiration," which becomes thereafter a special notion in the book signifying a patient spiritual or intellectual search or "quest" for the true and the good – as in the Socratic dictum, "the unexamined life is not worth living."

Chapter 10 then turns to the object of this quest, "wisdom in the ancient philosophical sense." Taking clues again from Aristotle, who identified "wisdom" (*sophia*) with "first philosophy" in his *Metaphysics*, I argue that there are two ends of ancient wisdom as conceived by Aristotle and other ancient thinkers: Understanding *objective reality* (or what is worth believing about the nature of things), and understanding *objective worth* (or what is worth striving for in the nature of things). (Thus, when I link "ethics" and "the quest for wisdom" in the title of this book, I mean by "wisdom" something more comprehensive than what Aristotle and other ancient philosophers called *phronesis* or "practical wisdom," though practical wisdom plays a role in the overall account of wisdom, as we shall see.[2]) In Chapter 10, I go on to explore the first of these ends of ancient wisdom (understanding objective reality) with the goal of seeking clues about how to achieve the second end (understanding objective worth).

Chapter 11 turns to the second end of ancient wisdom, understanding objective worth. I argue that the notion of "objective worth" involved in this second end is more complicated than is ordinarily realized and explore its nature in Chapter 11 by way of several thought experiments. The chapter also considers how the notion of objective worth is related to the dimensions of value discussed in Chapters 5–8, thus tying together the discussion of value in those chapters and the discussion of wisdom and philosophical inquiry of Chapters 9–11.

Chapters 12–14 then return to complete the argument for the ethical theory of Chapters 2–4 in the light of the intervening discussions of value and philosophical inquiry. I will not attempt to summarize here the arguments of Chapters 12–14 since they depend upon details of the discussions of values of Chapters 5–8 and philosophical inquiry of Chapters 9–11. Suffice it to say that the argument of Chapters 12–14 includes, among other things, an account of human flourishing in terms of the first three dimensions of value of Chapters 5–8. I argue, however, that such an account of human flourishing, though a necessary ingredient in a complete ethical theory, is not sufficient for such a theory. What is missing is spelled out in Chapters 9–11 on aspiration, wisdom and objective worth, which provide the additional ingredients necessary to complete the argument for the ethical theory of Chapters 2–4.

---

[2] Ryan 1999, 2007 and A. Benedikt (unpublished) provide useful overviews of historical and contemporary conceptions of wisdom. Tiberius 2008, Thiele 2006 discuss the implications of modern scientific research for our understanding of "practical wisdom."

In Chapters 15 to 17, I compare the theory developed in the preceding chapters to a selection of important alternative theories in contemporary normative ethics, arguing for its comparative merits. Chapter 15 considers intuitionist and Kantian ethical theories, Chapter 16, utilitarian and consequentialist theories of both act- and rule-varieties and Chapter 17, contractualist ethical theories. Chapter 15 begins with an overview of the theory of Chapters 1–14 before turning to the discussion of rival theories. Finally, the concluding Chapter 18 discusses practical applications of the theory for social ethics, political philosophy, law and moral education.

While Chapters 15–17 are the longest of the book, the engagement with rival theories is necessarily selective, given the complexity of contemporary ethical theory. A systematic critique of all alternative views would be a task for another book, or maybe several others; and to that extent, the defense of the view presented here is not complete, as I would freely acknowledge. I want to emphasize therefore that I am not claiming the view developed in this book is anything like the last word in ethical theory. I am too respectful of the complexity of modern ethical theory and of the sophistication of its theories to make such a claim. My goal, more modestly stated, is to introduce another option into current ethical debate, different from any familiar alternatives in the field, and to show that this option has sufficient merit to be seriously considered by philosophers as an alternative to existing theories.

The view developed has important Kantian themes, as seen in Chapters 4 and 15, but is not strictly speaking a Kantian ethics or a rationalist theory. Nor is it a version of utilitarianism or consequentialism, nor a contractarian or contractualist ethical theory, though it also borrows ideas from utilitarian and social contract theorists (J. S. Mill, for one, on the utilitarian side, as seen in Chapters 6 and 16). Virtues and excellences play an important role in the theory, as seen in Chapters 7, 8 and 13, but it is also not strictly speaking a "virtue ethics," in either ancient or modern senses of that expression, for reasons given in those chapters. Appeals to human nature also play a role, but the theory is also not a "natural law" theory in any traditional sense – and so on, for other familiar normative ethical views.

Because the theory does not fit neatly into any of the familiar categories of normative ethics, I proceed by developing it on its own terms, answering relevant objections as I go along, contrasting it at appropriate places with other ethical views and showing how it avoids many standard objections to other theories. But the task of defending the theory is only begun here, as noted. The late Robert Nozick remarked that in philosophy "there is room for words on subjects other than last words"[3]; and the chapters that follow have been written in this exploratory spirit.

### 3. PLURALISM AND THE MODERN FALL

The starting points of our inquiry are two of the "conditions of modernity" mentioned in Section 1 – namely, *pluralism* and *uncertainty* – which have played a pivotal role in raising doubts about the possibility of objective values and ethical standards in the minds of ordinary persons and in the human sciences and philosophy.

By "pluralism," I mean simply the fact that we live in a world of conflicting opinions, philosophies, religions, ways of life and points of view about fundamental matters, including good and evil, right and wrong. Some philosophers define pluralism about values as the doctrine that more than one view concerning the good, or the good life, is true.[4] But such a doctrine is controversial and is not what is meant by "pluralism" here. Whether a single view about the good and the right is true, and which view it might be, are issues to be addressed by an inquiry such as this one, not something to be prejudged at the outset. By pluralism in the present context, I mean something less controversial – the obvious fact that in our modern cultural environments we are daily faced with conflicting points of view about good and evil, right and wrong – a fact that leads us to *wonder* which view may be true, and whether our own is true.

Such a pluralism is made more insistent by two pervasive features of the modern world: the global village created by modern information-technology and the spread of democratic and pluralist societies. The first puts people in daily contact with views and values different from their own. The second allows and encourages differences of point of view within individual societies. The familiar image of a "global village" may be the wrong one for this new order of things since most villages of the past shared a common heritage of traditions and beliefs. A better analogy would be a global *city* in which different cultures and ways of life mingle and are forced to confront one another. In Nietzsche's image, seeing a thousand different tribes beating to a thousand different drums, we become the first people in history who do not believe we own the truth.[5]

How such wonder in the face of conflicting alternatives leads to doubts about which view of the good may be true is nicely illustrated by a scene

[3] Nozick 1974: xii.
[4] See, for example, Berlin 1965 and also Kekes 1993 for a sophisticated defense.
[5] Nietzsche 1966: sections 5, 749, 1011. Thanks to Kathleen Higgins for these references.

from C. S. Lewis's fantasy novel, *Perelandra* (1962), to which I will refer in subsequent arguments. Lewis describes the journey of a man named Ransom to the planet Venus – called "Perelandra" in the novel and described as an Eden-like world of islands floating on water and covered by exotic foliage. There Ransom meets a solitary human-like creature, a woman who tells him that her god, Maleldil, has commanded her to search for a man of her own kind who also inhabits this planet. Ransom's conversations with the woman are interrupted one day when he says that the floating islands on which they stand are making him feel queasy. He suggests they move over permanently to the "fixed land" – the land that does not float on water.

The woman is horrified by this suggestion, telling him that the one thing her god Maleldil has forbidden her or anyone to do is to stay over-night on the fixed land. Ransom's response then confuses the woman. For he says that in his own world, on Earth, everyone lives on the fixed land, night and day, and no one thinks it is wrong. In her confusion, the woman wonders whether there are different meanings of good and evil, right and wrong, and whether God may command one group of people to live one way and others to live a different way. In her confusion, she is tempted to go with Ransom over to the fixed land: If others can do it, she reasons, why can't she?

The thoughtful reader suddenly realizes that these two figures are reen-acting the Biblical story of the Garden of Eden, with Ransom playing the serpent, tempting this new Eve in her alien Eden to do the one thing her God has commanded her not to do. In the original Biblical story, the command is to not eat of the fruit of "the tree of the knowledge of good and evil." Eve eats of this fruit and Adam also; and by succumbing to temptation they come to "know good and evil" and are banished from the Garden. But in *Perelandra*, Lewis is suggesting a different, distinct-ively modern, version of the knowledge of good and evil. The new aware-ness that tempts and confuses us is the awareness that there may be more than one right way of living and that our way may not be the right one or the only right one. Like the woman on Perelandra, we may then say: If others can do it, why can't we?

Thus ends moral innocence – the secure feeling that the rights and wrongs learned in childhood are the only correct or true ones, unchal-lengeable and unambiguous. By knowing other ways of life and entertain-ing doubts about our own, we learn something about the complexities of good and evil. But the learning comes with a bitter taste. Having bitten into the fruit of the tree of knowledge of good and evil in this distinctively modern fashion, we live "after the modern Fall," so to speak. We have lost our moral innocence.

Not everyone lives in this condition of lost moral innocence, even in the modern world. Many persons, especially in traditional societies, still live (and many more wished they lived) before the modern Fall – never doubting that their own views are absolutely right and unchallenge-able. The difference between those who still believe in this absolute and unchallengeable way and those who do not is one of the great water-sheds separating modern from pre-modern modes of thought. These dif-ferent ways of thinking, the pre-modern and the modern, are now on a collision course throughout the globe, like geological plates scraping against one another, resulting in confusion and fear – and in our own time erupting into new kinds of violence. Yet those who live after the modern Fall, those who can no longer believe without hesitation that their own views are absolute and unchallengeable, can no more go back to pre-modern modes of thought than they can go back to believing the earth is flat or is at the center of the Universe. The question is: how do they go forward?

### 4. UNCERTAINTY AND THE DEEPER PROBLEM

The new "knowledge of good and evil" that tempts and confuses us, as it did the woman on Perelandra, is the awareness of different and com-peting ways of life and views of good and evil. But the experience of such pluralism alone is not the whole story. For the mere existence of diversity and disagreement, no matter how pervasive, does not rule out the possi-bility that one view is right and others wrong.[6] Pluralism in the sense of cultural and religious diversity was not unknown to ancient peoples. But the recognition of diversity did not lead in those times to a loss of faith or moral innocence (save among certain sophisticated thinkers such as the sophists of ancient Greece). Competing gods and ways of life were simply denounced as false or idolatrous.

Something else has happened in modernity. Realizing in the abstract that diversity and disagreement do not rule out the possibility that one view is right does not allay fears of pluralism, if we are also uncertain about how to show which of the competing views is right. In sum, the

---

[6] Shafer-Landau in his defense of moral realism (2003) argues persuasively that diversity and dis-agreement in moral matters, no matter how pervasive, does not necessarily rule out the existence of objective values or moral truths. See also Tersman 2006 on the implications of persistent moral disagreement for debates about moral realism.

source of lost moral innocence in the modern world is not pluralism alone, but pluralism *plus* an uncertainty about how to resolve fundamental disagreements between conflicting points of view, values and ways of life.

The uncertainty that conspires with pluralism to raise doubts about how to resolve such disagreements has its source in a deeper philosophical problem. To explain this problem, let me first say what will be meant here and in subsequent chapters when I speak of conflicting "points of view," "values," and "ways (or forms) of life."

The *points of view* of persons are defined by their beliefs (factual, evaluative and normative) along with their desires, intentions, emotions, feelings, preferences and other psychological attitudes that together tell us how the persons experience the world, what they believe about it and what their "values" are – where their *values* include what they care about, what they regard as good and bad, what purposes or ends they regard as worth pursuing or avoiding, what activities, accomplishments, and other things they regard as worthy of admiration or condemnation, and how, in general, they think persons ought to act and live their lives. *Ways (or forms) of life* are then plans of living implied by different points of view, so defined.

Note that what is meant here by the "values" of persons (or groups) is what they *hold* or *regard* or *believe* to be good or bad, right or wrong – which may or may not be what really *is* good or bad, right or wrong. This is the sense of "values" in which we may speak of a pluralism of conflicting values of different persons or groups and ask which of them, if any, may have the *correct* or *true* values or point of view about values.

The deeper philosophical problem alluded to in the previous paragraph concerns a troubling circularity involved in trying to prove the universal or absolute rightness of one's point of view in this sense *from* one's own point of view in a pluralistic world. To show that one point of view is right and other competing views wrong, you must present evidence. But the evidence will be gathered and interpreted from your own point of view. If the dispute is about values, some of the evidence will include beliefs about what is good or bad, right and wrong, that are not going to be accepted by those who have fundamental disagreements with your values in the first place. Your evaluative beliefs must be defended by appealing to other more fundamental evaluative and other beliefs that are also *yours*. Perhaps you will refer to the Bible or the Qur'an or the Bhagavad-Gita or some other sacred text, which is not going to be accepted by those who have basic disagreements with your point of view in the first place. (Even those who share your sacred text may not interpret it as you do.)

There is a troubling circularity in such debates, the circularity of defending your own point of view *from* your own point of view, of defending your values and beliefs in terms of other values or beliefs you hold, but others may not. The problem arises because we are finite creatures who always see the world from some particular point of view, limited by culture and history. This finiteness of point of view and the resulting circularity imply that claims to have the one true point of view about values are at least *dubitable* and hence not certain in the Cartesian sense of what cannot possibly be doubted. It is this Cartesian sense of certainty as *indubitability* that is intended here when I speak of "pluralism and uncertainty."[7] The uncertainty in question is the denial that claims to have the true point of view about values are "absolute and unchallengeable," in short, that they are beyond doubt.

Uncertainty in this sense does not rule out the possibility that some claims about the good and the right might be true or even that we might be able to know their truth in senses of knowledge (as justified or warranted true belief) that fall short of certainty (an issue to which we will return[8]). But the finiteness of points of view poses a problem about *how*, if at all, any such knowledge might be attained: How can we climb out of our historically and culturally limited points of view to find an objective standpoint above all the competing points of view in order to say what should be regarded as objectively good from all of them and not merely from our own?

This problem haunts the modern intellectual landscape. It is the source of trendy new theories, such as postmodernism and poststructuralism, among others, that make much of the fact that we always see the world from some limited point of view, a "conceptual framework," or "language game," a culture or tradition or a "form of life."[9] As a result, all judgments about good or evil, right or wrong – indeed all judgments about anything, some would argue – are *relative* to the point of view or framework or culture or history from which they arise. If this is the case, how is it possible to show that one way of viewing the world, our own or any other,

[7] Certainty in this Cartesian sense – we might call it *objective* certainty – should be distinguished from the *subjective* certainty or *certitude* that many people feel when they assume that what they believe could not possibly be false. Regarding the latter, we seem to have cognitive mechanisms that protect us from the debilitating effects of constantly doubting our everyday beliefs so that we can get on with living. Nonetheless, such subjective certainty or certitude does not guarantee the objective certainty of what is believed, for it does not show that what one feels subjective certitude about could not in fact be false. Lockhart 2000 is an interesting discussion of moral uncertainty that takes a different approach to it than I will take here.

[8] In Chapters 9–14.     [9] E.g., Lyotard 1987.

is universally right and others wrong, when we must assume the presuppositions of a particular point of view to support our claims? This question – prompted by pluralism and uncertainty – is the point of departure for the chapters that follow. A preliminary answer to it is suggested in the next three chapters.

# *Openness*

## I. OPENNESS AND RELATIVISM

This chapter presents an initial response to the problem of pluralism and uncertainty posed at the end of Chapter 1. The argument of this chapter is preliminary and incomplete, but it will serve as a template that will be progressively refined in subsequent chapters in response to questions and objections.

One natural reaction to the pluralism and uncertainty discussed in the previous chapter that is common in modern pluralist and democratic societies is the following. People think to themselves that since it seems impossible to demonstrate that their view is right from their point of view (because of the circularity problem mentioned) and since everyone else is in the same condition, the only proper stance to take in the presence of pluralism and uncertainty is an attitude of "openness" or tolerance toward other points of view. Judgments about good and evil, right and wrong, one might reason, are personal matters that should be made for oneself and not imposed on others against their will. Is it not true that much of the evil of human history has come from taking the opposite attitude, assuming one has *the* correct view and the right to impose it on others? "Evil takes root," as the late Russian poet Joseph Brodsky once said, "when one man begins to think he is superior to another."

But this attitude of openness, though it comes naturally to many who are reared in pluralist and democratic societies, is disparaged by some theorists and social critics. One such critic, Allan Bloom (1987: 26), argues that such openness to all points of view (an "openness of indifference" as he calls it) affects society, education and young people in perverse ways because it leads to a kind of *relativism* which supposes that no view is any better than any other, and hence to an indifference to objective truth and absolute right.[1] "Make judgments for yourself, not for others," this

---

[1] Bloom calls this a "relativism of indifference." Other notions of value relativism will be discussed later.

openness of indifference says, "and don't suppose your view is superior in truth or rightness to those of others." But such an attitude, Bloom argues, is a short step from supposing that no point of view *is* any better (or truer) than any other and that no one can take a universal point of view and say what is right or true for everyone. (Hereafter, as in Chapter 1, the *points of view* of persons are defined by their factual, evaluative and norma- tive beliefs, along with their desires, intentions, and other psychological attitudes that together tell us how they experience the world, what they believe about it and what their "values" are – in the sense of what they regard as good and right.)

The relativism of indifference Bloom decries may be a significant temp- tation in modern pluralist and democratic societies for reasons discussed in the previous chapter. But it is a mistake to think that relativistic con- clusions of the kinds he has in mind are the inevitable consequence of an attitude of openness toward other points of view. I now want to suggest that such an attitude of openness, when it is conceived *as part of a search for wisdom* (understood as the search for the objective truth about a given subject matter) need not lead to relativism or indifference, as critics such as Bloom fear. Rather openness, when it is so conceived as part of a search for wisdom, may point the way to belief in some objective and universal values.[2] We may begin to see how this might be so by engaging in a ser- ies of thought experiments. Those people who naturally think in terms of openness toward other points of view in response to pluralism and uncer- tainty are on to something important, I shall argue, though it is easy to misconstrue what they are on to.

To see why, the first step is to note that openness need not be an invi- tation to indifference. It can be a *way of expanding our minds beyond our own limited points of view.* It can be an effort to find out what should be recognized as true from every point of view (what is objectively or univer- sally true), not just what is recognized as true from our own point of view. Openness to other points of view, so conceived, would thus become a way of *searching* for the objective truth about what is good or valuable (i.e., a search for wisdom in matters of value) under conditions of pluralism and uncertainty rather than a denial of that objective truth. "Openness" functions in a similar way in other areas of human inquiry where there are conflicting theories and points of view. In the natural sciences, for example, where such openness functions well, it requires consideration

---

[2] Bloom mentions in passing (ibid.: 41) another potential attitude of openness (being open to learn- ing the truth) that need not lead to indifference, but he does not pursue this suggestion in the way that I shall in these chapters.

and testing of theories and evidence opposed to one's own theory as well as restricting undue bias in favor of one's own theory or mere authoritative appeals to one's own theory – all in the interests of *limiting narrowness of vision* and finding the *objective* truth about nature.

Why not think of openness in the search for objective *values* in the same way – as a way of expanding our minds beyond our own limited points of view and thereby limiting narrowness of vision – in order to find the objective truth about values? The thought seems strange at first because of obvious differences between fact and value and between theoretical and practical inquiry. (Here we begin to engage these "sunderings" of modernity mentioned in Chapter 1.) In the first place, systems of value, as great sages of the past, such as Confucius and the author of the Bhagavad-Gita remind us,[3] are not merely abstract theories that can be tested or experimented with in a laboratory. Systems of value are guides to *ways (or forms) of life* (i.e., to plans for living implied by different points of view, as defined in Chapter 1) that can only be ultimately tested by being lived. So openness to systems of value other than one's own (in the interests of finding out what should be recognized as good from every point of view) would mean initially *being open to other ways of life* in the sense of letting them be lived or experimented with, or tested, in a way that is appropriate for values, in action or practice.

## 2. THE MORAL SPHERE AND ITS LIMITS

But, once the matter is put this way, one can see why people have shied away from this line of thought. Would this mean being open to *every* way of life in the sense of allowing it to be lived or experimented with, which would amount to tolerating (among others) the ways of life of the Hitlers, Stalins, ruthless dictators, killers and other evildoers of the world? Then openness would amount to a relativism of indifference, as critics such as Bloom contend.

But the fact is that such openness does not imply tolerating every point of view and way of life. For, it turns out that you cannot open your mind to every point of view in the sense of allowing it to be lived or experimented with without hindrance or interference. There are situations in life (many of them in fact) in which it is impossible to be open to every point of view in this sense. So, while the initial attitude in the search for wisdom being suggested is to "open your mind to all other points of view

---

[3] Huang 1997: 6.22, p. 84; Malhotra 1999: chapters 2–4, 12.

in order to find the objective truth about the good and the right," the truth you find when you do so is not that "you should open your mind to all points of view." You cannot. Openness of mind is an initial attitude in the search for wisdom in these matters, but "relativism of indifference" need not be the final attitude.

Why not? Consider a situation in which you are walking down the street and see a man being assaulted and robbed in an alley. Suppose you are the first to see the event and the outcome will depend on what you do. If you stop to assist the victim by intervening or shouting for assistance, the assailant may see that he has been found out and will run. But if you just "walk on by," as wary city dwellers sometimes do, the man will be beaten and robbed. In such situations, where the outcome depends on your action, you cannot be open to both the points of view of the assailant and the victim, in the sense of allowing both persons to carry out their purposes or realize their desires (and so to pursue their ways of life) without hindrance or interference from others. If you do something to prevent the assault (by intervening or calling for help), you will be acting in such a way that the purposes and desires of the assailant are interfered with and not fulfilled. If you "walk on by" when you could have done something to help, you will be acting in such a way that the purposes and desires of the man being assaulted will be interfered with and not fulfilled (not directly by you, of course, but as a result of your acting in that way rather than otherwise).

In such situations, *where the outcome depends on what you do*, you cannot have it both ways. You cannot be open to both points of view (of assailant and victim) in the sense of allowing both to pursue their desired ends or purposes and ways of life without interference, *no matter what you do*. When pirates under the command of William Kidd attacked Philadelphia in the eighteenth century, pillaging and raping, some of the resident men with pacifist beliefs would not protect their women. These men were not thereby choosing a world in which everyone's purposes and ways of life would be allowed to be pursued without interference from others. They were choosing that it be the purposes of the pirates that would be so allowed and not those of their own women. They had not chosen a world without violence, but a world in which the violence would be directed at their women and not the pirates.

So there are situations in life in which one cannot be open to every point of view, no matter what one does. Let us say that in such situations the "moral sphere" has "broken down," where the *moral sphere* is defined as a sphere in which all persons can be *treated with openness* by all others in the sense of *being allowed to pursue and realize their desired ends or purposes, and hence to pursue their ways of life, without interference* (without being prevented, for example, from doing so by the pursuits of others). When the moral sphere "breaks down," all persons cannot be treated with openness in this sense. Some ways of life will be prevented from being pursued, no matter what one does. But which ones should it be?

An answer is to be found by returning to the original goal or end of openness. Recall that openness was not assumed to be the final truth about what is good or valuable, but was to guide us in the search for that truth. Montaigne once said that ideals are to us as the stars were to the ancient mariners: We never reach them, but we guide our path by them. Similarly, it is the persistent striving to maintain an ideal in which all persons can be treated with openness by all others (a moral sphere) to the degree possible in the face of obstacles that is to guide us in the search for what should be recognized as good or valuable *from all* points of view (i.e., objectively valuable). Such striving is meant to preserve us, to the degree that is within our power, from narrowness of vision that comes from viewing things only from our own points of view.

When the moral sphere breaks down, we cannot follow this ideal of openness to all to the letter ("cannot reach it"), no matter what we do. But we can continue to "guide our path by it" in adverse circumstances by trying to restore and preserve conditions in which *the ideal of openness to all can be followed once again by all*. That would mean trying to restore and preserve the moral sphere when it has broken down by stopping those who have broken it and made it impossible for others to follow the ideal. For it is the sphere in which the ideal of openness to all persons *can* be followed by all persons. Making efforts to restore this sphere when it has broken down is thus *as close as we can come to maintaining the ideal of openness to all points of view and ways of life in adverse circumstances* when we must depart from that ideal to some degree, no matter what we do. And maintaining this ideal to the degree possible is our way of expanding our minds beyond our own limited points of view to find out what should be recognized as good or valuable from all points of view, not merely from our own.

In our examples, stopping those whose ways of living would make it impossible for others to follow the ideal of openness to all means stopping the assailant and the pirates. We thus arrive at an answer to the original question of *who* is to be regarded as less worthy of being treated with openness when the moral sphere breaks down and it is no longer possible to treat everyone with openness, no matter what one does.

## 3. TWO WAYS OF SEARCHING

Needless to say, there are many complications and questions about this line of reasoning that will have to be addressed, and will be addressed, in this and subsequent chapters. But lest we miss the forest for the trees, at this point, let us consider another way of looking at the argument that provides further insight into its meaning. In a pluralist world of conflicting points of view and ways of life, one may argue that there are two distinct ways of searching for objective or universal values (those that are correct for all persons and from all points of view). An older way was to position oneself in one point of view – one's own – and argue that it was right and every other view wrong. This is the way people have thought about establishing the objective good and right for centuries.

But in a world of pluralism and uncertainty, this way founders over our finiteness and the circularity problem of Chapter 1. One could, of course, deny or ignore this problem – asserting the absolute or certain truth of one's own point of view about what is good or right *from* one's own point of view on authoritative or other grounds. In the face of the terrifying prospects of pluralism and uncertainty, one may engage in a kind of fundamentalist retrenchment, reasserting the old ways in the old way. We can understand this reaction and see why it has become an increasingly common means of coping with moral uncertainty in an age of pluralism – even as we fear the dogmatism and violence that may result from it.

But our question is a different one: What options are available to persons who, moved by the reflections about pluralism and uncertainty of Chapter 1, can no longer go back to the older way of establishing absolute values – merely defending the universal truth of their own points of view from their own points of view? Such persons can either abandon the search for objective or universal values altogether *or* they can try something new. They may succumb to subjectivism, relativism or skepticism, or look for a new way of searching.

When the problem is put this way, the preceding line of reasoning may be viewed as suggesting an alternative way of searching: the way of openness. Instead of trying to prove one's own point of view and way of life absolutely right from one's own point of view, try this: Open one's mind initially to other points of view and ways of life, allowing them to be pursued without interference *to the degree that one can do so* while maintaining a moral sphere in which all persons can be treated with such openness by all others; and make this a test of whether persons and ways of life are worthy of being treated with openness *by all others*, including oneself. Try this as a thought experiment and see what happens.

In this way, one lifts from oneself the burden of proving one's own way of life is right and every other wrong, and places the burden of proof on all persons equally to show their ways of life worthy of being allowed to be pursued by all others *by how they plan to act and live*. Some persons, such as the assailant and pirates, will then show their ways of life to be less worthy of being allowed to be pursued by all others by making it impossible to treat their ways of life with openness while treating all other ways with openness as well.

When put this way, the preceding argument can be seen to express a central theme of the book briefly stated in Chapter 1, which can now be more fully stated: "Inquiry into the truth about ethical matters and the nature of the good life must involve *practical engagement in the world*, including engagement with others.[4] But such practical engagement, if it is to yield ethical insight, must be *part of an overall search for wisdom*, in the sense of a search for what is *objectively* good and right and hence should be recognized as good and right from every point of view, not merely what is recognized as good or right for oneself or from one's own point of view."

The attitude of openness is an expression of this latter requirement. By opening one's mind initially *to all* points of view in an effort to find out what should be recognized as good *from all* points of view and by persistently striving to maintain conditions in which all persons can be treated with openness by all others to the degree possible in one's practical engagements with others, one finds the following: Some persons may make themselves less worthy of being treated with openness by virtue of their plans of action, which make it impossible for others to allow their ways of life to be pursued without interference, while allowing the ways of life of everyone else to be pursued without interference as well. *Practical inquiry* about the good is thus viewed as "experimental" in a way, like *theoretical inquiry* into nature. But practical inquiry is experimental in its own distinctive manner.

### 4. RESTORING AND PRESERVING THE MORAL SPHERE: VIOLENCE AND PACIFISM

What then is to be said about *our own* way of life, if we proceed in this way? It is to be treated no differently than the others. If *we* break the

---

[4] I owe to an anonymous reader the recognition of the importance of this notion of "practical engagement with others" to the arguments of this book.

moral sphere (making it impossible for other persons to treat us with openness and all others with openness as well), then we make *our* way of life less worthy of being treated with openness by others, i.e., less worthy of being allowed to be pursued without interference by them. So we are not entirely off the hook as a result of having distributed the burden of proof equally to everyone. We still have the burden of proving to others the worthiness of our own way of life by the same criterion we apply to them; and that is burden enough. For the "proof" (whether of our way of life or other ways) is not carried out merely by arguing in the abstract that one view is better than others, but in potential practical engagements with others, by how we plan to act and live.

Do we then have to wait until some persons actually break the moral sphere and show themselves less worthy before intervening – which would be disastrous in many instances? The answer is no, for the reason that, as noted, striving to maintain the ideal of a moral sphere in which all persons and ways of life are treated with openness by all others to the degree possible requires not only *restoring* that sphere when it has broken down, but also *preserving* it from future breakdown. The point is that it is by the persistent striving to maintain conditions in which the ideal of openness to all can be followed by all that we go about expanding our minds beyond our own limited points of view. We do so in an effort to find out what should be recognized as good or valuable *from all* points of view, not merely from our own. And we would not be respecting this ideal of openness to all to the degree possible if we failed to take reasonable steps to forestall future breakdowns of the moral sphere when possible. For that is the sphere in which the ideal of openness to all can be followed by all.

Thus, we punish criminals not only to stop them here and now (restore the sphere), but to deter them and others from committing similar acts in the future (to preserve the sphere). We do this because it is as close as we can come to preserving conditions in which the ideal of openness to all can be followed by all when we must violate that ideal to some degree, no matter what we do. Similarly, in the interests of preserving the moral sphere in the future, we can act preemptively if we see it is about to be broken. Those who read Hitler's *Mein Kampf* could see that his life-plan was a moral sphere-breaker and they had every right to intervene by force if they saw he was about to carry it out. Unfortunately, we know that too many of Hitler's contemporaries could not believe he meant what he said.

Consider pacifism. It may be the correct view *within* the moral sphere, but it fails when the moral sphere breaks down. Sometimes force is required to restore and preserve the ideal that normally prohibits force. Such a requirement is consistent with the goal of trying to maintain conditions in which the ideal of openness to all can be followed by all to the degree possible when that ideal cannot be followed to the letter, no matter what one does. When the pirates raided Philadelphia, every point of view could not be treated with openness. It was not a question of *whether* some view would not be treated with openness, but whose view it would be (the pirates or their victims). The point is revealed by a joke about pacifism common among members of the Society of Friends with whom I taught for a time in the Philadelphia area: A Quaker farmer finds a thief in his chicken coup. Aiming his shotgun at the thief, he exclaims, "I do not want to hurt you, sir, but I advise you to run, because you are standing where I am about to shoot."

The tensions of an extreme pacifist view are evident in tales of this kind: There are situations in which every point of view (including one's own) cannot be allowed to be pursued without interference from others. Yet even as we might be led thereby to question the universal truth of pacifism, it is worth noting that pacifism may be regarded in another sense as the "ideal" view on the above account. For pacifism would be the correct view *within* the moral sphere and the moral sphere is viewed as the *ideal* sphere. It is just that the world is not always perfect or ideal (indeed it rarely is); and so we find ourselves constantly trying to realize the ideal to the degree possible in an imperfect world. In a non-ideal world, the ideal view is not always the right view to follow.

### 5. EXCEPTIONS TO MORAL RULES: LYING

Pursuing the above line of reasoning would show something else of importance for ethical reasoning. It would show why there are commonly recognized *exceptions* to many traditional moral rules – thou shall not kill, lie, steal, cheat (exceptions, for example, such as self-defense and just wars in the case of rules against killing or engaging in violence). The existence of exceptions to traditional moral rules is a controversial matter, to be sure, and it is also a persistent source of confusion about objective ethical standards, along with relativism. For, a common thought is that if moral rules have exceptions, they cannot be universal or absolutely binding. Another fear is that once any exceptions are admitted, it will become problematic where the line on allowable exceptions is to be drawn. Disagreements will proliferate and the question of the woman on Perelandra will return: "If others can do it, why can't I?"

So it is interesting to note that exceptions to common moral rules would be dealt with by the reasoning of this chapter in the same way that relativism of indifference was dealt with. In the case of relativism of indifference, one starts with openness toward all ways of life as a thought experiment and finds that, at the point of moral sphere breakdown, one cannot be open to all ways of life in the sense of allowing them to be pursued without interference. But it is at just this point – *where the moral sphere breaks down* and a relativism of indifference fails in practice – that exceptions to moral rules also arise. Violence and force are not usually allowed (inside the moral sphere), but when the moral sphere breaks down (as in the case of assaults or warfare), violence or force may be needed to restore it. In such cases, we continue to serve the ideal of openness *to all* to the degree possible by striving to restore conditions in which it can be followed once again *by all*.

Or consider another traditional moral rule: Do not lie. To lie to others is usually to interfere in some way with their unhindered pursuit of their desired ends or purposes, often to one's own advantage, and this accounts for its usually being wrong within the moral sphere. But what happens when the moral sphere has broken down? Consider a familiar modern variant of Kant's "murderer at the door" example. In Nazi Germany, the secret police, the Gestapo, arrive at your door and ask whether you are hiding a Jewish family on your farm. You are in fact hiding a family; and the family is not likely to be found unless you reveal its presence. Nor, we may assume, is there danger you will be found out if you lie since the family is well hidden.

Here is a familiar example where most people feel an exception to a moral rule against lying is in order. But if so, why? Notice that the case is structurally similar to the assault in the alley. The moral sphere has broken down because you (the farm owner) cannot treat all persons involved with openness in the situation in the sense of allowing their desired ends or purposes to be pursued and realized without interference. If you tell the truth to the Gestapo, you are choosing to favor their purposes and desires over the Jewish family's. If you lie, you favor the Jewish family's purposes and desires, but not the Gestapo's.

Once again, you cannot have it both ways in the situation. The only question is whose purposes and ways of life will be treated as less worthy of being pursued, not whether someone's will be so treated. And, as in the assailant and pirate examples, those who should be treated as less worthy are those whose purposes or plans of action have made it impossible for others to treat everyone in the situation with openness. That would be the Gestapo in the present case, whose plan it is to harm the Jewish family, as the assailant and pirates planned to harm their victims – which means you should lie. It is not that lying is merely permissible in such a case. It would be the right thing to do, just as the right thing to do would be to stop the assailant if you could. The same ideal that tells you lying is usually wrong – inside the moral sphere – tells you that it can be the right thing to do in cases like this when the moral sphere breaks down and you are no longer "inside" it. So it would be also, if someone forced you to play a game of cards threatening to kill your children if you lost. Cheating is usually wrong (inside the moral sphere) but in this case, where the moral sphere has badly broken down, it would be right to cheat in any way you could.

### 6. CONCLUSION: MILL

As noted earlier, many complications and questions about this line of reasoning will have to be addressed in subsequent chapters. Among them are questions about the exact criteria for moral sphere breakdown and for distinguishing guilty from innocent parties. (I am well aware that much further argument is needed on these and many other matters.) But, looking at the broader picture again for the present, one can see how this line of reasoning might support many traditional ethical rules endorsed by the major world religions and wisdom traditions (do not kill, lie, steal, cheat) and commonly recognized exceptions to these rules. Moreover, the exceptions would not be arbitrary or ad hoc. They would follow naturally from the line of reasoning that leads to the rules themselves, once one understands the limitations imposed by imperfect conditions.

In addition, the above line of reasoning would lead to another traditional and widely acknowledged moral principle, the Golden Rule ("Do unto others as you would have them do unto you") in one of its traditional readings – allowing the ways of life of others to be pursued without interference by others, as you would want your own way of life to be allowed to be pursued[5] – *up to the point of course where the moral sphere breaks down.* And from the same reasoning, one could also derive Lockean-inspired Jeffersonian rights to life, liberty and the pursuit of happiness that lie at the foundations of modern free and democratic societies: To be open to others' ways of life in the sense of allowing them to be pursued without

---

[5] I am not claiming this is the only interpretation of that rule, or even the most common one historically, but it is a possible one. Wattles 1996 is an excellent historical study of various interpretations of the rule.

interference is to *allow others to live and pursue happiness as they choose* – up to the point once again where they would break the moral sphere.

These are interesting results. Starting with an attitude of "openness" to all points of view and ways of life – an attitude that might seem to lead to a relativism of indifference – one arrives instead at certain traditional ethical rules and commonly recognized exceptions to these rules, at a particular version of the Golden Rule and a recognition of certain human rights (to life, liberty and the pursuit of happiness). All this comes from a starting point (openness to all points of view) that seems decidedly "modern" and may appear to be subversive of beliefs about objective or universal values.

What makes things otherwise is that openness is conceived *not as the final truth about the good and the right*, but as a method of *searching* for that truth (searching for wisdom in matters of value) under conditions of pluralism and uncertainty. The traditional way of searching for what should be recognized as good and right from every point of view – i.e., positioning oneself in one point of view and trying to prove it absolutely right and every other view wrong – is thwarted by pluralism and uncertainty. One may either give up the search in response or try some other method.

The way of openness as an alternative suggests itself for two reasons. First, it takes seriously the conditions of pluralism and uncertainty that thwart other attempts to find objective or universal value. Second, the way of openness focuses attention on the fact that it is objective or universal value – what should be recognized as good or right from every point of view – that one is looking for. If you want to find out what should be recognized as good or right from every point of view, open your mind initially to all points of view and ways of life; and make the ability of yourself and others to sustain such an attitude of openness to all persons a test of whether persons are worthy of being treated with openness by yourself and all others. When you do so, you find that some ways of living fail this test by making it impossible to treat them with openness and to treat all other ways of life with openness as well.

But paradoxically, you find this out by *initially* being willing in principle to open your mind to all persons and every point of view and by trying to sustain such an attitude of openness to all to the degree possible in an imperfect world. It is the persistent striving to maintain this ideal in the face of obstacles that leads to ethical insight. In his classic treatise, *On Liberty*, John Stuart Mill expressed the belief that by maintaining a condition of openness and allowing all points of view to be heard, the truth would emerge.[6] This claim was, of course, part of Mill's classic defense of freedom of speech. But the above argument gives it a new twist: By being initially open to all points of view, the "ethical" truth emerges that one cannot be open to all points of view and ways of life and must regard some as less worthy of being treated with such openness than others. We begin to address many questions posed by this argument in the next two chapters.

[6] Mill 1956: chapter 3.

CHAPTER 3

# *The retreat*

## I. ANOTHER LOOK

To further develop the argument of Chapter 2 and address additional objections to it, I am going to introduce a thought experiment in this chapter that will play an important role in subsequent chapters. Suppose we have organized a retreat at some remote mountain site – say a monastery in the foothills of the Himalayas (for symbolic value) – inviting people from all over the world representing different cultures, religions, points of view about values and forms of life. The attendees are given the collective task of coming to some kind of understanding before the retreat is over about which point of view or form of life is the right one – or which are the right ones, should there be more than one (where "points of view" are understood as in Chapters 1 and 2, and "ways or forms of life" are understood as plans for living implied by different points of view).

To make matters as difficult and realistic as possible, let us add to the mix of Christian, Jewish, Muslim, Hindu, Buddhist, Taoist and other religious believers at this retreat, a sampling of non-believers who think all the religious views are misguided, as well as agnostics and persons representing various secular ideologies, positivists (who believe that only science provides objective knowledge or reliable evidence), secular humanists, social Darwinists, Marxists, Aryan supremacists, Satanists, new age channelers, Nietzschean elitists, postmodernist relativists and numerous others – the learned and the unlearned, the wise and the foolish. The aim is to represent the modern world in all its pluralism. We include the foolish as well as the wise in the spirit of a legendary Texas politician who said that "if there were no fools in the state legislature, it would not be a representative body."[1]

We can imagine that many of the representatives present from the various religions of the world and some others representing secular ideologies

---

[1] Carl Parker, a long-time state senator from Houston, said this.

will try to persuade others of the absolute rightness of their respective points of view and the wrongness of all others. They will see the task of reaching agreement as one of proselytizing or converting others to their beliefs and will try hard to do this. For the goal, as they see it, is to seek the truth and they believe they already have the truth. Others may not place such a high priority on proselytizing or conversion, but will be prepared to defend the rightness of their views when challenged.

Now let us assume, for the sake of argument, what is most likely to be the outcome of this retreat, if many groups proceed in this way. After days or weeks of heated discussion, perhaps some people will be converted to this or that religion, and some religious believers will lose their faith in the presence of secular and scientific challenges. But most people present are likely to stand firm with their respective world-views and ways of life, having failed to persuade others or to be persuaded by others. (Would we expect any different outcome from even a modicum of experience of human beings?) The collective task of finding general agreement on the right way of life, or right ways of life, will have failed. What then?

Well, some people, discouraged by, or cynical about, the fruitless bickering will simply leave. Let us assume (which seems likely) that on one side, those who leave will include many of those who are certain they already have the truth – the dogmatists, let us call them. (Some religious people will be in this group, but it will not include all or only religious people. We should expect no scarcity of dogmatists and ideologues, or their opposites, on all sides, if this is truly a representative body.) Having failed to convert or persuade others of their views, the dogmatists will chalk up their failure to the irrationality, ignorance, perversity, sinfulness or downright stupidity of the others present, and will see no point in continuing.

At the other end of the spectrum will be subjectivists, relativists and skeptics of various stripes, who do not believe there is any such thing as objective or universal truth about the right way of life to be searching for or reaching agreement about. To them, the fruitless bickering has another meaning; it is evidence that the objective good does not exist. This group too is likely to leave the retreat (though we might guess that a few of them will stay around to make cynical comments on the proceedings).

Let us now imagine that all those who intend to leave have departed. Why would anyone stay? Because, we may suppose, there are some present at this retreat who, while they are not certain that their own point of view or any other is objectively or universally right, have not given up believing there is such a thing as universal truth or rightness; and they desire to find what it is and whether their view or any other has it. They are neither dogmatists believing with certainty that they already have the truth nor relativists or skeptics who believe objective truth about matters of value does not exist; and they have not given up the search for it. Indeed that *search* is what the retreat was all about; and those who remain choose to continue it.

Now suppose that when all those who intend to leave have packed their bags and departed, some wise persons stand up and address those remaining. The message they convey goes something like this. "We have come here to search for the right and the good from every point of view. We have failed to convince each other because we have been appealing to fundamental beliefs and values that we cherish but others do not share. But we are not for that reason going to give up the search. Let us try something new. Let us in our imaginations draw a large circle around all of us here present, as well as around all others who have departed and all other persons whatever. This circle represents our willingness to allow all to pursue their ways of life without interference to the degree that we can do so while maintaining a world in which all persons can be allowed to pursue their ways of life without interference by all others.

"By drawing this circle and acting toward others in this way, we need not thereby concede that other ways of life besides our own are objectively good or right. We do not know that. Neither do we know that our own is the right one, though we would like to continue believing it is. That is what we are trying to find out. The point of drawing this large circle and acting in the way suggested is to shift the burden of proof from our particular points of view and distribute that burden equally to all persons, allowing them to show by how they plan to act that their points of view and ways of life are worthy of being allowed to be pursued by all others. Let us draw this circle and act in this manner as a thought experiment and see what happens."

This suggestion recreates the argument of Chapter 2. The attitude being suggested to the participants is *openness*. The circle drawn around those to whom the attitude of openness is to be initially accorded is the *moral sphere*. Those who stay behind at the retreat and proceed in this manner (hereafter I shall simply call them "the retreatants") will find that some persons may subsequently show themselves to be less worthy of being treated with openness by all others by making it impossible for others to allow their ways of life to be pursued and at the same time to allow the ways of life of all others to be pursued as well. And by such reasoning, the retreatants will be led, in the manner of Chapter 2, to ethical principles – not to lie, steal, cheat, etc. – that obtain within the moral sphere and to commonly recognized exceptions to those principles, to a version of the Golden Rule and to a recognition of certain rights to life, liberty and the pursuit of happiness that obtain up to the point of moral sphere breakdown. These are substantial results for their efforts.

Moreover, those who stay at the retreat and proceed in this way are those to whom the argument of Chapter 2 was addressed. Troubled by pluralism and uncertainty, they can no longer be dogmatists, believing they already know with certainty what is objectively good and right. But, not having abandoned the idea that there is an objective good and right to be sought, they are not yet ready to embrace relativism or skepticism either. Such persons live "after the modern Fall," so to speak, having lost moral innocence, *but not the love for wisdom*. They are still searching for the objective good.

## 2. THE SEARCH AND UNIVERSALITY

We can now see from this story of the retreat more clearly why the attitude of openness of Chapter 2 is a choice and what kind of choice it is. *It is the choice to stay at the retreat and to keep searching for the right and the good from every point of view despite conditions of pluralism and uncertainty.* It is a choice to accept neither dogmatism nor skepticism as a final resting place in one's search for the objective good, but rather to act out of a love of wisdom (*philosophia*), which is skeptical of dogma, yet not dogmatic about skepticism. But once the matter is put this way, an obvious objection looms. Since those persons who stay behind and try openness are only a subset of all those who attended the retreat, many of whom have left, how can the results they attain be universal – true from *all* points of view? How could their results apply to everyone?

The first part of an answer to this question is that to find what is true from all points of view, all points of view do not have to participate in the search. If quantum physics should turn out to be the true theory about the physical world, it will be true for Russians and Americans, Chinese and Sudanese, Navajo Indians and Maori tribesmen, whether or not each of these participated in the search *or* would agree to its results. Analogously, in the case of values and ways of life, what counts for the universality of the results is not whether all ways of life have participated in the search or whether those in all ways of life agree, but whether those who have participated in the search *have taken into account all ways of life*. This is done by the retreatants by drawing the large circle representing openness around all ways of life whatever – not only of those still present at the retreat, but also of those who have departed and all others as well.

This is crucial. For, if those who stayed at the retreat had drawn the initial circle of openness only around themselves, their results would have been valid only for themselves. If those who stayed had chosen to make an agreement or social contract among themselves to respect only each others' rights and ways of life, that again would have been valid and binding only for themselves.[2] But this is not what these retreatants are doing. They are engaged in a philosophical search for what is objectively right and good for everyone and should be recognized as right and good from all points of view.

If such a thing required agreement from everyone and from every point of view, they would have already lost at the point where so many left the retreat and would not even participate. But if those remaining at the retreat gave up the search for that reason (because many had left), they would have mistaken the nature of their goal, just as physicists would be mistaken to give up their belief in quantum physics because they could not convince some primitive tribesmen or members of the flat-earth society that it was true. Similarly, what counts for the universality of the results of the retreatants' inquiries is not whether all ways of life have participated in the search, or whether all would agree, but whether those who *have* participated in the search have taken into account all ways of life, allowing each to be tested or experimented with. And this is done by drawing the large circle representing openness around all ways of life, *including* those who have left the retreat and do not agree with them. That is the test of the sincerity of their attempt to find an objective truth that will have universal application. (Analogously, the test of the sincerity of those who participate in the search for a theory of the physical world that will have universal application is whether those who participate in the search, whether they be flat-earthers or quantum physicists, are willing to allow all theories, including their own, to be put to an experimental test.)

Such a requirement means in practice that the retreatants will say to one another: "In our continuing search for the truth, we shall apply these ethical principles at which we have arrived, such as a certain version of the Golden Rule and rules not to lie or cheat. And we will *initially* accord openness to everyone, not merely to those who agree with us, allowing all to show us by how they plan to act and live that their ways of life are

---

[2] As a consequence, I argue in later chapters (particularly 17) that the ethical theory presented is not a contractarian or contractualist theory of any kinds familiar to modern ethical theory.

worthy of being allowed by everyone to be pursued. This does not mean we will be helpless in the face of evil-doing by those who left the retreat and do not agree with these principles or do not follow them. For we are committed by our own principles of openness only up to the point where others break the moral sphere. At that point, we cannot treat them with openness and at the same time maintain a moral sphere in which everyone is treated with openness by everyone else; and we can take measures to restore and preserve the sphere in which the ideal of openness to all can be followed once again by all.

"So if it should happen that some persons who have left the retreat – say, a group of dogmatists who do not believe in openness – subsequently persecute others or make war on neighbors in the name of their faith or ideology, or try to impose their beliefs on others forcibly, that is where the line on openness for their ways of life will be drawn. It will be impossible at that point for us to treat with openness the persecutors and those whom they are persecuting. But until that point is reached, even dogmatists will be allowed to pursue their ways of life without interference, though they may not themselves believe in openness. And what applies to them applies as well to all others who left the retreat or stayed behind. If they should persecute others or try to impose their wills on others forcibly or by deceit or manipulation, that is where the line on openness to their ways of life will be drawn."

### 3. FURTHER OBJECTIONS

But these claims lead to a further objection the retreatants must address. Suppose some recalcitrant and aggressive group that has left the retreat does subsequently persecute, exploit or make war on its disagreeing neighbors. And suppose the retreatants have the power to intervene and do forcibly intervene to restore and preserve the moral sphere. Are the retreatants not then imposing *their* view coercively on this recalcitrant group, which does not happen to agree with the retreatants' principles? And if so, are the retreatants not doing precisely what they claim the recalcitrant groups have no right to do to *their* disbelieving neighbors? What gives the retreatants any more right to impose their ("moral sphere") view on others who do not agree with them than any other persons or groups have to impose their views on others?

These are good questions and the answers to them provide further insight into the meaning of the retreat and the argument of Chapter 2. When such questions are raised among the retreatants, after some reflection, they realize how they must reply. "To believe as we do that we have the right to forcibly intervene *only* when the moral sphere has broken down and only to restore and preserve it, is to believe that the only thing that gives persons the right to impose their wills on others is that *they have tried their hardest not to* do so. For the point where the moral sphere breaks down is the point at which one can no longer treat with openness every way of life, *no matter what one does* or no matter how hard one tries. To restrain oneself until such a point is reached is what is meant by the persistent striving to maintain conditions in which the ideal of openness to all can be followed by all to the degree possible in an imperfect world. So long as one is doing this, one is seeking an objective good that is worthy of being recognized as such by all; and one will only intervene or force one's will on others after trying one's hardest to avoid doing so and finding that it is no longer possible.

"Consider, by contrast, those groups mentioned who persecute their neighbors. They accept no such constraint. If they did, they would not impose their wills forcibly until they had exhausted other options. They would look first for an accommodation or resolution of their conflict that both they and their neighbors could agree upon from their respective points of view before persecuting them. We assumed, in our example, that the persecutors did not do this. If they had been among the dog-matists who left the retreat, they may have believed they had a right to impose their views on their neighbors because their beliefs were the correct or superior ones. Or, if they were relativists or skeptics, they may have believed there was no objective right or wrong in the matter, so that 'might makes right' or one can persecute one's neighbors when it serves one's self-interest. But, whatever their motive, they would not merely be trying to restore the moral sphere when it has broken down. They would not have been trying to avoid imposing their wills on others until it was no longer possible to avoid doing so."

So there is a difference in the retreatants' actions and the persecutors'. What the retreatants believe is not that they have rights that others do not possess. Rather, they believe that the only thing which gives any persons the right to impose their wills coercively on others is that they have tried their hardest not to do so and found it is no longer possible, no matter what they do. To try one's hardest to treat all ways of life with openness and to fail to do so only as a last resort is a difficult ideal, to be sure, and it may be that we can only approximate it in everyday life. Is it always clear when we have tried our hardest to treat all ways of life with openness before intervening – or even clear what this requirement *means* in every circumstance? Is it always clear when the moral sphere has broken down or whether it has broken down, or who is responsible when it does? These questions and others will be addressed in the next chapter.

### 4. FINAL THOUGHTS: OPENNESS AND RESPECT

But before addressing them, I want to conclude this chapter with some final thoughts about the implications of the retreat for the argument of Chapter 2 and for the arguments to follow. Those who stay at the retreat to continue their search realize they have crossed a divide between the older way of seeking objective or universal values and a newer way of openness they have chosen. Those pursuing the older way, of positioning oneself in one's own point of view and trying to convince others that it was right and all other views wrong, soon left the retreat. Their way led to endless bickering.

Yet the newer way of openness the retreatants had chosen did not require that they abandon their particular points of view and ways of life. They realize that, as finite beings, they must inevitably search for the good *from* some particular point of view in which they find themselves. *One cannot search for the good from no point of view whatever.* Nor does practicing openness require that the retreatants give up believing in the correctness of their own points of view. Most of them could scarcely do that and continue to live in accordance with those views after they left the retreat. What openness requires is rather a recognition of the limitations of their own and other points of view. It requires recognizing the finiteness of their human condition.

Consider, for example, that among those who stay at the retreat, many may be religious people who will continue to adhere to the beliefs of their respective religious traditions after the retreat is over. Like others who stayed at the retreat to go on searching, including non-believers, these religious believers are moved by pluralism and uncertainty. But it is not faith they have necessarily lost, only certainty and innocence. They know that most of the religious traditions of which they are a part emphasize the finiteness of the human condition and the need for faith. Given this human condition, they infer that they see only through a glass darkly, if they see at all. If this is so, they reason, then our finiteness extends to our condition of knowers as well; and pluralism and uncertainty are not merely modern conditions, but human conditions.

When these believers who remain at the retreat proceed in this fashion, they are doing what the others who remain are also doing: They are trying their hardest to get beyond their own limitations, to overcome narrowness of vision by opening their minds initially to all points of view and seeing what happens. Taking such an attitude does not mean they must believe that other views to which they take this attitude will turn out to be true. It is even consistent with taking such an attitude of openness that they believe their own view will ultimately prevail in the search for truth or that their own view will be an indispensable part of the final truth. But they do not know this for certain; and initially according openness to all points of view is a way of ensuring that the competition to find out will be fair and open.

By taking such an attitude toward others, therefore, the retreatants (unlike the dogmatists who left the retreat) are thereby according to others a kind of initial *respect* that I shall hereafter refer to as "respect in the sense of openness," or "openness respect."

To accord *respect in the sense of openness* (or *openness respect*) to persons is to treat them with openness to the degree that one can do so while maintaining a moral sphere in which all persons can be treated with openness by all others, and to do this as a way of allowing persons to show by how they plan to live in relation to others that they are worthy of being treated with openness by all others, including oneself.

"Treating with openness" in this definition in turn has the meaning given to it in Chapter 2, which may be summarized as follows:

To *treat persons with openness* is to allow them to pursue their ways of life and realize their desired ends ("to live and pursue happiness as they choose") without interference (without being prevented, for example, from doing so by the pursuits of others).

To accord "respect" in this sense of openness to persons is therefore (as noted at the end of Chapter 2) to accord them rights to life, liberty and the pursuit of happiness ("to live and pursue happiness as they choose") – but only *provisionally*, up the point where they would break the moral sphere (that is, "to the degree that one can do so" while maintaining a moral sphere in which all are similarly treated).

To treat persons in this way, even if only provisionally, is to accord them a kind of respect, which dogmatists who left the retreat were not willing to accord. But respect in this sense of openness must be distinguished from other notions of respect common in the philosophical literature, despite some similarities.[3] It must be distinguished, for example, from what some philosophers call *"appraisal respect"* (Darwall 1977) and

---

[3] This literature on respect is vast. Thoughtful overviews and guides to it include Hudson 1980, Buss 1999, Dillon 2007.

others *"evaluative respect"* (Hudson 1980, Dillon 1992) – the respect to be accorded to persons, deeds, ways of life and other things that are regarded as praiseworthy or excellent in some way and hence worthy of such favorable attitudes as esteem or admiration. Openness respect does not require such favorable attitudes toward other points of view and ways of life, but neither does it rule them out. Its point is rather to keep an "open mind" about the ultimate worthiness or unworthiness for appraisal or evaluative respect of other points of view and ways of life – allowing persons to show this through the living of their ways of life. (How one might go about determining which ways of life *are* worthy of appraisal or evaluative respect in various senses is one of many issues to be considered in subsequent chapters.[4])

Openness respect *may* be viewed as a kind of what some philosophers call *recognition respect* (Darwall 1977) and others *consideration respect* (Frankena 1986, Cranor 1982). But it is recognition or consideration respect of a special kind. Generally understood, recognition or consideration respect involves a disposition to give appropriate weight or consideration in one's practical deliberations to certain facts about others and to regulate one's behavior accordingly. By taking an attitude of openness to others, the retreatants are disposed to give weight or consideration in their practical deliberations to the ways of life of others and to regulate their behavior accordingly. But the recognition or consideration thereby accorded (treating others with openness) is provisional. Its goal is to find out whether others are ultimately worthy of the recognition or consideration initially accorded to them – of being allowed to pursue their ways of life without interference by others.

Thus, to avoid confusion with other notions of respect commonly cited in the literature, I am giving respect in this sense of openness a special name. When I talk about respecting persons, points of view and ways of life hereafter without qualifying the kind of respect involved, I will mean respect in this sense of openness. When other notions of respect are discussed, appraisal respect or others, I will designate them accordingly. What I want to emphasize, however, is that respect in this sense of openness is a kind of respect, despite its differences from other familiar notions. To keep an open mind about the ultimate rightness or praiseworthiness of other points of view and ways of life – even provisionally – is to respect those views and ways in a manner that many of those who left the retreat were not willing to do.

---

[4] Notably, in Chapters 5–8, 11, 13 and 14.

It is instructive to compare scientists who take an analogous attitude of "openness" to theories of the physical world that are different from their own. Taking such an attitude need not imply that the scientists think competing theories are ultimately correct or true. They may believe their own theory will turn out to be the ultimately correct or true one. But keeping an "open mind" with respect to competing theories means that competing theories are regarded as worthy of being "tested" or "experimented with" to find out whether or not they are correct or true. Such an attitude is essential to the pursuit of wisdom in the theoretical sciences; and it does involve a kind of respect for other theories – deeming them worthy of being tested – whatever one's view may be about their ultimate truth. It is quite different from assuming one's own theory is obviously superior or certainly true, say on authoritative grounds, and dismissing rival theories out of hand as not even worthy of being tested.

Similarly, taking an attitude of openness to other points of view about values and ways of life, as the retreatants do, does not entail believing that other views and ways are ultimately good or worth pursuing. It means only that other views and ways of life are worthy of being allowed to be pursued (to be "tested" or "experimented with") to find out whether or not they are ultimately worth pursuing. Such an attitude, I am suggesting, is as essential to the pursuit of wisdom *in practical inquiry* as in the theoretical sciences. To say this, however, is not to deny that there are fundamental differences between the ways in which one might experiment with, or "test," scientific theories, on the one hand, and value theories and ways of life, on the other. There are obvious differences. But there are also revealing similarities between scientific and value experimentation that will be discussed in Chapter 6 in terms of J. S. Mill's seminal notion of "experiments in living." If practical inquiry is "experimental" like theoretical inquiry, as noted in Chapter 2, it is nonetheless experimental in its own distinctive way.

# CHAPTER 4

# *The moral sphere*

## I. INTENTIONS, PURPOSES AND PLANS OF ACTION

In this chapter, the ethical theory implied by the arguments of Chapters 2 and 3 is spelled out in greater detail and additional objections to it addressed. In the process, a comparison is made between the theory and certain features of Kantian ethics. The theory that emerges from the reasoning of Chapters 2 and 3 has some revealing similarities to Kantian approaches to ethics, I argue, but some equally revealing differences. Important moral issues are explored in the light of this comparison, including the need for a distinction between ideal and non-ideal ethical theory. I begin by addressing some questions left unanswered in Chapters 2 and 3 about the role of the moral sphere and its breakdown, questions that will lead to the main themes of the chapter.

The retreatants chose to treat others with openness up to a point where the moral sphere has broken down. But is it always clear when this point has been reached? Is it always clear when, or whether, the moral sphere has broken down and who is the guilty party when it does? These questions were not fully addressed in Chapters 2 and 3, where the examples of moral sphere breakdown were simple ones in which the guilty parties were easily identified (assailants, Gestapo, pirates, persecuting neighbors). Starting with simpler cases before moving on to complex ones is not uncommon in ethical discussion. But there are troubling questions to be asked, even about the simplest cases of moral sphere breakdown cited in Chapters 2 and 3, before considering more difficult cases.

In the example of the assault in the alley, for instance, a person playing devil's advocate might object that it is merely a conflict between two different and competing ways of life. The assailant is thwarting the victim's interests and purposes by force. But can we not also say the victim is thwarting the assailant's purposes by forcibly resisting the attack? Call this "the symmetry objection." It prompts one to ask questions like the following: On what grounds do we treat the parties differently in such cases, calling one guilty and the other innocent? On what grounds do we say one has broken the moral sphere and not the other, so that the way of life of one of them is less worthy of being treated with openness by those involved? Such questions, in cases such as the assault, pirates and Gestapo, may seem from a common-sense perspective hardly worth asking, and even a bit grotesque. But they force us to think more carefully about the criteria for moral sphere breakdown in a general manner that can be extended beyond the simplest cases. If we are justified in treating the parties differently in such conflicts, why is this so?

It turns out that the first response that comes to mind in the assault case is not quite adequate. It is natural to think that the assailant is the one who broke the moral sphere because his actions *initiated* the conflict and so created the situation in which both parties could not be treated with openness. ("He or she started it" is the schoolyard version of this response.) Such a response may point in the right direction, but it cannot be the whole story. For one thing, initiation of conflict cannot be defined merely by asking who was the first to act in time or the first to act physically. Suppose the victim in the alley, suspecting the intentions of his assailant, had initiated physical contact by punching the assailant in the midsection and then running away before the other man could pull out his knife. Though the intended victim acted first in this instance, we would not for that reason count him the guilty party, *if* his suspicions about the assailant's intentions were well-founded.

This thought suggests that we must attend to the *intentions* of agents as well as to their actions in order to adequately understand moral sphere breakdown. In the courtroom, as in everyday life, questions of intent enter the picture when trying to determine guilt or innocence. Now intentions (as emphasized by recent philosophers of action such as Michael Bratman (1987) and Alfred Mele (1992)) embody our life-plans or *plans of action* of varying degrees of complexity expressed in our *purposes* or *ends* and the *means* by which we carry out those purposes. To focus on intentions therefore is to focus on the agents' plans of action, of which their particular actions may be merely a part. Viewed from this perspective, different *ways of life* or *forms of life* – notions that played a crucial role in the argument of Chapters 2 and 3 – may be viewed as the most comprehensive life-plans or plans of action. And I want to suggest that plans of action in general (including ways of life) are the key to understanding moral sphere breakdown.

## 2. MORAL SPHERE-BREAKING PLANS OF ACTION

When the moral sphere breaks down, plans of action and ways of life intersect and conflict. To identify a guilty party, one has to find a difference in the plans of action of the parties that brought them into conflict. Suppose the man who was assaulted in the alley had planned to leave work that afternoon, do some shopping and go home to dinner. Nothing in this plan of action, or in his intentions or purposes generally, required or licensed him to impose his will on others, or to force others to do what he wanted, regardless of their desires or interests in the matter.

This is not the case for the assailant. His plan of action that day ("to assault and rob someone") by its nature required him to force his will on some unsuspecting other, whatever the desires, interests and purposes of the other might be. So while both assailant and victim might have encountered obstacles and conflicts in the pursuit of their intentions or plans that day, there was an important difference. The assailant's plan of action was a moral sphere-breaker *by the very nature of what he planned*; his victim's was not. Accordingly, we may say as a first approximation that *moral sphere-breaking plans of action* or *ways of life* are those that "require or license the agents acting on them to *impose their wills on others*, or make others do or undergo what they want, whatever the desires, interests, concerns or purposes of those others might be in the matter."

The life-plans of Hitler's *Mein Kampf* and of the pirates who pillaged Philadelphia are of this moral sphere-breaking kind: The plans required those who would follow them to impose their wills on others whatever the desires or interests of the others might be. The man assaulted in the alley may in fact resist the assailant when the trajectories of their plans cross. But it is the nature of the assailant's plan that caused the conflict and moral sphere breakdown, if his intention or plan was indeed to assault the victim. So the assailant is the guilty party, even if the victim acts first to preempt the attack. The assailant's guilt, however, resides not only in the action, but in the intention and plan of action that led to it.

The above condition, however, is only the first step of a two-step account of moral sphere-breaking plans of action and ways of life. A second condition must be added to deal with the symmetry objection. *Before* their plans of action intersect, the assailant's plan is moral sphere-breaking in the above sense, since it requires him to impose his will on some other person that day. The assault victim's plan, by contrast, is not, since he plans only to go shopping and return home to cook dinner. But *after* their plans intersect, it is another story. For if the assault victim resists the assailant – or when third parties, such as passers-by or the police, intervene to subdue the assailant – they are also acting on plans of action that "require or license the agents acting on them to impose their wills" on some other person (namely the *assailant*) "whatever the desires, interests, concerns or purposes of that other person might be in the matter." Something else must account for the asymmetry in the plans of the assailant and those who resist him, after their plans intersect.

The clue needed for this further condition is to be found in the argument of Chapter 3. By taking an attitude of openness or respect (in the sense of openness) toward other ways of life, the retreatants had chosen not to impose their wills on others *except as a last resort*, when all ways of life could not be treated with openness, no matter what they did. Expressing this point in another way, one may say that the retreatants accepted the following constraint on their plans of action as a result of their argument from openness: Imposing one's will on others is permissible only when by doing so *one is doing what one can do* to maintain a moral sphere in which all persons can be treated with openness by all others when one must depart from that ideal to some degree, no matter what one does.

The retreatants accepted such a constraint as a consequence of their argument, whereas the persecuting group that had left the retreat and later aggressed against its neighbors (in the example of Chapter 3) accepted no such constraint. Failing to conform to this constraint provides the further condition needed to define moral sphere-breaking plans of action and ways of life:

*Moral sphere-breaking plans of action* or *ways of life* are those that (i) require or license agents acting on them to *impose their wills on others*, or make others do or undergo what they want, whatever the desires, interests, concerns or purposes of those others might be in the matter, (ii) in situations where the agents are *not doing what they can do* to maintain a moral sphere in which all persons can be treated with openness by all others when they must depart from the ideal of treating all persons with openness to some degree, no matter what they do.

The plans of action of the assailant and the persecuting neighbors satisfy both these conditions and are therefore moral sphere-breaking. The assailant is not in a situation in which he cannot treat all persons with openness, no matter what he does. For it is open to him to allow his victim and others to pursue their plans of action that day without interference, by simply not pursuing his plan to assault and rob someone. So the assailant is "not doing what he can do to maintain a moral sphere in which all persons can be treated with openness by all others" and his plan satisfies condition (ii). Since his plan also satisfies condition

(i) (requiring him "to impose his will on another person, whatever the desires or purposes of that other might be"), his plan is moral sphere-breaking. Similarly, the persecuting neighbors satisfy both conditions for moral sphere-breaking plans when they engage in unprovoked aggression against their neighbors.

By contrast, when third parties, such as passers-by or police, intervene to subdue the assailant in order to restore the moral sphere, their plans of action fail to satisfy condition (ii) for moral sphere-breaking plans and are not moral sphere-breaking. By intervening to restore the moral sphere, they are "doing what they can do to maintain a moral sphere in which all persons can be treated with openness by all others," when that sphere has broken down due to the actions of the assailant. The plans of those who intervene are then not moral sphere-breaking even though those plans require them "to impose their wills on another [the assailant] whatever the desires or purposes of the other might be in the matter" – and so satisfy condition (i). What saves the agents from moral sphere-breaking in such cases is that they are doing their best to sustain an ideal in which all persons are treated with openness by all others, even as they must depart from that ideal to some degree.

### 3. TREATING AS ENDS AND AS MEANS

The means by which agents may "impose their wills on others," or "make others do or undergo what they want" may take many forms; and hence moral sphere-breaking plans of action may take many forms. Physical force and intimidation are two of the most common ways of imposing one's will on others, but manipulation and deception are others.

A woman who is persuaded by a con man to invest her life savings in a fraudulent scheme may consent to invest her money and go along with the plan (though she would not have consented if she had known what the man's plan really was). But even though the victim consents in this case, the con man's life-plan is the "moral sphere-breaker" by the above account and he is the guilty party. For his plan of action requires him to "impose his will" on the victim, or "make her do or undergo what he wants, whatever her interests or concerns" may be in the matter; and by so acting, he is "not doing what he can do to maintain a moral sphere in which all persons can be treated with openness by all others." For he could in principle treat all persons in the situation, including the woman, with openness by not pursuing his scheme, though he chooses to pursue it anyway. In more familiar language, we can say that the con man's intent in imposing his will in this way is to use the victim as a *means* to promote his own *ends*, regardless of the desires or interests of the victim.

This language of "means" and "ends" is, of course, familiar from one of the formulations of Kant's Categorical Imperative, the so-called Formula of Humanity: "Act so that you treat humanity, whether in your own person or in that of another, always at the same time as an end and never as a means only."[1] Those who break the moral sphere violate a similar principle as interpreted in the previous paragraph. They treat some other persons as mere means to their own ends, as does the assailant or the con man. The similarities to the Kantian principle make it instructive, I believe, to attempt to interpret "treating persons as ends" in terms of the notions of "treating with openness" and "openness respect" of Chapters 2 and 3 and to interpret "treating persons as means only" in terms of the account of "moral sphere-breaking plans of action" of the previous section. The result of such an interpretation would not, I believe, be the same as Kant's Formula of Humanity, for reasons to be discussed. But the differences from Kant's principle (as well as the similarities to it) are instructive.

If we attempt such an interpretation, "treating persons as ends" could appropriately be interpreted as "according persons respect in the sense of openness," as defined at the end of Chapter 3. Adapting that definition gives us the following:

To *treat persons as ends* (=to accord them *respect in the sense of openness*) is to treat persons with openness to the degree that one can do so while maintaining a moral sphere in which all persons can be treated with openness by all others, and to do this as a way of allowing persons to show by how they plan to live in relation to others that they are worthy of being treated with openness by all others, including oneself.

As noted earlier, "treating with openness" in this definition has the following meaning:

To *treat persons with openness* is to allow them to pursue their ways of life and realize their desired ends ("to live and pursue happiness as they choose") without interference (without being prevented, for example, from doing so by the pursuits of others).

To treat persons as ends in this sense would thus commit one (as noted in Chapter 3) to according persons rights to life, liberty and the pursuit of happiness ("to live and pursue happiness as they choose"), but only provisionally – up to the point where the moral sphere breaks down.

[1] Kant 1959: 47.

"Treating persons as *means only*" could then be interpreted in terms of the *moral sphere-breaking plans of action* of the previous section. Such an interpretation has the advantage of allowing one to make an important distinction, in the spirit of Kant, between "treating persons as means" (simpliciter) and "treating persons as means *only*" or "as a *mere* means." Treating persons as means (simpliciter) would involve satisfying *condition (i)* of the account of moral sphere-breaking plans of action of Section 3:

To *treat persons as means* is to impose one's will on them, or make them do or undergo what one wants, whatever their desires, interests, concerns or purposes might be in the matter.

Treating persons "as means *only*" or "as *mere* means" would, by contrast, involve satisfying both *conditions (i) and (ii)* of moral sphere-breaking plans and would therefore be equivalent to "engaging in moral sphere-breaking plans of action" or "breaking the moral sphere":

To *treat persons as means only* or as *mere means* (=to engage in *moral sphere-breaking plans of action* or to *break the moral sphere*) is (i) to treat persons as means in the above sense (ii) in situations where one is *not* doing what one can do to maintain a moral sphere in which all persons can be treated with openness by all others.

One may then treat persons as means (simply) without necessarily engaging in moral sphere-breaking plans of action. Such is the case of the police or retreatants, who attempt to thwart the plans of assailants or persecuting neighbors. They "impose their wills" on those they are thwarting and thus treat them as means, but not as means *only* or as *mere* means, so long as by so acting, they are "doing what they can do to maintain a moral sphere in which all persons can be treated with openness by all others."

## 4. KANT, KORSGAARD, AND THE SUPPOSED RIGHT TO LIE FOR ALTRUISTIC MOTIVES

I am not claiming these are the meanings Kant gives to "treating persons as ends" or "as means only" in his Formula of Humanity. Indeed, there are several reasons for thinking the meanings are not Kant's, despite some superficial similarities. Kant's idea is that humans are to be treated as "ends in themselves" because they are rational beings or persons capable of acting on principles that they legislate for themselves. As self-legislating or autonomous agents (i.e., persons) capable of freely choosing their own ends and the principles on which they shall act, humans have an ultimate worth for Kant that must be respected in all situations.

By contrast, "treating persons as ends" in the sense of openness respect just defined, while it imposes constraints on one's behavior toward others, involves keeping an open mind about who is ultimately worthy of being allowed to pursue plans or action or ways of life without interference. Indeed, the purpose of treating all persons as ends, or respecting them in the sense of openness, is to allow persons to show by how they plan to live whether they are worthy of the recognition or consideration of being treated with openness that was initially accorded to them. Having a rational nature or being a self-legislating or autonomous agent alone is not enough to make persons worthy of such consideration. It depends on how persons *exercise* their rational nature and autonomy – on what ends or purposes they choose to pursue and on what principles they choose to act.

As a consequence, the requirement to "treat all persons as ends and no one as means only," interpreted in terms of the preceding definitions, would allow exceptions to common moral rules, "Don't lie," "Don't cheat," Don't coerce," "Keep your promises," and the like. When assailants, pirates, Gestapo, persecuting neighbors, etc., treat others as "mere means" – or, equivalently, when they "engage in moral sphere-breaking plans of action" or "break the moral sphere" – they make it impossible for others to allow them to pursue their ways of life without interference while allowing all others to pursue their ways of life as well. They may then be treated as means in the interests of restoring and preserving the moral sphere.

Note, however, that when interpreted in this way, the general requirement to "treat all persons as ends and no one as means only" would not itself have exceptions. It would be a universal requirement. But it would entail that *common moral rules*, such as "Don't lie" and "Don't steal," have exceptions. By contrast, whether Kant's Formula of Humanity and other versions of his Categorical Imperative allow exceptions to such common moral rules is a much-disputed issue in Kant scholarship. There are certainly passages in Kant's writings where he seems to be arguing that exceptions to such common rules are not allowed, most clearly in his much-discussed essay "On the Supposed Right to Lie from Altruistic Motives."[2] It is instructive to compare what Kant says in this essay about treating all persons as ends with the interpretation of that requirement given here in terms of openness.

In a penetrating article on Kant's essay about lying, Christine Korsgaard (1998) concedes that it does seem to be Kant's meaning in this essay that the Formula of Humanity allows no exceptions on lying. Kant offers as

---

[2] Kant 1976.

an example in the essay an original version of the Gestapo example of Chapter 2. A murderer comes to the door and asks whether a person, whom you know to be the murderer's intended victim, is hiding in your home. Kant says (to the dismay of Korsgaard and other sympathetic readers of Kant) that you are obligated not to lie (out of "altruistic motives") even in such a case. In defense of this conclusion, Kant says:

After you have honestly answered the murderer's question about whether his intended victim is at home, it may be that he [the intended victim] has slipped out so that he does not come in the way of the murderer and thus that the murder may not be committed. But if you had lied and said he was not at home when he had really gone out without your knowing it, and if the murderer had then met him as he went away and murdered him, you might justly be accused as the cause of his death. For if you had told the truth as far as you knew it, perhaps the murderer might have been apprehended by the neighbors while he searched the house and thus the deed might have been prevented. (1976: 348)

As Korsgaard notes, Kant seems to be saying in this passage that if you lie and the murder is committed anyway as a result of the lie because of a series of unlikely events, then you are partly responsible and share the blame due to your lie. But if you follow the requirement of (perfect) duty never to lie in this instance, things *may* turn out well after all by a series of coincidences (however unlikely). And if things do *not* turn out well, and the murder is committed, you have at least done your duty by telling the truth and so are not to blame for the bad consequences.

Korsgaard is troubled by Kant's reasoning in this essay and she thinks his view must be modified in some way to avoid his conclusion. She wisely comments that, on Kant's approach in the essay,

Your share of the way the world is well-defined and limited, and if you act as you ought, bad outcomes are not your responsibility. The trouble is that in cases such as that of the murderer at the door it seems grotesque simply to say that I have done my part by telling the truth and the bad results are not my responsibility. (p. 300)

This feature of Kant's deontological morality has troubled many readers of Kant (sympathetic and unsympathetic), as it troubles Korsgaard. Defenders of Kant have tried to respond to it in various ways. It is hard to believe that you are not in any way responsible for the outcome, if you tell the truth to the murderer at the door and the *most likely* result (the murder) does in fact occur. Yet, Korsgaard concedes that Kant's Formula of Humanity can lead to this conclusion because, as she puts it, "the formula of humanity gives us reason to believe that all lies are wrong" (p. 293).

Why is this so? The formula says that you should "Act so that you treat humanity, whether in your own person or that of another, *always* as an end and never as a means only." And, as Korsgaard notes, to treat the "humanity" in a person as an end is to respect that person's rational nature and the person's "capacity to determine ends through rational choice" (p. 287). When you lie to others or coerce them in order to realize some end or purpose of your own, you make it impossible for them to freely *choose* whether or not to "assent to" and go along with your purposes.

If the woman who was conned into investing in a fraudulent scheme had known of the con man's purpose, she would not have assented. But he deceived her, thereby taking away her freedom to choose whether or not to go along with his true purpose. He thereby treated her humanity (her capacity to determine her ends through rational choice) as mere means to his ends. Similarly, the coercer "makes" the coerced person do as he wants, thus treating the coerced person's humanity as a means to the coercer's ends. But, as Korsgaard notes, the Formula of Humanity seems to say that you can never do this: "Act so that you treat humanity, whether in your own person or that of another, *always* as an end and never as a means only." The imperative is after all a *categorical* imperative. And this seems to imply that one must tell the truth to the murderer as well, or one will not be treating *his* humanity "as an end" but "as a means only."

What has gone wrong in this reasoning may, I think, be explained as follows. Korsgaard and other contemporary Kantians plausibly argue that the basic theory of value underlying Kant's Formula of Humanity (and perhaps all Kant's formulations of the Categorical Imperative) is that "your rational nature is the source of justifying power of your reasons and so of the goodness of your ends" (p. 293). But, even if we grant this claim (as many of Kant's critics would not), so that every good end is so because it is a chosen end of some rational being, the converse would not follow (as Korsgaard and other Kantians would surely agree). That is, it would not follow that every chosen end of a rational agent is thereby a *good* end.

Rational nature and free choice may indeed be good things, as Kant holds, and a source of other goodness. But persons can exercise their rational nature and free choice to choose bad ends as well as good ends. So it would not follow (even if we were to grant that rational nature is "the source of the goodness of ends") that we must treat persons as ends in themselves by virtue of their rational nature and capacity for choice *irrespective of the plans of action and purposes* they actually choose to pursue by employing their rational nature. To tell the truth to the murderer at the door out of respect for his humanity or rational nature, even though he has used that rational nature to choose an evil end, is grotesque, as Korsgaard says. It is, one might say, a kind of "idolatry of reason."

## 5. THE ENDS PRINCIPLE: IDEAL
### AND NON-IDEAL THEORY

Korsgaard is not happy with this feature of Kant's view for good reasons. So she suggests that Kant's view must be modified by adding special principles for "dealing with evil" (p. 282). Her suggestion involves appealing to a distinction, which she borrows from John Rawls, between *ideal theory* and *non-ideal theory* in ethics. The Formula of Humanity tells us how to behave in an ideal world (something like a Kingdom of Ends) in which no one is choosing evil ends. But in the real world where people do sometimes choose evil we need other principles – a non-ideal theory – to tell us how to behave. Korsgaard does not attempt to give a systematic account of what non-ideal theory would involve beyond suggesting the need for it to supplement Kant's theory. But I think in suggesting it she is on the right track. Though I would argue that pursuing this suggestion would take us farther away from a distinctively Kantian ethics than she and other Kantians would perhaps like.

For it is worth noting that just such a distinction between *ideal* and *non-ideal* theory in ethics follows from the arguments of Chapters 2 and 3. We can see this if, as those arguments suggest, we substitute for the Formula of Humanity an alternative principle that makes use of the definitions of "treating persons as ends" and "as means only" of Section 3 of this chapter. The resulting principle would not be the same as Kant's Formula of Humanity, as I indicated, though it would be couched in similar language. To avoid any confusion on the matter, therefore, I will give this alternative principle its own name and will hereafter call it the

*Ends Principle* (*EP*): "Treat all persons as ends in every situation, and no one as means only (or as mere means)."

The key terms in this principle have the meanings given them in Section 3, which I repeat here in summary fashion for convenience.

To *treat persons as ends* (or with *respect in the sense of openness*) is to treat them with openness ("to allow them to pursue their ways or life without interference") to the degree that one can do so while maintaining a moral sphere in which all persons can be treated with openness by all others, and to do this as a way of allowing persons to show by how they plan to live in relation to others that they are worthy of being treated with openness by all others, including oneself.

To *treat persons as means only* or as *mere means* (=to engage in *moral sphere-breaking plans of action* or to *break the moral sphere*) is (i) to impose one's will on persons, or make them do or undergo what one wants, whatever their desires, interests, concerns or purposes might be in the matter (ii) in situations where one is *not* doing what one can do to maintain a moral sphere in which all persons can be treated with openness by all others.

When "treating as ends" and "treating as means only" are so interpreted, the above Ends Principle allows for a distinction between ideal and non-ideal ethical theory along the following lines:

*Ideal Theory* would apply *when the moral sphere obtains* ("inside" the moral sphere) and would require that we "treat all persons with openness" (allowing them to pursue their ways of life without interference) and not "break that moral sphere" which does obtain by "engaging in moral sphere-breaking plans of action."

*Non-ideal Theory* would apply *when the moral sphere has broken down* and would require that we do what we can do to maintain a moral sphere in which all persons can be treated with openness by all others to the degree possible, restoring it when it has broken down and departing as little as possible from the ideal of treating all persons with openness, when we must depart from that ideal to some degree, no matter what we do.

Viewed in this way, the Ends Principle ("Treat all persons as ends in every situation and no one as means only") would be an analogue (though only an analogue) of Kant's Formula of Humanity; and the moral sphere (the sphere in which everyone *can* treat everyone else with openness) would be an analogue (though only an analogue) of Kant's ideal Kingdom of Ends. Moreover, it would be by making efforts to maintain this ideal sphere to the degree possible when it has broken down that we would learn how to act in non-ideal circumstances. Principles of non-ideal theory would require us to depart as little as possible from conditions in which all persons can be treated with openness by all others when we must depart from such conditions to some degree.[3] Thus conceived, principles of *ideal* and *non-ideal* ethical theory would both follow from the general requirement to "treat all persons as ends in every situation and no one as means only."

In the remainder of the chapter, I want to consider further what specific principles of non-ideal theory would be, if viewed in this way.

## 6. NON-IDEAL THEORY WITH AND WITHOUT GUILTY PARTIES

Since non-ideal theory concerns how we should proceed when the moral sphere breaks down, one central principle of non-ideal theory has already emerged in the arguments thus far. When the moral sphere breaks down, "Restrain or stop the guilty parties (those whose plans are moral

---

[3] Korsgaard makes a similar suggestion (1998: 297) and again I believe she is right.

sphere-breaking), not the innocent," where "restraining or stopping the guilty" means interfering with or thwarting those who would break the moral sphere in the pursuit of their plans of action and ways of life.

This requirement leads to a question, however, that has not been previously addressed: Must there always *be* a guilty party when the moral sphere breaks down? The answer, as it turns out, is no; and the question thus forces us to delve more deeply into the nature of moral sphere breakdown and the requirements of non-ideal theory. When moral sphere breakdown occurs, it may simply be the case that there are *conflicts of interests*, such that all parties cannot have all their desires, interests or purposes fulfilled, though none is yet guilty of using others as mere means. "The ends of human beings are many," as Isaiah Berlin has said, "and they often come in conflict with one another."[4] Two nations may have reasonable claims to the same piece of land. One man wants to practice the trumpet all afternoon while his neighbor wants to sleep. A husband would like to play golf while his wife wants him to mow the lawn.

Strictly speaking, the moral sphere has broken down in such situations, since the desired ends or purposes of both parties cannot be realized, no matter what is done. Yet neither side may *yet* be guilty, if no one has thus far decided to "impose his or her will on the others, whatever the desires, interests or purposes of the others may be." It would be a different story if one nation decided to take the land by force, or the neighbor went to his next-door neighbor with the intention of destroying the trumpet. These would be moral sphere-breaking plans of action. Such disputes may come to that, if other options fail. But prior to that point, the parties merely have conflicts of interests, all of which cannot be satisfied.

What does the preceding account of moral sphere breakdown have to say about conflicts of interests of such kinds, when there is as yet no discernible guilty party? For the two parties (persons or groups) involved in the conflict, say the trumpeter and his neighbor, to "treat each other as ends," according to the Ends Principle, would mean "doing what they can do to maintain a moral sphere in which each is treated with openness by the other." That in turn would imply that each should do what he can to allow the other to pursue his way of life and realize his desired ends (the trumpeter to practice, the neighbor to sleep) to the degree possible in resolving the conflict. The ideal solution would therefore be for them to reach a compromise to which both can voluntarily (i.e., knowingly and non-coercively) consent – a compromise in which neither "imposes

---

[4] Berlin 1965: xl.

his will on the other, or makes the other do what he wants, whatever the desires, interests or purposes of the other may be in the situation." The trumpeter might agree to practice only during hours when the neighbor is not sleeping. The two nations might agree to a negotiated settlement in which the disputed land is divided between them; and the husband may consent to mow the lawn if he can play golf tomorrow. To do so in each case would be what it would mean for the parties in such conflict situations to "treat each other as ends and not as means only," as the Ends Principle would require.

But we know that many real-world conflicts of interest are not so ideally resolved. Often it is not possible to split the disputed objects, like a piece of land or pieces of a pie, or to reach compromises that will satisfy all parties. The biblical story of King Solomon and the baby claimed by two women was meant to remind us of this truth. (Suggesting the baby be cut in half was no ideal solution, but a means of revealing the true mother.) In addition, parties involved in conflict situations often cannot resolve them face to face; emotions run deep or suspicions may exist that others are not bargaining in good faith.

In such cases, we usually resort to "second-best strategies" for resolving conflicts of interests – third-party arbitrators, judges, juries, majority vote, choosing by lot, and other procedural methods, private, legal and political. These second-best strategies will often produce less than ideal solutions. Yet they may be ethically justified, on the above account, to the extent that they depart as little as possible from a moral sphere in which all persons are treated with respect (in the sense of openness) in non-ideal circumstances in which all cannot pursue their ways of life and realize their desired ends to the degree that they would wish.

Majority vote as a method of settling conflicts in social and political contexts is instructive in this regard. A vote of the majority will produce an unhappy minority that does not have its desired ends or purposes fulfilled; so it is not an ideal solution. But democratic theorists tell us that in many real-world situations, majority vote is the fairest procedure one can devise for settling many disputes. For it respects the voice of each party equally in deciding which view will prevail, when one view must prevail over others, no matter what is done. When such situations arise, majority vote departs as little as possible from the ideal of treating all persons with openness, when the desired ends of all persons cannot be fully realized. Of course, even where this is true, we would be talking about majority vote under fair voting conditions – no fraud or manipulation of the results to favor one outcome, and so on. Any such fraud or manipulation would involve one group "imposing its will on others, whatever the desires, interests or purposes of those others might be in the matter."

## 7. NON-IDEAL THEORY CONTINUED: LIFE-BOAT SCENARIOS

Additional examples of conflict situations further illustrate the goal of departing as little as possible from the ideal of treating all parties with openness when the moral sphere has broken down without a guilty party. Particularly instructive are examples of "life-boat scenarios," which are familiar in discussions of ethics. After a disaster at sea, ten persons find themselves on a life-raft that can support only eight. Or, five men find themselves on a disabled airplane with only four parachutes and the parachutes will not support more than one man. The moral sphere has badly broken down in such situations, since the desires and purposes of all parties cannot be realized, no matter what is done. (We assume they all want to live.) Yet no one of the parties is guilty, if the disasters were accidental and no person involved was responsible. The world has simply turned rotten for these people through no fault of their own.

Consider the five men on the airplane with four parachutes. What should they do? They might, of course, fight over the parachutes and settle the matter by force. But, while it may come to that eventually, the question is: What "ethical" or "moral" options are available to them before force prevails? An answer is provided by the idea that guides us in other cases of moral sphere breakdown: Depart as little as possible from a moral sphere in which all persons can be treated with openness by all others, when the ends or purposes of all parties (to live in this case) cannot be fulfilled, no matter what one does. A number of possibilities are suggested by this criterion in the present case.

Suppose, for example, that one of the five men were to volunteer to sacrifice himself and become a hero to save the others. Though such sacrifice is not required (since respecting each in the sense of openness means respecting their freedom to choose) our intuitions suggest that it would lead to an ethically favorable solution. Why? Note that if someone did voluntarily take this heroic step, *the moral sphere would be immediately restored* because everyone would now be allowed to pursue their ends or purposes without interference – staying alive in the case of the four who would now have their parachutes and freely choosing a heroic course in the case of the volunteer. If the volunteer's choice was genuinely voluntary and un-coerced, then no one would be "imposing his will on the others." In this way, heroic acts may restore the moral sphere when the world has deteriorated to such a degree that maintaining the ideal of openness to all is at its most difficult. Heroism is more than duty requires – it is supererogatory – yet it may *serve the ethical ideal* in many circumstances by restoring and preserving the moral sphere when it has broken down.

Suppose, however, that in the case of the disabled airplane, the heroic solution is not available. No one volunteers to sacrifice himself. What then? One suggestion that naturally comes to mind is that, if time permits, the men should draw lots to see who will get the parachutes. In the absence of other clear options, this suggestion has merit. But we should try to understand why it has merit. While someone is going to die unwillingly, if they all want to live, choosing by lot means that all will be treated equally in deciding who it will be. By deciding in this way, the men would therefore come as close as they can to maintaining a moral sphere among them in which all are treated with openness by all others, since each would have an equal chance of having his purposes fulfilled, when they must depart from this ideal to some degree. Centuries ago, Aristotle noted that choosing by lot would be the fairest solution to some difficult social and political problems that could not be fairly resolved in any other way. Our reasoning supports this claim.

Suppose finally that in this downward spiral of events, the men on the airplane do draw lots and the loser refuses to abide by the outcome. What then? It appears they have now reached a stage at which force is all that remains. If the lottery loser tries to grab one of the parachutes by force, the other four are justified in subduing and restraining him. But this is the case because they have reached a point where, by following such a procedure to decide who would survive, they have done as much as they can do in the circumstances to maintain the ideal of a moral sphere in which all persons can be treated with openness by all others.

It is important to recall in this connection the retreatants' requirement of Chapter 3 – that the only thing which gives one the right to forcibly impose one's will on others is that one has tried one's hardest not to. This constraint, which the retreatants' imposed on themselves by taking an attitude of openness to all persons, can now be seen to be related to a general principle of non-ideal theory: In non-ideal circumstances of moral sphere breakdown *with a guilty party or not*, it is the persistent striving to maintain to the degree possible a moral sphere in which all persons can be treated with openness by all others that guides one in the search for the ethically correct answer.

## 8. LEVELS OF THE MORAL SPHERE: MIGHT AND RIGHT, WAR AND PEACE

These results may be summarized in a simple diagram.

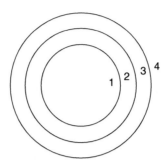

The inner circle (1) represents the moral sphere in which all persons can be treated with openness by all others. Circle 2 represents situations of the kind just considered where the moral sphere has broken down without a guilty party, including conflicts of interest; and circle 3 represents situations of moral sphere breakdown *with* a guilty party. Finally, level 4 represents the point where ethical options have been exhausted and force prevails, as when the lottery loser on the plane refuses to abide by the result and must be subdued by the others.

Level 4 represents the most morally degraded of conditions, which Hobbes called the "state of nature" – a state of war of "all against all" in which no moral laws obtain.[5] No further circle is drawn around 4 because it is not strictly speaking a *moral* sphere at all, as Hobbes suggests. Whereas in the inner three circles, we retain a measure of respect for the ideal moral sphere, at level 4 the world is reduced to a point where we have lost it altogether. Imagine the situation in this way: As we move outward from the center in the diagram, the moral condition of the world gets worse, but the ethical goal remains the same – to try to restore and preserve as much of the original ideal of a moral sphere in which all persons can be treated with openness by all (circle 1) as is possible in deteriorating circumstances until we no longer can (level 4).

I noted in Chapter 2 that pacifism might be the right view if the moral sphere never broke down, if we were always in circle 1. We may now add that the opposite doctrine of "might-makes-right" might be correct in

---

[5] Hobbes 1958: chapter 13.

many instances, if a Hobbesian state of nature always prevailed, if the world were always at level 4. But we are not always at either of these levels. When the moral sphere breaks down, it is not the case that one is thrown immediately into level 4 where "anything goes" or "might makes right." To the extent that one continues to be guided by the ideal of a moral sphere in non-ideal circumstances, moral constraints emerge between levels 1 and 4, such as restraining the guilty (those whose life-plans are moral sphere-breaking) rather than the innocent, and seeking the fairest resolution of conflicts – constraints that one should seek to satisfy before the state of nature prevails.

Viewing the matter in this way suggests another principle of non-ideal theory: "When the moral sphere breaks down, use minimal force to restore and preserve it." The assailant in the alley whose life-plan broke the moral sphere should be restrained. But neither the passers-by nor the police have the right to shoot the assailant through the heart, if he can be subdued with less force. What is the rationale for such a requirement? By using minimum force to restore and preserve the moral sphere, we accord to the guilty party as much *residual* recognition in the form of openness as we can, consistent with the fact that we must restrain him. And doing that is a further example of departing as little as possible from the ideal of a moral sphere in which all are treated with openness when that ideal cannot be perfectly realized. Similarly, prison inmates retain some rights and should be treated with some measure of the recognition required by treating them as ends, even as they have forfeited the full measure of such recognition.

Consider as further illustration of these principles the rules of just warfare embodied in international conventions, such as the Hague and Geneva conventions. One can see operating behind these familiar conventions of warfare the two rules we have identified for moral sphere breakdown at level 3 of the diagram: "Restrain the guilty, not the innocent" and "Use minimum force to restore and preserve the moral sphere." The first rule is exemplified by Geneva conventions against harming innocent non-combatants and indiscriminate saturation bombing of civilian populations, among many other restrictions. The second rule is exemplified by rules protecting prisoners of war or mandating medical care for captured enemy soldiers, among many other requirements. Both these rules ("Restrain the guilty, not the innocent ..." and "Use minimum force ...") are consequences, as we have seen, of striving to maintain the moral sphere to the degree possible in non-ideal circumstances. *Innocent* non-combatants are to be treated with as much recognition of their desired ends (staying alive, not being harmed) and combatants are to be treated with as much *residual* recognition of their desired ends as is consistent with the needs of battle.

What happens if *both* (or multiple) parties are guilty? What if both of two warring nations are guilty of being overly aggressive in settling their dispute or if different factions in a civil war are both brutalizing each other and innocent civilians? (These are more extreme cases of level 3 breakdowns, i.e., breakdowns with a guilty party.) The goal that is consistent with prior reasoning in such cases would be to try to restore the ideals of fair conflict resolution like those of circle 2. In other words, attempt to return, if possible, to a level closer to the moral center (circle 1) – from level 3 to level 2. Not surprisingly, fair conflict resolution is more problematic and difficult when there are many guilty parties than when none is yet guilty. But the goal is the same – resolution of conflict that respects all parties in the sense of openness to the degree possible.

With this in mind, familiar methods suggest themselves. One might try to talk the parties (warring nations, factions in civil war) into a voluntary cease-fire, to cool down emotions. Then one might try to get them to sit down with each other at the negotiating table. If face-to-face negotiation fails because of distrust or lack of bargaining in good faith, one might try third-party arbitrators or judges (i.e., second-best strategies). These are common diplomatic procedures. But we can also recognize them as ethically justified efforts for good reasons, however difficult they may be to carry out in practice. For they all involve staying as close as possible to the ideal of a moral sphere in which all parties are treated with openness to the degree possible under extremely difficult conditions.

If each of these successive efforts fails, the situation edges closer to level 4 where force may become the only option. At a certain point, other nations may have to stand back and let warring factions fight while taking what steps they can to protect innocent non-combatants. Or, other nations might try to impose a cease-fire by force, if they have the power to do so without unreasonable costs and without causing more bloodshed than would otherwise occur – especially if such a cease-fire were a prelude to subsequent negotiations between the warring parties themselves.

Imposition of force by other nations is fraught with practical and long-term political dangers, as we know from the history of the past century; and it should be engaged in with great caution. Yet it may often be ethically justified. Similar practical and political obstacles attend humanitarian interventions within nations, where one group is brutally persecuting others, even though humanitarian interventions can also be ethically justified in principle by the above reasoning. But it should not be surprising that moral sphere breakdowns with many guilty parties would be more difficult to resolve than those without guilty parties, and many such conflicts may not be resolvable at all without bloodshed. Yet the ethical goals remain the same, even in such degraded conditions – to try to restore and preserve the moral sphere to the degree possible.

## 9. NON-VIOLENCE AND "EXPERIMENTS WITH TRUTH"

Such goals also tell us something important, in conclusion, about the ethical significance of non-violence movements, pioneered in the twentieth century by figures such as Mohandas Gandhi and Martin Luther King. Humans are prone to assume too quickly that the moral sphere has broken down and prone to leap to violence too soon as a means of resolving conflicts. We often use more force when less force will do. But how can we know how much force is needed unless we are willing to experiment with less? Non-violence movements may teach us how to experiment with less. It is noteworthy that when Gandhi undertook his efforts to make the British relinquish control in India without resort to violent revolution, he tellingly referred to his practices of non-violence as his "experiments with truth."[6] (*Satyagraha* is the Sanskrit term, which literally means "truth-force.")

This idea of *practical* "experiments with truth" is especially important for the argument of the past three chapters in which the motivation for striving to maintain the moral sphere to the degree possible in an imperfect world is to discover the objective truth about values. If we need scientific experimentation for technological progress, then why not moral experimentation for moral progress? What would be meant by "moral progress" in this context, by contrast with technological or other kinds of progress, is expanding the moral sphere (circle 1) so that it encompasses more areas of life – so that more conflicts can be settled by persuasion rather than by coercion.

It is instructive to think of the moral sphere in general as the sphere of *persuasion*, in contrast to *coercion* (which comes into play when the moral sphere breaks down). But this would not be accurate if the category of persuasion includes the manipulative persuasion that is so common in modern societies through political spin doctoring, public relations, propaganda and other means. For the goal of such manipulative persuasion is

[6] Gandhi, Selections in Somerville and Santoni 1963: 500–10.

usually to impose the persuaders' wills on others, and often, in doing so, to use others as a "mere means" to the persuaders' ends. In contrast to such manipulative persuasion, a useful expression for the kind of persuasion intended in the moral sphere is the Quaker expression *friendly persuasion* – a persuasion that respects the values, purposes and ways of life of others, allowing them to freely choose from their own points of view. By saying moral progress lies in expanding the moral sphere, so that more conflicts are settled by persuasion rather than coercion, we mean friendly persuasion in this sense.

Viewed from this perspective, non-violence movements like those of Gandhi and King are among the most important moral experiments of modern times. They contribute to moral progress by showing that we often use more force when less will do, so that non-coercive methods can work in areas of life where they were never previously thought possible. The moral sphere is thereby expanded beyond where it had been before.

### 10. SUMMARY: MORAL SPHERE THEORY (MST)

In summary, non-ideal theory would deal with moral sphere breakdown and how we should proceed when the moral sphere breaks down. So conceived, it may be viewed in terms of the diagram of nested circles at the beginning of Section 8, which describes levels of moral sphere breakdown, with guilty parties and without. Principles of non-ideal theory would emerge at these different levels: "Restrain the guilty, not the innocent" and "Use the minimum force necessary to restore the moral sphere," when there is a guilty party (level 3); and where there are conflicts of interest, but as yet no guilty parties (level 2), "Try to find as fair a compromise as possible, to which all parties can voluntarily consent." Or, where such compromise is not possible, "Try to find second-best strategies that will respect the interests, concerns and purposes of all parties to the degree possible."

All such principles of non-ideal theory (and others mentioned when there is more than one guilty party) are guided by a unifying goal: Striving to depart as little as possible from the ideal moral sphere in which all persons can be treated with openness by all others (circle 1), when one must depart from this ideal to some degree. It is this unifying goal that makes non-ideal theory an ethical *theory* rather than a collection of ad hoc pronouncements. The same goal also makes non-ideal theory a natural extension of ideal theory since both follow from the Ends Principle ("Treat all persons as ends in every situation and no one as means only") which requires maintaining the moral sphere *to the degree that one can* in every situation.

In subsequent chapters, I will refer to the theory developed in the past three chapters as a "moral sphere theory" of the right, or right action. While the theory has been developed in this chapter beyond its initial statements in Chapters 2 and 3, it is still not a complete ethical theory, much less a complete theory of the good. The next four chapters will attempt to situate it in a broader account of value or the good.

# CHAPTER 5

## *Fact and value*

### I. DIMENSIONS OF VALUE

This chapter and the three following begin the task of situating the argument of Chapters 2–4 in a broader theory of value and eventually in a theory of philosophical inquiry. This task will involve, among other things, considering yet another of Hegel's "sunderings" of modernity cited in Chapter 1 – the sundering of *fact* from *value*.

Let us suppose the retreatants of Chapter 3 have gone through all the reasoning of the previous chapters, when skeptical members among them rise to make the following objection.

"We have been talking about being open to other ways of life in order to find the objective truth about values and have learned much in the process. We have arrived at some ethical principles that are shared by many of our respective traditions and have agreed on the conclusion that some ways of life are less worthy than others of our unqualified respect in the sense of openness. But these results cannot be the whole story of what we came here to learn. For suppose we strive to create a moral sphere in which all persons can be treated with openness and in which we are allowed to pursue our ways of life without interference from others. These measures alone would not tell us how we should go about living our lives in other respects. They will not tell us, except in a very general way, what sorts of lives we should live; and so they do not give us a complete answer to the question of what "the good life" is. Nor do they show which of our differing points of view about value and differing ways of life is the right one or whether our own view is the right one. Yet these are the things we came here to determine. Our task is not complete."

Indeed, their task is far from complete. You might say the retreatants have at best arrived only at a fragment of a theory of value or the good. They have arrived at what some persons would call an account of *moral* or *ethical* value that concerns "how we should treat one other" or, in T. M. Scanlon's expression, "what we owe to each other." But that is neither a complete theory of the good nor a complete account of "how we should live." (I shall argue later that it is not even a complete account of moral or ethical value, though it represents an important part of what we call moral or ethical value.[1])

To seek such a complete theory of the good or the good life, the retreatants would also have to consider what other goods and ends are worth pursuing – beauty? truth? happiness? among many others; and they would have to ask themselves the question: In what do these other goods consist? W. H. Auden once wryly remarked that we were put on this Earth to help other people. He then added "what those other people were put here for, I don't know."[2] There is more than humor in this remark. If morals or ethics concerned only how we should treat one another or what we owe to each other, then it would be far from a complete theory of the good, much less a complete guide to life.

A number of philosophers, including Bernard Williams (1985), have noted the tendency in modern times to think of morality in this narrow way – as a matter of obligations or duties we have towards ourselves and others; and they have contrasted this view with that of the ancient philosophers who meant by the study of ethics an inquiry into the nature of the good and the good life generally. The questions of the ancients were not only "What obligations or duties do we have to each other?" but "How should we live?" "What should we strive for?" "What is the best form of life?" "What ends or goals are ultimately worth pursuing?" Similarly, the retreatants in their search for wisdom about which of their ways of life is best are seeking an answer to these broader questions. In this respect, their inquiry is incomplete. But how should it go forward?

To go further, one must address questions about the nature of value or the good in general; and this task, I shall argue, is not one that can be accomplished in one fell swoop.[3] I suggest that we first need to take seriously Aristotle's claim that "'good' is said in many ways." The notion of value, I shall argue, is no simple thing with a single definition. The good has multiple dimensions each of which has to be understood before one can adequately address the question of what the good life is. To begin the task, I will argue in this chapter and the next three that we consider human value in four dimensions. Each higher dimension of value would include, but go beyond, lower dimensions as, say, a three-dimensional space includes two-dimensional surfaces and one-dimensional lines. This

[1] See Chapters 7, 12, 15.
[2] From a lecture at Yale University, March 1963.
[3] For excellent overviews of the issues about value that I will be addressing, see Schroeder 2008 and Chappell 1995, as well as the essays in Honderich 1985.

spatial metaphor is crude, but we shall see that it is instructive. The first three dimensions of value are familiar to us, as are the three familiar dimensions of space, while the fourth dimension of value is more elusive, though no less important.

### 2. THE FIRST DIMENSION: BASIC VALUE EXPERIENCES

The first dimension of value is *experiential*. Spinoza pointed us in the right direction, I believe, when he noted that our first encounter with good and evil is through experiences of certain characteristic kinds, such as joy (*laetitia*) and sadness (*tristitia*).[4] (One does not have to accept Spinoza's entire theory of value, much less his metaphysics, as I will not, to make use of some of his prescient insights about these experiences, or "affects" of the mind, as he calls them, in Books III and IV of his *Ethics*.[5]) Let us call positive experiences of these characteristic kinds (such as joy) "basic value experiences" and the negative ones (such as sadness) "basic disvalue experiences." Basic value experiences would include joy, delight, amusement, pride, sensory pleasure, enjoyment, comfort, exhilaration, romantic love, contentment, ecstasy, and the like, while basic disvalue experiences would include sadness, loneliness, frustration, pain, boredom, grief, humiliation, anxiety, embarrassment, fear, disappointment, despair, and others.

We may think of these basic value and disvalue experiences as *prima facie* good or bad respectively, which is to say that they are good or bad in the first instance, *unless they are overridden in some higher dimension of value.* Thus, the delight a small child experiences when first seeing a squirrel is one thing, the delight a terrorist takes in torturing a prisoner quite another. Spinoza and many others would say that in the latter case, the delight of the torturer is not a good at all, but an evil.[6] Using our dimensional metaphor, we would say that the torturer's delight is overridden and becomes bad when viewed from a higher dimension.

Spinoza's way of describing such overriding was to say that many of our ordinary experiences of joy or delight, such as the torturer's, are based

---

[4] Spinoza 1996: 76–77 (originally published 1677).

[5] Among my departures is that Spinoza believes all experiential goods are ultimately only apparent goods (involving "confused" perceptions). I will argue that experiential goods need not all be merely apparent.

[6] For excellent discussions of these issues, with views differing from mine, see Lemos 1994, M. Zimmerman 2001. Other works on value that have informed my thinking in these chapters, despite differing views, include Bond 1983, Griffin 1986, Broome 1991, R. Miller 1992, Mi. Smith 1994, Sumner 1996, R. Adams 1999, Hurka 2001, Bloomfield 2001, Railton 2003, Shafer-Landau 2003, Helm 2001, Oddie 2005, Crisp 2006, Kraut 2007, Kupperman 2007.

on "inadequate" or "confused" ideas, which distract us from higher or true goods. We tend to value present goods over future ones, for example, because the present ones bring immediate joy or pleasure, even when the present goods may in truth be the cause of much greater future evils.[7] In such cases, the immediate experiential joys or pleasures are overridden when viewed from a broader perspective and become bad. I mention Spinoza's view here not to endorse its details, but to illustrate what "overriding" of experiential values would be like. Claims about overriding must be justified by some arguments or other; and such arguments will be considered when we consider higher dimensions of value.

But why are these basic value experiences viewed by many persons as initially good (or bad) so long as they are *not* overridden? Spinoza again provides a clue when he notes that our first encounter with good and evil is through basic value and disvalue experiences and we initially learn what good and evil mean in terms of them. "The knowledge of good and evil," he says, "is nothing but an affect of joy or sadness, insofar as we are conscious of it."[8] We might say that basic value experiences (such as the child's delight at seeing the squirrel) are like windows through which value first enters our human world.[9] They are the first word on good and evil, though not necessarily the last word. Friedrich Schiller made this point for basic value experiences when, in his "Ode to Joy," he called joy "the beautiful torch of the gods, daughter from Elysium." The image is of joyful moments in this life as sparks of light in an otherwise dark world, providing fleeting glimpses of the good. This was an image captured by Beethoven in his Ninth Symphony, in which Schiller's Ode was set to some of the most joyous music ever written.

In a different place and time, Siddhartha Gautama, known as the Buddha, made a similar point about basic *dis*value experiences: They are the experiences, he intimated, through which *evil* first enters our human world. Shortly after undergoing enlightenment, the Buddha enunciated "four noble truths" for his followers, the first of which was that all existence was suffering, where suffering was experiential evil in one form or another – sadness, frustration, grief, pain, loneliness, and so on. Again I want to emphasize that one does not have to accept everything these figures, such as the Buddha or Spinoza, say about value, much less their

---

[7] Spinoza 1996: 149. If our ideas were not confused, we would see things from the perspective of eternity and "the mind would want the good it conceives as future just as it wants the good it conceives as present."

[8] Ibid.: 120.

[9] I have defended such a view of these experiences in Kane 1988, 1997, 1998.

(very different) metaphysical outlooks, to appreciate their insights about value of this experiential kind: Our first intimations of good and evil come through certain characteristic basic value and disvalue experiences, such as joy and sadness, that we regard as good or bad in the first instance and are like windows through which value enters our human world. Such experiences constitute what I am calling the first or experiential dimension of value.

### 3. PRIMA FACIE, OR DEFEASIBLE, GOODS

There are several things of importance to note about value in this basic experiential dimension. First, at this elementary level, value is already *plural*. Many thinkers want to reduce all basic value and disvalue experiences to "pleasure" and "pain" respectively. But this oversimplifies these experiences. Feelings of delight, amusement and pride are quite different from each other and from the pleasures of taste or smell; yet all are basic value experiences. Boredom is not the same thing as sensory pain, nor is either quite like loneliness, humiliation or grief; yet these are all basic disvalue experiences. In short, there are different modalities of value experience, positive and negative; and it is worth emphasizing that value is pluralistic, even at this most elementary level. The inherent plurality of value is effectively defended with different qualifications by a number of recent philosophers; and I think it is important to emphasize, as some of these authors do, that plurality may extend even to this experiential level of value.[10]

A second issue of note about this experiential dimension of value concerns the question of whether the value in it is "merely subjective" or whether there is some objectivity to it as well. This is an intriguing question. For, there is an obvious sense in which basic value and disvalue experiences are subjective: They are conscious experiences that (like other conscious experiences) are directly accessible only to the subjects who have them (leaving aside unusual phenomena such as telepathy). But there is an interesting, if qualified, sense in which the value of such experiences can also be said to be objective on the above account of them. To explain this, we must consider a familiar sense in which it has sometimes been

---

[10] Kekes 1989, Stocker 1990, E. Anderson 1993, Milgram 1997, Raz 2003, among others. Berlin 1965 is a classic defense. Chang 1997 is an excellent anthology on the topic. Crisp 2006 (p. 102) argues that even hedonists should avoid the too narrow language of pleasure and pain and use the broader language of enjoyment and suffering. Mayerfeld 1999 argues in interesting ways for the moral importance of suffering broadly conceived.

claimed that all values (not merely basic value experiences) are "merely subjective."

*Subjectivism* about values in this familiar sense is the view that *there are no matters of fact in the world to which judgments or statements of the form "x is good (or bad)" or "x is right (or wrong)" correspond*, that is, no objective facts or features of the world for such judgments or statements to be *true* of. Subjectivism so understood is thus a *non-realist* or *anti-realist* view about values and there can be both cognitivist and non-cognitivist versions of it. Certain non-cognitivist versions of subjectivism, such as emotivism, insist that judgments, such as "x is good or bad," "x is right or wrong," express feelings, attitudes or sentiments (of approval or disapproval) of those making the judgments rather than claims about the world that could be true or false. Cognitivist versions – such as the "error theory" of J. L. Mackie (1977) – allow that evaluative or ethical judgments can be true or false, but insist that all such judgments are in fact false, since there are no evaluative or moral facts in the world for them to be true of.

Return now to basic value and disvalue experiences in the light of these remarks. If John experiences joy at the reception of a gift, it would be true to say that "<The experience John is now having> is (a first-dimensional) prima facie good for John." This statement is true by virtue of the nature of the experience John is having, specifically by virtue of the felt quality of that experience. If he were experiencing pain or humiliation at failing to receive a gift, rather than joy, the claim would be false.[11] So the statement is saying something true about John's experience and not merely expressing attitudes (of approval or disapproval) of those making the statement. The good ascribed to experiences in such statements is highly qualified, to be sure. But, if "good" may be said in many ways, as Aristotle noted, evaluative statements or judgments will often be qualified in various ways: "X is good (or bad) (in some respect or manner) (for some purpose) (in certain circumstances) (for some person) ..." And first-dimensional value *is* a qualified kind of value.

First, John's experience is only said to be *prima facie* good for John – good if not overridden in some higher dimension or when viewed in some broader context of John's life. It may turn out to be bad when viewed in a broader context. It is thus a *defeasible* good. Yet, in saying the experience of

---

[11] The statement would also be false if his experience were value neutral, not accompanied by any positive or negative "affect," and neither true nor false, if John were not having any experience, in which case the subject term would not refer.

joy is prima facie good, we are saying something objectively true about its *potential* or *conditional* value: The experience of joy is objectively good for John *unless* it is overridden in a higher dimension. And if the experience is not in fact overridden in a higher dimension, we are also saying something that would be true about its *actual* value: If it is not in fact overridden in any higher dimension, the experience would be objectively good for John.

It is instructive to compare the notion of a prima facie *good* in this respect to W. D. Ross's notion of a prima facie *duty*. (One does not have to endorse Ross's intuitionism about moral duties, as I do not, to see the virtues of the analogy.[12]) For Ross, the duty, say, to tell the truth, is only a prima facie duty. In cases where it may come in conflict with other prima facie duties (such as the duty of beneficence), it may be overridden. Thus, we may not need to tell the truth to the Gestapo when they come to the door, out of beneficence for the Jewish family we are protecting. Ross's intuitionist view is often criticized for not providing an adequate account of which duties should override others, and why they should do so, when prima facie duties conflict. He leaves the matter to moral intuitions. But it is the *idea* of prima facie duty that is of interest here and not Ross's intuitionist moral theory in general.

According to this idea, a prima facie duty may not in fact be our actual, all things considered, duty in certain situations when it is overridden. Yet, to say we *have* a prima facie duty, e.g., of beneficence, for Ross, is nonetheless to say something true and important *about our obligations to others*. It is to say that we have an obligation to act out of beneficence, *whenever* that obligation is not in fact overridden by some other obligation. Similarly, a basic value experience may not turn out to be an actual, all things considered, good for a person, since it may be overridden. Nonetheless, to say it is a prima facie good for a person is to say something true and important about *what is good for that person*. It is to say that the basic value experience is an objective good for that person, *when* it is in fact not overridden by other more important goods.

This point is especially important because I will argue later that, as one moves to higher dimensions of value, some basic value experiences may be overridden, but many will not be. The everyday joys and pleasures of receiving a gift or delighting in a visit to the park, and many more basic value experiences, may be significant ingredients or parts of good lives more broadly conceived. Aristotle said as much when he said that, while

---

[12] Ross's intuitionism and the views of some of its modern defenders, such as Audi 2004, McNaughton and Rawling 1998, Stratton-Lake 2000, and others, are discussed in Chapter 15.

pleasure is not the ultimate good, pleasurable experiences will normally be a part of the good life. Basic value experiences, qua prima facie and defeasible, are only the first word on value, not the last. Yet, if not overridden, they may also be significant features of the last word on value as well.

There is another, equally important, way in which value in this first experiential dimension is qualified. Basic value or disvalue experiences are also said to be good or bad *for* the subjects who have the experiences. John's joyful experience is prima facie good for John. The experience may also be good for some others as well (e.g., for those who may care about John), but that is not required insofar as the experience is merely a first-dimensional good. Value *qua* first-dimensional is thus not only prima facie, but also *relative*, value – that is, good (or bad) *for* those who have the basic value or disvalue experiences (and perhaps also for those who care about them). The experiences may turn out in some higher dimension to be more than "merely" relative values, but that question remains an open one. Values, I shall argue, may be relative (i.e., good *for* certain beings) without being "merely" relative.

In summary, values in this first experiential dimension are experiences of various kinds (basic value or disvalue experiences), such as joy and sadness, that are prima facie good or bad by virtue of their affective or felt qualities, though the experiences themselves may be directly accessible only to the subjects who have them. Every time you or anyone feels pain, the gap between fact and value has *potentially* been bridged – even if only initially *for you*. The good or evil of the experience is still only relative for you and it is prima facie, or potentially, overridable when placed in a broader context. The pain, for example, may be necessary to attain some higher good. But when not so overridden, it may be objectively bad for the being who has it.

## 4. MOORE AND THE NATURALISTIC FALLACY

One may object that these claims follow because we have defined basic value and disvalue experiences as good and bad respectively (even if only in a prima facie sense). And in doing so, it may seem that we have run afoul of G. E. Moore's well-known "naturalistic fallacy"[13] – the fallacy of defining the good in terms of natural facts. By natural facts Moore meant those that are "the subject matter of the natural sciences and also of psychology," including facts about the preservation of the species, about

[13] Moore 1903: 13.

the greatest happiness of the greatest number, about the objects of human appetites or desires and – of special interest for present purposes – about psychological experiences, such as pleasure and pain.[14]

To show it is a fallacy to define the good in such terms, Moore appealed to his well-known "open question argument," which would take the following form when applied to basic value experiences: Psychological facts about human beings, such as their experiencing joy or pleasure, cannot be good by definition. For, of any such psychological fact, such as John's now experiencing pleasure, we can know that it is a fact and yet sensibly ask "But is it really good (that John is now having such an experience)?" The answer to this question might be yes or no, depending on the circumstances – what the pleasure was taken in, what implications it might have for John's behavior, etc. Yet this question would not remain an open question, Moore argued, if such experiences were good by definition. Simply knowing that John was having such an experience would be sufficient to ensure that it was really good.

Philosophers have raised a number of potent objections to this open question argument.[15] But I want to raise a different objection here specifically related to basic value experiences. Moore's argument is pointing to something important about such experiences, but I think he draws the wrong conclusion from it. The reason the question "Is it really good?" remains open in cases of joy, pleasure, and other basic value experiences, I would argue, is that such experiences are by definition only prima facie or defeasibly good – good in the first instance, if not overridden. Their value is in principle overridable in other dimensions of value; and so they may not be "really" good in the sense of "all things considered" good. This thought is borne out by considering examples of basic value experiences where the answers to Moore's question "Is it really good?" may be negative: To say that John's experiencing joy is not good if taken in the misfortunes of others or that pleasure taken in overeating is not really good, is to say that the joy and pleasure in these cases is overridden by some greater good, such as long-term health or ethical duties to others, and it is thus not all things considered good.

Simply to say therefore that someone is having these experiences is not sufficient to ensure that they are "really" good in an all things considered sense. We need to supplement Moore's thoughts with some insights altered

[14] Ibid.
[15] Frankena 1939; Harman 1977: 19–20, among others. A. Miller (2003: chapter 2) provides an excellent overview of debates about the argument, as does Baldwin 1990.

and adapted from Spinoza. Basic value and disvalue experiences, such as joy and sadness, are prima facie good or bad because it is through such experiences that we first learn what good and evil mean; it is through them that the notions of good and evil first enter our human world. But, at the same time, such experiences are only the first word on the meaning of good and evil, because value has no single meaning. What is good *in* the first dimension may also be good in higher dimensions, but it may not be.

In this way, we may acknowledge that Moore's open question argument is pointing to something important without drawing his conclusion from it. The conclusion Moore draws is that the good is not definable in naturalistic (including experiential) terms, whereas the conclusion I think we should draw from the argument is that "good" cannot be defined *in one fell swoop*. The good must rather be defined in stages – in different dimensions, with various qualifications. If value is viewed in this way, the possibility is left open that value in some of these dimensions may be definable in naturalistic or experiential terms, even if all values are not; and this possibility of being definable in naturalistic or experiential terms would turn out to be particularly likely for the first and most elemental dimension of value through which, as Spinoza noted, we gain our first intimations of good and evil.

### 5. OPEN QUESTIONS AND GUIDANCE OF ACTION: DARWALL, GIBBARD AND RAILTON

A further advantage of looking at Moore's open question argument in this way is that one can see why the argument is important for understanding value, while acknowledging the force of certain philosophical objections to it. One such objection, made by Frankena, Harman and many others, is that the open question argument is question-begging.[16] Moore mistakenly assumed that if anything were a correct definition (e.g., "pleasure is good"), every competent speaker of the language must immediately be convinced of its truth and so would have no reason to ask "Is this experience of pleasure really good?" But if every competent speaker must immediately be convinced of the truth of any definition, it would be impossible for an *analysis* of the meaning of a term or concept to be informative, as analyses of concepts often can be. Moore's open question argument, as Harman puts it, rests on an arbitrarily narrow conception of philosophical or scientific definition.

---

[16] Frankena 1939: 465; Harman, ibid.

Yet, many prominent philosophers who acknowledge the force of such criticisms continue to believe that Moore's open question argument has something important to tell us. For example, Darwall, Gibbard and Railton, in their influential essay, "Toward a *Fin de Siecle* Ethics" (1992) concede to Moore's critics that the open question argument "rests upon an arbitrarily narrowed conception of philosophical or scientific definition" (p. 115). But they add that "it seems impossible to deny that Moore was on to something" with his open question argument. Moore, they suggest, "discovered not a proof of a fallacy, but an argumentative device that implicitly but effectively brings to the fore certain characteristic features of 'good' … that seem to stand in the way of our accepting any known naturalistic or metaphysical definition as unquestionably right" (pp. 115–16).

I think these remarks of Darwall, Gibbard and Railton point in the right direction with regard to Moore's open question argument. What is needed, they say, is an explanation of why the open question argument remains so often "compelling for otherwise competent, reflective speakers of English," even if it is not the "proof of a fallacy." The above account of basic value experiences may be viewed as providing such an explanation with regard specifically to experiential goods, such as joy, delight, enjoyment and pleasure. The reason Moore's open question "Is it really good?" so often seems appropriate for such basic value experiences is that they are only prima facie or defeasibly good; and hence they are only "really" (i.e., all things considered) good, if not overridden in some higher dimension of value.

This explanation is consonant, I believe, with Darwall, Gibbard and Railton's own suggestion as to why Moore's question "Is it really good?" so often seems appropriate. They suggest that Moore's question alerts us to the fact that "attributions of goodness have a conceptual link with the guidance of action" (p. 116).[17] For example, when persons ask of natural facts, such as experiences of pleasure, whether they are "really" good, what they are asking, according to Darwall, Gibbard and Railton, is something like the following question: "Is it clear that, other things being equal, we really ought to, or must devote ourselves to bringing about experiences of pleasure?" (p. 116). And the answer to *such* a question, they suggest, will normally be: "It depends." It depends on what persons take pleasure in (gambling? addictive drugs? torturing?), on whether the objects of pleasurable experiences are themselves good, on whether such experiences inhibit or enhance the pursuit of other long-term goals or distract from the pursuit of more important or comprehensive goods, and so on.

---

[17] Rosati (2002) also insightfully links the Open Question argument to issues about agency and guidance of action.

But, as we shall see in subsequent chapters, these are just the sorts of questions that arise when we ask whether the value of basic value experiences is or is not "overridden" in higher dimensions of value. Whether experiential goods are or are not overridden normally depends, as Darwall, Gibbard and Railton suggest, on what role such experiences play in "the guidance of action" and more generally, as I shall argue, on what role such experiences play in "plans of action" and "ways or forms of life." We pursue this and related thoughts in the next three chapters.

## 6. EPILOGUE: OVERRIDING AND INTRINSIC VALUE

Before turning to these matters, however, I want to consider one final objection that may be raised to the account of overriding presented in this chapter. It should be noted, first, that the general idea that experiences which are good in some contexts may be overridden and become bad in other contexts is not unique to this account, but is commonly expressed in the philosophical tradition. To cite examples, Aristotle says that "the pleasure proper to a morally good activity is good, the pleasure proper to a bad activity evil."[18] Thomas Aquinas says that "something may be good according to a particular judgment which is not good according to a wider judgment, and conversely."[19] Kant denies that pleasure is good when experienced by someone who lacks a good will (for example, one who takes pleasure in the misfortunes of others). And Ross holds that the pleasure experienced by persons as a result of their wicked acts is undeserved and therefore bad.[20]

This common view has occasionally been challenged, however, and a particularly instructive objection to it is made by Noah Lemos in his perceptive work, *Intrinsic Value* (1994). Lemos directs his objection against Ross, though he makes clear that it applies to all other philosophers, including those just mentioned, who make similar claims. What Ross *et al.* miss, according to Lemos, is that we can meaningfully say of the wicked man who takes pleasure in the suffering or misfortune of others that "he has a *good* that he deserves not to have" (p. 44). But this fact suggests that the wicked man's experiencing pleasure remains a good even in contexts where the pleasure is taken in the suffering or misfortune of others, rather than becoming bad, as Ross and others suggest.

This is a subtle dispute, but I think light can be thrown on it if we think of the good dimensionally. To see why, consider two facts about a sadist, call him "Sad," both of which obtain at a time t:

[18] 1983: 1175b.    [19] Aquinas 1950: vol 1, question 19, articles 6 and 10.
[20] Ross 1930: 136.

(1)   Sad experiences pleasure in torturing an innocent man.
(1*)  Sad experiences pleasure.

Ross *et al.* and Lemos do not disagree about (1). They agree that the fact
described by (1) is bad. Their disagreement is a more subtle one about the
fact described by (1*), which in Lemos' terms is a part of, or ingredient in,
the larger or "total" fact described by (1). Lemos thinks the fact described
by (1*) remains a good even when it is part of the larger fact, which is bad,
because one can meaningfully say that in (1), Sad has "a *good* (an experience of pleasure) that he deserves not to have." By contrast, Ross and others in the tradition say that Sad's experiencing pleasure (1*) in the context
of (1) is bad *because* the pleasure is undeserved. (Compare Aristotle's claim
that "the pleasure proper to a bad activity is evil.")

There are conflicting intuitions here, each of which has some weight.
But they have weight I believe because "good" and "bad" are being used
in different ways. We should remind ourselves here as elsewhere that
"'good' is said in many ways"; and if we think dimensionally about the
ways that "good" may be said, as I am suggesting, then things may be (i)
good *in a dimension* of value without being (ii) *all things considered* good.
Something is good all things considered when it is good in a dimension
of value, d, *and is not overridden* (becoming bad) *in any higher dimension*
than d. With this distinction in mind, one can meaningfully say of Sad's
experiencing pleasure (1*) in torturing an innocent man (1) both that in
this context he has "a good (a *first dimensional* good) he does not deserve
to have" and that his experiencing pleasure in this context "is bad (*all
things considered*) because the pleasure is undeserved." Both claims are
meaningful, but different senses of "good" and "bad" would be involved.

In Sad's case, the two senses – good in a dimension and good all things
considered – come apart. But they need not always do so. Consider the
similarly related facts that (2) <Mary (an abandoned child) experiences
joy when found and comforted> and that (2*) <Mary experiences joy>.
If Mary's experiencing joy (2*) in the context of (2) is deserved and is not
overridden in any higher dimension than the first, then (unlike Sad's
experience of pleasure) Mary's joy is both good in a dimension (the first
dimension) *and* all things considered good. Likewise, something may be
bad in the first dimension and all things considered bad as well, e.g., the
innocent man's experiencing pain in the context of being tortured by Sad.

Finally, the distinction between good in a dimension and all things
considered good has implications regarding the notion of *intrinsic value*.
Intrinsic value has been interpreted in different ways in philosophical discussions of value, but two meanings have been central. On the first of

these, something is intrinsically good when it is good "in itself" independently of its relations to other things – hence good by virtue of its *intrinsic* or non-relational properties alone rather than by virtue of its *extrinsic* or relational properties. On the second meaning, something is intrinsically good when it is good "in itself" in another sense, namely, good *for its own sake* and not merely good as a *means* or *contribution* to some other goods.

It turns out that basic value experiences, such as pleasure and joy, are intrinsic *first-dimensional* goods in both senses: As first-dimensional goods, they are good by virtue of their intrinsic (felt) qualities alone (for the agents who have them) and good for their own sake, not merely as a means or contribution to some other goods. But it does not follow that such experiences are intrinsic *all things considered* goods. If a basic value experience, such as Sad's pleasure in torturing, is overridden in a dimension higher than the first, then it is not an intrinsic all things considered good because it is not all things considered good at all.

By contrast, non-overridden basic value experiences, such as Mary's joy, are both good in the first dimension and all things considered good. But it is important to note that insofar as such experiences are *all things considered* good, they would not be so *merely* by virtue of their intrinsic properties (how they feel to the agents who have them), but also by virtue of the contributions they make to more comprehensive goods, such as a happy life or a moral community. A distinction is thus in order for non-overridden basic value experiences, such as Mary's joy. *Qua first-dimensional goods*, they are good by virtue of their intrinsic, non-relational properties alone and good for their own sake, not merely as a means or contribution to other goods. But *qua all things considered goods* (which they also are), non-overridden basic value experiences are not merely good by virtue of their intrinsic (or non-relational) properties or merely good in themselves or for their own sakes for the agents who have them. They are also (all things considered) good by virtue of their relations and contributions to more comprehensive goods. The nature of these more comprehensive goods is the subject of the next three chapters.

# CHAPTER 6

# *Value experiments*

## I. THE SECOND DIMENSION OF VALUE

In what I shall call a second dimension of value, value expands outward from mere subjective experience into the realm of action and *practical engagements* with the world, including *activities* in the pursuit of purposes or interests and *attachments* to things and persons we care about. Some basic value experiences may be momentary, analogous to points on a plane, while others, such as enjoying a horseback ride, will be stretched out over time, like lines in a plane. Experience stretched out in this way is sentient life; and when this life involves purposive activity with practical goals and attachments to things cared about that go beyond mere enjoyment or pleasure, we arrive at a second dimension of value.

This second dimension of value includes not only experiences, but also activities undertaken by individuals in the pursuit of plans, intentions, interests and purposes. If horseback riding is merely an enjoyable pastime for Jane, then the value of it for her is merely first-dimensional. But if the riding also has some further purpose, such as rounding up cattle or delivering mail, then we are into a second dimension of value. Jane may also enjoy the riding for its own sake in addition to its serving a useful function; and in that case she experiences value in both the first and second dimensions. Such "fusing" of value from different dimensions is especially satisfying and is one reason why people put such importance on having a job or work they enjoy doing.

Value in this second dimension is a measure of the success or failure of the practical engagements we pursue and the attachments we care about (say, to friends or family). We build houses to shelter ourselves or impress our neighbors, plant seeds to grow food or to adorn our environment with flowers, play games to win, cultivate friendships, and so on. The value (or disvalue) here lies in the fulfillment (or non-fulfillment) of the purposes and interests of the agents undertaking the activities and in the persistence of the attachments they care about. It follows that value in this second dimension is also *plural*, indeed more evidently so than in the first dimension. In the words of Isaiah Berlin quoted earlier, "the purposes or ends of human beings are many and they often come in conflict with one another."

## 2. INCLUSION AND OVERRIDING

Note that this second dimension of value so conceived *includes* the first dimension, insofar as practical engagements in the world, such as purposive activities and ongoing relationships, involve a succession of experiences through time. Purposive activities and relationships are "lived through" and, as such, include diverse (first-dimensional) value and disvalue experiences such as enjoyment, exhilaration, exhaustion, pride, sadness, frustration, disappointment, and the like, as one-dimensional lines are included in two-dimensional spaces.

In addition, second-dimensional value can "override" first-dimensional experiences, as when short-term enjoyments or pleasures, such as eating a piece of cake, are sacrificed to attain longer-term goals, such as losing weight. What is prima facie good in the first dimension becomes bad in the second dimension. Similarly, what is prima facie bad in the first dimension, such as the pain of stretching a damaged ligament, may be a necessary means to a valuable long-term purpose, the rehabilitation of a surgically repaired leg.

Yet value in the second dimension can itself be overridden and is therefore also *prima facie* or *defeasible*. Suppose a man plans a fishing trip with friends. He has a number of purposes in mind – to get some much needed rest and relaxation from a stressful job; to bond with old friends; the chance to fish in mountain streams, and so on. Alas, he learns that his daughter's high school graduation is scheduled the same week as the planned trip and she will be devastated if he does not attend. Since the fishing trip cannot be rescheduled, he chooses to forego it. Its value is overridden by something more important to him, his daughter's welfare and his family commitments. ("The purposes or ends of humans are many and often they come in conflict with one another.")

In this and other ways, activities and undertakings that may fulfill purposes or interests of agents in the second dimension of value may in principle be overridden when viewed from a broader perspective. Yet, as with first-dimensional value experiences, if such second-dimensional activities are *not* overridden by more important goods or in higher dimensions of value, they too can be objective goods for the persons undertaking them. If the daughter's graduation had not conflicted and the man had gone on his trip and his purposes were fulfilled – if he managed the needed relaxation, bonded with his friends, etc. – then the trip would have been objectively valuable for him. Of course, the trip may also have turned out to be a disaster: It may have rained the whole time, the friends may have quarreled, reviving old grievances, in which case the above statement would be false.

Value in the second dimension thus depends on more than not being overridden. It also depends on how activities or undertakings turn out, whether they succeed or fail in fulfilling the agent's purposes and interests. Second-dimensional value is thus also *relative* value, like first-dimensional value, since it is a matter of fulfilling or failing to fulfill the purposes or interests *of* particular agents. But that does not preclude its being objectively good for the agents involved and those who may care about the agents or for whom they care, *if* not overridden in any higher dimension. If a woman succeeds in building a workbench that will please her husband, the fulfillment of her purpose and the activity through which she fulfilled it are second-dimensional goods for her and for those who care about her and for whom she cares, such as her husband.[1] These are relative goods *for* the particular persons involved; but it remains an objective matter of fact whether or not these goods do fulfill the purposes and interests of those persons. In this way, value in the second dimension, like value in the first, *when it is not overridden*, can be both objective and relative – "objectively relative."

### 3. "EXPERIMENTS IN LIVING": MILL AND OTHERS

Central to this conception of second-dimensional value is the notion of a *value experiment*. If I undertake a regimen of exercise and a special diet to lose weight, I am undertaking a value experiment. Success or failure of the experiment lies in the fulfillment or non-fulfillment of the purpose of losing weight and the extent to which the fulfillment of the purpose satisfies my desires and interests. This is where the second-dimensional value lies as well.

---

[1] There can thus in principle be *intrinsic* second-dimensional values (as well as intrinsic first-dimensional values). Examples would be fulfilling careers, happy marriages, satisfying friendships, which may be good for their own sakes, even if they may also be instrumentally good for other things (raising well-adjusted children, etc.). There may be *instrumental* second-dimensional goods as well, such as the workbench if it contributes to a happy marriage.

Recall that one of the contentious issues about fact and value has to do with this issue of experimentation. It is often said, or assumed, that one can perform experiments about matters of fact (as in the empirical sciences), but not about values. I think this assumption ought to be viewed as a mistake. We experiment with values all the time. Any plan of action or way of life put into practice is a value experiment whose results can be tested against prior expectations, purposes and interests, like the diet regimen just mentioned. A career is a value experiment in this sense, as is a marriage, a vacation, a party, a date, a fishing trip with old friends, a business enterprise, a research project, an economic policy, a political program, and so on. Any one of them may turn out to be a success or a failure when measured against the desires, interests and purposes of those undertaking them.

Value experiments, so conceived, are the stuff of life. John Stuart Mill called them "experiments in living" and they play a significant role in the social and political theory of his *On Liberty*.[2] Mill claimed that persons were generally happier when they were free to choose their own value experiments, or experiments in living; and he considered this an important argument in favor of free societies. Elizabeth Anderson, in an insightful essay on Mill's experiments in living, says that "John Stuart Mill thought that we learn about the good through 'experiments in living.' As an empiricist, he rejected the traditional view that we know about the good through a priori intuitions. Conceptions of the good must be tested by the experiences we have in living them out" (1991: 5).

I think Mill is on to something important here to which Anderson directs our attention. We cannot determine what the good life is in an a priori fashion. We must do it by engaging in experiments in living, or (as I put it earlier) through our *practical engagements in the world*." Note that *this idea was already at work in the argument of Chapter 2*, where openness to various ways of life meant initially "letting them be lived or experimented with or tested in a way that is appropriate for values, in action or practice." I now want to emphasize that this theme of testing values through practical engagements in the world extends beyond the ethical arguments of Chapters 2–4. It also includes the testing of plans of action and ways of life generally through what Mill called "experiments in living." As noted in Chapter 4, Gandhi called his own value experiments with non-violence in India his "experiments with truth." His *Satyagraha* movement, whose goal of making the British relinquish control of India

---

[2] Mill 1956: 75–81.

without resort to violent revolution was largely realized, was one of the most significant value experiments of the twentieth century.

Clearly, value experiments of such kinds differ in significant ways from scientific experiments, partly (but not only) because value experiments take place in daily life, while scientific experiments usually take place in a laboratory under controlled conditions. Yet the similarities are revealing and instructive. One way to bring out the similarities is to consider a disputed criterion about what makes scientific experiments genuine. I have in mind Karl Popper's much-discussed view that genuine scientific experiments must be capable of falsifying or refuting or disconfirming the hypotheses or theories they are testing as well as providing evidence in their favor.[3] Theories are genuinely scientific, on Popper's view, if they are capable of being falsified by experience or experiment.

In criticism of this much-discussed "criterion of falsifiability," historians and philosophers of science have often pointed out that widely accepted scientific theories are not always definitively refuted or falsified by one or even a few disconfirming observations or experiments. Theories are often adjusted in the face of contrary evidence rather than abandoned entirely. Or their adherents may wait for some future explanation of the unexplained facts rather than completely abandoning an otherwise successful theory.

These and other criticisms of Popper's criterion of falsifiability are widely accepted. Yet, there remains a kernel of truth to the criterion that most of its critics do not wish to deny. Confirmations of a theory should count as genuine only if (in Popper's words) "they are the result of *risky predictions,*" predictions that could in principle *fail* as well as succeed.[4] In other words, genuine experimental tests of a theory must take a risk; they must be capable of providing evidence that counts against the theory as well as for it. This makes sense, for if we put forth theories that cannot be falsified by *any* possible experience, then we are merely spinning ideas in our heads and not making *objective* claims about the world at all. If our theories claim to be about objective facts, then the world ought to be capable of fighting back by showing the theories false as well as true.

But it is interesting that "value experiments" can take such a risk of failure as well. Consider the examples given earlier: a diet regimen, a career, a marriage, a vacation, a party, a date, a business enterprise, a research project, an economic policy, a political program. All of them take risks and all can fail in various ways to fulfill their intended purposes or satisfy

[3] Popper 1965.   [4] Popper 1965: 36.

the desires of those involved. Gandhi's experiments with non-violence in India might well have failed; they were in fact extremely risky. With value experiments, the world also fights back and objective evidence can count against their success as well as for their success.

## 4. VALUE EXPERIMENTS AND PLANS OF ACTION: NOZICK'S EXPERIENCE MACHINE

The differences between value experiments and scientific experiments, I would suggest, lie elsewhere. The important differences have to do with the fact that value experimentation is *personal* in a way that scientific experimentation is not. What experiments with values test (as noted in Chapter 4) are *plans of action* and *ways of life* of particular persons or groups (which correspond to the *theories* or *hypotheses* tested in scientific experimentation). And success or failure of value experiments is measured in the first instance in terms of the fulfillment or non-fulfillment of the purposes and interests of agents that were to be realized by the plans of action and ways of living.

This introduces a personal and agent-relative element into value experimentation that makes it different. But objectivity is not thereby excluded. For, once the purposes and interests defining the plans of action are specified, there are objective facts of the matter about whether or not these purposes and interests are realized. It is an objective matter whether the diet regimen succeeds in its goals or the British do leave India without violent revolution. And it is an objective matter of fact whether or not the man's fishing trip provides the needed rest, relaxation and bonding with friends. Wishing will not make it so.

As a consequence, second-dimensional value, which is bound up with plans of action that are tested as value experiments, has a measure of objectivity, though second-dimensional value remains to some degree subjective and relative as well. Indeed, there is greater objectivity in the second dimension of value than in the first. For people can be mistaken about the objective success of their plans of action. The woman may believe she has made a sturdy workbench that will please her husband and may feel quite satisfied with herself for doing so. Yet the bench may in fact be unstable and her husband will be disappointed. She is thus mistaken about the objective success of her experiment. By contrast, basic disvalue experiences such as humiliation, shame, or anxiety, are first-dimensional disvalues even if their subjects have no good objective reasons to feel humiliated, ashamed or anxious.

This difference between first- and second-dimensional value is the first hint of a general theme of some importance. As we move to higher dimensions of value, value becomes more objective, and less subjective, even though some elements of subjectivity and relativity may remain. At each higher dimension we *move further beyond our own subjectivity* and out into the wider world beyond ourselves. In the second dimension, we are not merely interested in *experiencing* something, but in *doing* something – in making a mark upon the objective world. Hence there is greater risk of failure, but also greater hope of satisfaction and meaning.

This greater objectivity in the transition from first- to second-dimensional value is nicely illustrated by Robert Nozick's well-known example of an "experience machine."[5] By electronically stimulating the brain, Nozick's experience machine can give one the illusion and there-fore the pleasure of any activity whatever, even though one is not actually engaged in the activity. In such an experience machine, all value would be *first dimensional*. There would be no value in the second and higher dimensions. Nozick himself thought life in such a machine would be deeply impoverished because he argued that we desire more than just to have experiences in life. We desire to *do* something, accomplish things, and make a mark upon the objective world. Whether or not one agrees with Nozick on this point, his experience machine provides a nice illus-tration of the distinction between the first and second dimensions of value. In a Nozickian experience machine, all value would be merely "one dimensional."

5.  SUCCESS AND FAILURE

I have been arguing that second-dimensional value, which is bound up with plans of action and ways of living that are tested as value experiments, has a measure of objectivity that goes beyond the first dimension of value. But is it always so easy to determine when or whether a particular value experiment has failed or succeeded? And if it is not, might judgments of success or failure (and hence judgments about second-dimensional value) be "merely" subjective after all? Objective success or failure of the diet regimen is clear enough; and Gandhi either does succeed in getting the British to leave India on his terms or he does not.

But other examples are not so clear. Careers and marriages were said to be examples; and heaven knows many of them fail. But how do we know

5  Nozick 1974: 42–5.

definitively that a career or marriage has been a failure or success? The simple answer is that we do not always know definitively, if that means with finality or certainty. (It seems that careers and marriages, like many other things in modern life, are plagued by pluralism and uncertainty – in this case, pluralism of choice and uncertainty of outcome.)

Consider careers. A young lawyer may be unsatisfied with her work, but at first she adjusts. She changes law firms, gets new colleagues, turns to a different area of the law that suits her talents better. But over time, as dissatisfaction mounts and these changes continually fail, she may conclude that a career in law was a failed value experiment for her. She may abandon it and become a teacher. Such career changes need not be the result of merely subjective judgments. The woman's judgment that her talents and interests were not well suited to the law – and that she went into it for the wrong reasons, perhaps to please others – may in fact be true. Her talents and temperament may be better suited to teaching; and she may find success and happiness as a teacher. (Ethical considerations might also be involved. She may have a family to support requiring a higher income. But in that case the decision would be viewed from a higher dimension that would override even the practical and personal considerations of the second dimension.)

This pattern is a familiar one, and we also see it in marriages. Persons usually do not give up on marriages with the first signs of trouble or dissatisfaction. More often than not, only an accumulation of difficulties over time that seem to have no resolution lead to the abandonment of a marriage (or a career), since long-term investments are involved. How do the partners know when such a point has been reached? They do not know with certainty, any more than the young lawyer does; nor should they jump too soon to the conclusion that this point has arrived (which is an analogue of deciding too hastily that the moral sphere has broken down). Divorce is as much a value experiment as a marriage and fraught with as much risk for all concerned. (Ethical considerations may also be involved, as with careers, especially where children are concerned. But in that event also, the decision would be viewed from a still higher dimension that overrides the personal and practical considerations of the second dimension.) If we could be certain of the outcome or rightness of our value experiments before we undertook them, life would be easier, but would it be *human* life? Indeed, would it be *life*?

One may object that marriages are undertaken with a "commitment" ("till death do us part") that makes the term "experiment" inappropriate to describe them. "Living together" prior to marriage (or in lieu of it) may more appropriately be termed an experiment. But marriage, it might be said, is a sacred bond, involving a prior commitment inconsistent with the thought that parties are just "trying it out." But even if this is true, it is consistent with saying that marriage is a value experiment or "experiment in living," in Mill's sense intended here. For, what is crucial to value experiments in the Millian sense is that people "learn from experience" through undertaking them and the undertakings may be successful or unsuccessful to varying degrees when measured against the interests and purposes of those undertaking them; and these things can be true of marriage even when undertaken as a sacred and unbreakable commitment. What makes value experiments "experimental" is not how, or with what commitments, we get into them, but rather that the commitments with which we get into them are no guarantee of how they will turn out.

### 6. VALUE VERSUS SCIENTIFIC EXPERIMENTATION AGAIN

Let us return then to the point that, even when abandoning a career or a marriage is an option, people do not usually give up with the first signs of trouble or dissatisfaction. Usually, it is an accumulation of difficulties over time, which seem to have no resolution, that leads to the abandonment of a career or marriage, since long-term investments are involved. What is noteworthy, however, is that these features of value experiments also have analogues in scientific experimentation. Recall that objections to Popper's falsifiability criterion were made on the grounds that in the history of science theories are not always definitively refuted or abandoned on the basis of one or even a few disconfirming observations or experiments. Such hesitation to abandon a theory is especially strong if the scientific theory has been successful in other areas and in cases where no clearly better alternatives exist. Adjustments are made to the threatened theory; or one waits for some future explanation of the discomforting anomalies.

Reluctance to abandon a theory in such circumstances is quite rational. Over time, however, the accumulation of disconfirming evidence and failed adjustments, and the availability of alternatives, may lead to a rational judgment that the theory is a failure and thus to its abandonment. Ptolemaic astronomers did not immediately abandon their theory when Copernicus came along, but drew more epicycles to explain anomalies in the planetary orbits and only abandoned their theory after a century of contrary evidence had accumulated. (Some of the contrarians simply died, but that's another story.) Interestingly, we see a similar pattern with complex value experiments, such as careers, marriages, business enterprises, social policies, and so on. They are not abandoned in one fell swoop, but only after the accumulation of difficulties (anomalies) that resist adjustments and appear to have no resolution. Even then, they may only be abandoned in the presence of potentially better alternatives.

Actually, this similarity of pattern should not surprise us. Scientists often have a significant *investment* in their theories, an investment very like our investment in long-term life-plans and value experiments. So we should not expect scientists to abandon their theories too easily either. Nor need there be a clear or definitive cut-off point at which they say "that's enough" (fifty epicycles? one hundred?), just as there is often no such clear point in careers and marriages. Yet, in the end, failure may come to be acknowledged for good reasons.

The differences between value and scientific experiments do not therefore lie in the fact that it may take an accumulation of evidence over time (and not necessarily a single failed experience or experiment) to refute the life-plans or theories being tested; nor do the differences lie in the fact that there is no pre-established cut-off point where one must say "that's enough." The difference, as suggested earlier, lies rather in the fact that the success or failure of life-plans or plans of action that value experiments test is related in a more personal, or agent-relative, way to the purposes and interests of the subjects or groups who are testing them.

As a consequence, the results of value experiments are not so easily generalized. The woman who left a career in law to go into teaching was not passing judgment on the goodness or badness of the practice of law in general. (That would be a different debate.) Rather she came reluctantly and gradually to the conclusion that a career in law was a bad thing *for her*, given her talents, temperament and interests. And about this conclusion she may have been objectively right, even though the result could only be generalized to other persons with relevantly similar talents, temperaments and interests. Second-dimensional value is in this respect objective, notwithstanding the subjective and personal element in it. We should not be surprised that physicists can generalize more thoroughly from their experiments, since the electrons and protons they deal with are alike by comparison with persons.

If the success or failure of value experiments is related in a more personal way to the purposes and interests of agents who undertake them, then, there will be one final reason why success or failure will be difficult to assess: Different and conflicting purposes and interests have to be considered. Success or failure of the diet regimen is easier to assess because it involves one reasonably clear goal. This is not so with more complex value experiments, which include not only careers and marriages, but long-term projects, business enterprises, political programs, and so forth. They may be satisfactory in some ways, not in others. Trade-offs must be considered between desires and interests that are satisfied and others left unsatisfied – for different parties involved. "The ends of human beings are many, and often they come in conflict with one another."

When Berlin said this, he did not have in mind only the conflicting purposes of different persons, but also (and very importantly) the conflicting purposes and interests *within* a single person. We often want things that cannot be simultaneously obtained and we only find this out by painful experience (that is, by value experimenting). This is especially true of the young, who often think they can "have it all" without significant trade-offs – marriage, career, children, adventure, romance, excitement. Dealing with such trade-offs is another way in which value experimentation can show us – by succeeding or failing – what purposes and desires can and cannot be simultaneously realized. When desires and purposes cannot be simultaneously realized, we have to go back and reassess which of them should be modified. In such cases, the world fights back against our plans and projects. They bump up against an objective reality; and the assessments we make are not merely subjective. If we delude ourselves about success or failure, we risk paying a heavy price.

## 7. PRACTICAL REASONING AND PRACTICAL INQUIRY: HAPPINESS

A final point about value experiments that must be mentioned is that they can and often do take place "in the head" – imagining scenarios, considering possible outcomes and consequences of actions in the attempt to decide which plans or intentions are worthy of being pursued in reality. (There is a scientific analogue to this feature also in the "thought experiments" of scientists.) Indeed much of what we call *practical* reasoning or deliberation takes this form of what we might call "vicarious value experimenting" – weighing possible consequences of plans of action in order to determine which ones are *worthy* of being tried in practice. Elijah Milgram makes a persuasive case for thinking about practical reasoning in this way in his insightful book, *Practical Induction* (1997).[6] A good deal

---

[6] Milgram also argues persuasively that we can engage in practical reasoning about what *ends* are worth pursuing, as well as about means. Richardson (1994) makes a strong and wide-ranging case for this as well, as does Vogler (2001) in her brilliant study of Mill's views about value and practical reasoning.

of what is called "practical wisdom" (*phronesis* to the ancient Greek think-ers) is knowing enough about ourselves and about others and the world around us to aptly choose which experiments in living are likely to be ful-filling and which are not. The capacity for such value experimenting "in the head" is a distinguishing feature of rational agents.

The ultimate test of success for value experiments of individuals in the second dimension of value is *happiness* or *flourishing* understood in the sense that the ancient philosophers described as "satisfaction with one's life as a whole." But what exactly happiness amounts to in this general sense is a contestable matter; and its specific nature was highly con-tested even among the ancient thinkers who proposed it as the goal.[7] To understand what happiness is, one would have to consider how the many purposes and interests of life fit together in a meaningful way and what *purposes* and *interests* are ultimately *worth* pursuing. But the answers to such questions would move us beyond the second dimension of value to higher dimensions where the question is not only about what happiness may consist in, but whether it alone – or something else – is the ultim-ate goal of life. In this way, the second dimension of value, like the first, poses questions that can only be fully addressed by going beyond it.

---

[7] Annas 1993 is a comprehensive study of debates among ancient philosophers concerning this notion of happiness.

# CHAPTER 7

# *Virtues, excellences and forms of life*

## I. THE THIRD DIMENSION OF VALUE

When we turn to a third dimension of value, we find that it includes the other two, but transcends and can override both. In the third dimension, activities and experiences are not merely viewed practically in terms of what we get from them – but more importantly, in terms of how they define what we *are*. In this dimension, the hunter in a primitive tribe does not merely hunt for food (a second-dimensional concern), but takes pride in his skill with the bow because of what it says about his standing as a human being. The activity signifies that he is an *excellent* archer, a *good* provider for his family and a *loyal* member of his tribe. It defines what he is and his status in the world and in the community of which he is a part. We may say in general that the value of activities and experiences in this third dimension derives from their role in "*forms of life*" (to use Wittgenstein's expression) which give them meaning or significance; and it involves the pursuit of various *virtues* or *excellences* characteristic of those forms of life.

The third dimension of value thus includes what Charles Taylor (1982) calls "strong evaluations" (those that define our *ideals* rather than merely our *interests*) and also what Alasdair MacIntyre (1981: 187) has called the values embodied in "practices" and "traditions." By a practice, MacIntyre means "a socially established ... human activity" through which we strive to realize goods by achieving "standards of excellence appropriate to that activity." As examples, he cites architecture, physics, medicine, law, painting, violin-making, music, farming, chess, football, politics, wine-making, teaching and the making and sustaining of family life, among many others. Each of these practices has its own standards of excellence; and the excellences achieved in each are instances of third-dimensional value – a fine painting, a well-played chess game, a new scientific discovery, a beautiful-sounding violin.

When the pursuits of human goods in practices extend through many generations, they become *traditions* and *cultures*, which are also the embodiment of third-dimensional value. (*Religions* and religious traditions count as well, insofar as they are not merely systems of beliefs, but entire forms of life with ritual practices, observances and ideals of spirituality and sainthood.) Virtues, according to MacIntyre, are those human qualities (excellences) that allow one to achieve the goods distinctive of practices.

Through the pursuit of practices, traditions, and forms of life, humans seek a number of ends that are central to this third dimension of value. Among these ends, four are particularly worth mentioning – expression of meaning, mastery, contribution with commitment, and excellence or virtue. Rom Harré remarks that a substantial proportion of human behavior in all known cultures serves expressive ends (1980: 5). As soon as basic utilitarian needs for food and shelter are fulfilled, even the most seemingly primitive of peoples turn to expressive activities such as storytelling, myth, dance, art, ritual practices and public discourse, through which they express to themselves and others what they are and what gives meaning to their existence.

By "mastery," I mean simply the experience of doing something well, and by "contribution," the fact that what one does is important to – plays a valued and indispensable role in – the community or form of life with which one identifies. The psychology of the homeless and unemployed is interesting in this regard. They worry about not having enough to eat (which is a second-dimensional concern). But they worry also about the loss of self-respect that comes from believing society has no need for them and there is no valued role for them to play (a third-dimensional concern).

Finally, the capstone of third-dimensional value is excellence of action or achievement in various practices and forms of life (*arete*, to the ancient Greek philosophers). The excellence may be manifested in the practice of the virtues appropriate to a form of life or in the attainment of the highest achievements recognized in that form of life – great painting, music, statesmanship, and so on.

## 2. INCLUSION AND OVERRIDING: INTERNAL AND EXTERNAL GOODS

Note that third-dimensional value so conceived, includes the other two dimensions of value while at the same time transcending them. Pursuing ends of meaningful expression, mastery, contribution and excellence involves engagement in (second-dimensional) purposive activities that in turn involve successions of (first-dimensional) experiences – much as three-dimensional spaces include two-dimensional planes and one-dimensional lines. But the activities and experiences of the first two dimensions are "transfigured" or "raised up" in the third dimension to a higher level, where they have a meaning and significance that transcends whatever practical ends they might otherwise achieve, or whatever enjoyment or pleasure they might afford.

Such transcending of practical ends and pleasures implies that there is also "overriding" in the third dimension. Enjoyments, pleasures and practical goals may be part of the pursuit of excellence, but some of them may divert or distract from that pursuit as well. A performance-enhancing drug may be a good thing if a runner has to get a message as quickly as possible to a neighboring village. But in the context of a competition meant to demonstrate athletic excellence or *arete*, where the drug gives the runner an unfair advantage, taking the drug undermines the practice, even though the runner may in fact run faster.

A distinction drawn by MacIntyre between two kinds of goods is important for understanding practices and third-dimensional value generally (1981: 188). He distinguishes goods that are *internal* to practices from those that are *external*. If a violin-maker takes pride in his craftsmanship in producing an instrument of magnificent sound, then he is seeking a good that is internal to the practice of violin-making, a good that is distinctive of this practice. By contrast, if the violin-maker's interest is in the money or prestige his work will bring, he is interested in goods that are external to the practice. It is common to be interested in both kinds of goods, but external goods, such as prestige, status or money, can be realized in many different ways, whereas internal goods are specific to the practice in question: The skills and excellences distinctive of violin-making can only be fully realized by making violins.

There is a social point behind this distinction for MacIntyre. Like other social critics, he bemoans the tendency of modern commercial cultures to emphasize external goods over internal ones. Examples of this emphasis are not hard to find: Physicians who may be more interested in money and status than in the true ends of the practice of medicine, craftsmen and repairmen more interested in a fast dollar than in taking pride in their work, politicians more interested in their own power and survival than in serving the public's interests, professional athletes more interested in the size of their latest contract than in the success of their team, a general fascination with fame and celebrity at the expense of genuine merit and excellence of achievement.

The public unease and distaste inspired by these trends suggests a confusion of priorities, according to critics like MacIntyre. Societies that emphasize external goods over internal goods impoverish the means by which humans go about cooperatively seeking the good. He notes that external goods are "characteristically objects of competition in which there must be losers as well as winners." By contrast, "internal goods are indeed the outcome of competition to excel, but it is characteristic of them that their achievement is a good for the whole community who participate in the practice" and who can appreciate its achievements (ibid.). With internal goods there is a sense of excellence that transcends personal pleasures and possessions and has worth to a wider community of persons beyond oneself. In this manner, third-dimensional value takes us a further step beyond the subjectivity of the first dimension.

### 3. PRACTICES, TRADITIONS AND EXCELLENCES (ARETAI): MACINTYRE, RAZ

It should be evident from the above examples that value in the third dimension is also *plural*, even more evidently so than in the first two dimensions. There are many practices and traditions through which humans pursue meaningful expression, mastery, contribution and excellence. If this were not so, the possibilities for pursuing human goods would be immeasurably impoverished.

MacIntyre's list of practices is only a beginning: architecture, physics, medicine, law, music, painting, chess, teaching, and so on; and each practice has its own distinctive kinds of excellence. Mozart's achievements are quite different from Shakespeare's, and the excellence of both differs markedly from those of Michelangelo or Einstein, to take a few clear examples. To fully appreciate these diverse excellences or *aretai*, we have to understand the practices and traditions of which they are a part. You have to know something about physics and its history to fully understand Einstein's achievements. To fully appreciate Michael Jordan's greatness as a basketball player you have to know the nuances of the game of basketball. If you do not know anything about Zen Buddhism, you cannot fully appreciate the practice of poetry that the Japanese call *haiku*.

In this way, practices, traditions and forms of life provide the contexts in which excellences have meaning. Shakespeare's *distinctive* greatness could not have been realized without the English language, nor Mozart's, if there were no violins. Yet even where we cannot fully appreciate the value of a practice from the inside because we do not share its distinctive traditions, we can acknowledge that there is such value from others who do appreciate it. Calligraphy is an art of writing practiced in China for centuries. I do not fully appreciate it, but I trust the judgment and expertise of my friend Shepard Liu when he shows me the work of acknowledged masters of the art; and I glimpse the beauty in their work. Excellence is to some degree in the eye of the beholder, but not only in the eye of the beholder. There is an objective excellence to behold, if there is an audience fit to render it.

This does not mean that judgments of excellence in practices are incontestable or that the standards are always clear and fixed. MacIntyre emphasizes the idea that practices can change and develop; and when they do they become *traditions* (pp. 221ff.). The trial lawyer's standards of excellence are not merely connected to arbitrary rules of transitory legal practice. They are embedded in a longer tradition of common law that is supposed to serve the interests of justice, respect for evidence, fair representation, and so on. When particular standards of practice no longer serve these ends, they are subject to change. The same is true of musicians exploring the boundaries of musical traditions, such as jazz, or opera, or of chemists working within the traditions of modern chemistry.

A tradition, as MacIntyre puts it, is a continuing argument about what is *worth* pursuing. Judgments about what is worth pursuing continue to be rooted in human purposes, desires and interests, to be sure, but the purposes and interests are elevated in the third dimension to the level of ideals that transcend personal needs; they become goods for an entire community or form of life with which one identifies; and they thereby invest one's activities with greater significance. There is more to argue about because there is more at stake.

Other recent philosophers have emphasized the importance of what I am here calling third-dimensional value. Joseph Raz, for example, in his Tanner Lectures on Human Values, emphasizes, like MacIntyre, that many values arise from, and are dependent on, "social practices" (2003). Raz goes further, arguing that almost all important human values depend on social practices. (He exempts only "sensual and perceptual pleasures," which I have been calling first-dimensional values, and "enabling or facilitating" values, such as freedom and health.) One does not have to agree with Raz that most important values depend on social practices to acknowledge that many human values require for their realization the context of specific practices, traditions and forms of life that give them meaning and significance. Such values are an important part of what I am here calling the third dimension of value. Raz adds the supporting thought that ideas of humor, opera, and other artistic genres are themselves normative ideas because the nature of such things is partly determined by their specific norms of excellence.

### 4. VIRTUES AND FORMS OF LIFE: TAYLOR, ANDERSON

We have been talking about exemplary forms of excellence or *arete* in arts and culture that are contestable, but also recognizable. Yet third-dimensional value includes much more than that. It also includes playing roles well and fulfilling functions well within cultures, cooperative enterprises and forms of life: being a good accountant, auto mechanic, police officer, carpenter, nurse or engineer, a loyal employee, caring parent, courageous soldier, generous donor, fair judge, honest shopkeeper, patient arbitrator, grateful friend or responsible citizen.

These are all examples of third-dimensional value as well; and they show how the *virtues* enter into third-dimensional value: loyalty, courage, generosity, fairness, honesty, gratitude, trustworthiness, responsibility, and the like. These are traits that make good employees, parents, soldiers, judges, friends, citizens, and so on, thereby contributing to the flourishing *not only of the individuals who possess the traits*, but to the flourishing of various "forms of life" and to other persons who participate in those forms of life.

Ascriptions of virtues and excellences of these kinds are called "strong evaluations" by Charles Taylor (1982: 113). Strong evaluations express not merely our *interests*, but our *ideals*, in the sense of traits of character and excellences of accomplishment that define what we are and what kinds of persons we think we should be. Citing Taylor as a precedent, Elizabeth Anderson is another philosopher who has emphasized the importance of ideals in this sense to the theory of value. "The core of an ideal," Anderson says, "consists in a conception of qualities of character, or characteristics of a community, which the holders regard as excellent and as central to their identities ... a U. S. marine is supposed to be patriotic ... a connoisseur of fine art is supposed to cultivate an appreciation of the subtle qualities in painting and sculpture and to be appalled by the damage done to great works. A labor union activist is supposed to build solidarity with fellow members of the working class" (1993: 7).

Since third-dimensional value also includes ideals of these sorts as well as various forms of excellence in practices, traditions and forms of life, there is a plenitude of value in the third dimension; and value is plural in this dimension as well. Despite this plurality, however, there is a further measure of objectivity in the third dimension because third-dimensional value is no longer related merely to subjective experiences or to personal and practical needs, as in the first two dimensions of value. One may well be wrong or deceived about whether one really is a good mechanic, calligraphist, courageous soldier or loyal friend by the standards of the practices, traditions and forms of life in which one participates and to which one contributes.

Yet we may continue to wonder about the standards of the practices, traditions and forms of life themselves. Are these standards themselves ultimately "worth pursuing"? This is the deeper question about ultimate ends to which third-dimensional value gives rise. If, as MacIntyre says, traditions and forms of life are continuing arguments about what is worth pursuing, are there standards for judging which traditions and forms of life are objectively right and worthy – standards that go beyond, or transcend, the traditions and forms of life themselves?

MacIntyre himself was deeply troubled by this question because he was convinced that if human value was not a meaningless abstraction, it had to be rooted in concrete human experiences, practices and forms of life.[1] Humans have always sought the good in the contexts of their particular experiences and activities within communities and traditions into which they were enculturated; and it is hard to see how they could do so in any other way. Being initiated into a culture begins with learning a language and social conventions that shape our sensibilities and influence the way we interpret and value things around us; and this shaping accelerates as cultural learning proceeds. But such cultural shaping would seem to suggest that all human value must be inevitably *relative* after all – relative to cultures, traditions and forms of life in the third dimension of value, no less than in the first two dimensions. How then can we make judgments about the objective rightness or worth of cultures, traditions and forms of life themselves?

### 5. RELATIVISM AGAIN: THE RETREATANTS REVISITED

It is not difficult to see that this is the problem the retreatants were struggling with in Chapter 3. How, if at all, they asked, can we climb out of

---

[1] MacIntyre pursued this problem in other works, e.g., 1988 and 1990. Discussion of his efforts to resolve it appear in two instructive anthologies: Horton and Mendus 1994 and M. Murphy 2003.

our historically and culturally limited points of view or forms of life to reach a higher standpoint above them all, from which to judge which of our conflicting points of view and ways of life is objectively right and ultimately worth pursuing? To reach such a higher standpoint would mean going beyond the third dimension of value to a fourth dimension. Such a fourth dimension would be a higher dimension of value from which persons could say not merely that their ideals, virtues, excellences and ethical standards were good from their own points of view, but were good *period* – and so should be recognized as good by all persons from all points of view.

Yet the very existence of such a fourth dimension of value is problematic. We know that most peoples and societies of the past believed there was such a higher dimension of value from which one could make absolute and not merely relative judgments about the ultimate worth of forms of life. Indeed, they naturally tended to believe their own forms of life represented this absolute perspective. They assumed their beliefs about the gods and the cosmos and the virtues and excellences they recognized, the practices and traditions they followed, were not only true and right *for them*, but true or right *simpliciter*, in the nature of things. If others in different societies or cultures disagreed, those others were simply mistaken.

People of the past who thought this way were in effect projecting their third-dimensional forms of life *into a fourth dimension*, assuming their beliefs, virtues and excellences transcended their own forms of life and were universally or non-relatively good. The fourth dimension, so conceived, would be such a standpoint above all different and conflicting third-dimensional cultures, traditions and ways of life. It would be a kind of God's-eye point of view, to use Hilary Putnam's expression, from which we could look down upon the conflicting ways of life in the third dimension and say which is right and which is wrong from a standpoint above them all. But how would one arrive at such a standpoint, if it exists at all?

Framing the problem in this way provides further insight into the nature of value *relativism*. Relativists about values insist that all value judgments of the form "X is good or bad, right or wrong ..." must be qualified by adding "good or bad, right or wrong, *for* some person or group, society or culture, or *from* some perspective, point or view or form of life." On such a view, there can be no grounds for saying that something is good or right period, without adding "for whom?", "from what point of view?", "in what form of life?" But taking such a position, I want to suggest, amounts to claiming that *we cannot get beyond the first three dimensions of value* in order to ascend to a fourth dimension above all the competing perspectives. We can no more ascend to a fourth dimension of value than we can get beyond the first three familiar dimensions of space to a fourth dimension of space. Indeed, for value relativists, there is no such higher dimension of value to ascend to. Any such dimension is illusory because, as finite beings, we are necessarily embedded in historically and culturally limited (third-dimensional) points of view and forms of life and cannot rise above them.

There are other versions of value relativism that are more easily refuted, as we shall see in the next chapter. But this is the kind of relativism, I think, that troubles most ordinary persons and social theorists when they worry whether "all values are relative." They fear that we may not be able to justify claims that some things are right or wrong for everyone and should be recognized as such from every point of view, because there can in principle be no higher standpoint from which to make such claims. Viewed in this way, value relativism presents a powerful challenge to modern thought that cannot be answered by simple or facile arguments. The challenge can only be adequately addressed by asking how, if at all, one might get beyond the first three dimensions of value to something higher.

# CHAPTER 8

# *The fourth dimension*

## I. INCLUSION AND TRANSCENDENCE: NON-RELATIVE VALUE

To many moderns, the first three dimensions of value exhaust the dimensions of human value – as the three familiar dimensions of ordinary experience exhaust the dimensions of space. What might be meant by a fourth dimension of value is not so easily described and many thinkers would deny it exists at all. But, while the existence of a fourth dimension of value may be controversial, it seems to be presupposed by much of what humans have had to say about the good and the right.

Without such a dimension, for example, what we call *ethical* or *moral* value would not be what most people take it to be. This is not to say that all fourth-dimensional value is ethical or even that all value people call ethical lies in the fourth dimension. The virtues and excellences that comprise third-dimensional value (loyalty, friendliness, trustworthiness, and the like) are an important part of many ancient and modern views of ethics. But a crucial part of what we call ethical or moral value does I think lie in the fourth dimension – including (of special importance) that part explored in Chapters 2–4, which implies that each person is to be treated as an end by every other person and no one as a mere means. Fourth-dimensional value, to put a name on it, is *non-relative* (absolute or universal) worth – not merely what is thought to have worth from this or that particular point of view, in this or that form of life, for this or that person or society or culture, but worth that should be recognized by everyone from every point of view.

Conceived in this way, fourth-dimensional value (if it did exist) would include the other three dimensions of value, yet would also transcend them. To see how it would transcend them, suppose there are persons who agree with you across a broad spectrum about what is necessary to live a happy or flourishing human life. The problem is that these people care only about whether they and their group or society or culture attain such a life and do not care whether you do. Their society attains high degrees of excellence in science, art and civic life among themselves (third-dimensional value) while marginalizing or exploiting other groups, including yours.[1] (Perhaps your marginalized group is the product of ethnic cleansing.)

You may have no disagreement with these people about the nature of human flourishing (as defined in the other three dimensions of value) or about what makes them and other humans happy. It is just that they have a good measure of what is needed to attain such happiness and you do not, *and they do not care that you do not.* They do not acknowledge any "right" of yours to be treated as an end or with respect in any sense by others, or to be allowed to pursue happiness as you choose. Such acknowledgment of worthiness for consideration by others, independently of what you could do for them, is an example of the recognition of fourth-dimensional value.

We can see from this example how fourth-dimensional value transcends the third dimension. Third-dimensional value may tell us what a flourishing or happy life would be for individuals or groups. But it is not evident that persons living such a life, as a condition for their flourishing, must recognize the worthiness of other individuals or groups for a flourishing life as well. If such recognition of others' worthiness should be required for one's own flourishing, it would have to be shown by further argument; and that argument would project us from the third dimension into the fourth.

Perhaps the flourishing of certain individuals and groups might depend on the flourishing of *some* particular other persons or groups who could assist them significantly or cause them harm. Then, enlightened self-interest would demand a concern about *those* other persons or groups. But that would be a selective and self-interested concern of the sort that sociobiologists and evolutionary psychologists call "reciprocal altruism" (cooperating with others for mutual benefit); and thus it would be a *relative* (third-dimensional) interest based on what others could do *for them* and for the flourishing of *their* form of life.[2] It would not be a universal

---

[1] Hardin 1995 is an instructive study of the genesis and dangers of such groups, whose adherents Kai Nielsen calls "classist amoralists." In a subtle work, Vogler (2002) argues in similar vein that, while we may have reasons to be moral, it does not follow that we have "all things considered" reasons, so that it is possible to be both reasonable and vicious. Astute reviews of Vogler that agree on this particular point include Driver 2004, p. 847 and Buss 2008, p. 478.

[2] See Wright 1994, Kitcher 2006, for overviews. E. O. Wilson 1975 is a seminal study. In an important work, Sober and D. S. Wilson 1998 relate altruism to group selection.

(fourth-dimensional) concern based on the objective worthiness of the others in themselves for consideration from all other persons.

Many biologists and evolutionary psychologists now tell us that such reciprocal altruism is the basis for the evolution of cooperation in the human species; and reciprocal altruism is also made the basis for some well-known modern contractarian theories of ethics, such as those of Kurt Baier, David Gauthier and others, that take their inspiration from Hobbes as well as from modern game theory.[3] On such views, enlightened egoists (or groups) would seek to avoid living in a Hobbesian state of nature of continual conflict with other individuals and groups by making a tacit or explicit social compact in which they agreed to cooperate with one another for mutual benefit.

A social contract of such a kind may be a step in the direction of ethics, but it still expresses a relative, third-dimensional, concern based on self-interest. It expresses the rational concern of enlightened self-interested persons to protect themselves from harm and to promote the flourishing of their own ways of life. If some persons or groups were too powerless to help or hurt them, there would be no reason in the logic of reciprocal altruism alone why the powerless groups have to be included in the contract – no reason why they could not be marginalized or exploited.[4] There remains a troubling gap here between what is good for one's own self or group or for the flourishing of one's own form of life, and what is good, period; and that is the gap between the third and fourth dimensions of value.[5]

## 2. HUMAN NATURE, NATURAL LAW AND CLASSICAL VIRTUE ETHICS

One may think this gap between the third and fourth dimensions might be bridged in another way, if one could show that what was good for oneself and one's own form of life was in fact good for all humans. That is, one may think the gap might be bridged by an account of human

---

[3] Baier 1958, 1995; Gauthier 1986; Kavka 1986; Skyrms 1996; Axelrod 1984; Kitcher 2006; Alexander 2007; Hampton 2007.

[4] These points have been made by many critics of contractarian views. See perceptive overviews by Sayre-McCord 2000, Ashford and Mulgan 2007 as well as essays in Paul, Miller and Paul 1988 and Vallentyne 1991.

[5] In an important work, Joyce (2006) makes a related argument in a different way. He makes a strong evolutionary case for individual and group benefits of tendencies to make moral judgments, but argues that this evolutionary explanation falls short of justifying the "practical clout" we assign to moral judgments, which leads him to challenging skeptical conclusions about morality. Hauser (2005) also makes a case for the evolutionary origins of our moral sense.

happiness or flourishing that was *universal*, applying to all humans and not only to oneself or one's group. For then it seems one would have an account of the absolute good from all points of view that the fourth dimension requires.

Finding such universal requirements for human happiness or flourishing was, to be sure, the goal of some *natural law* theories of ethics as well as many classical versions of *virtue ethics* that have their roots in Aristotle.[6] Such theories sought to establish what forms of life were best for all humans by appealing to a common human nature and the ends and virtues essential to the fulfillment of that nature. In some natural law theories, including many modern ones, doing this would involve identifying goods sought by all humans based on common human traits, needs or ends in all cultures and identifying the kinds of lives that would best satisfy beings with such traits, needs or ends.[7]

Many versions of *virtue ethics* similarly seek to identify common traits of character that would lead to flourishing lives for all humans.[8] Rosalund Hursthouse, a modern proponent of the classical approach to virtue ethics along with Philippa Foot and others, defines a virtue as "a character trait a human being needs for eudaimonia, to flourish or live well."[9] The assumption of classical virtue ethics, as Julia Annas (another of its defenders) has pointed out, was that, given our human nature, the cultivation of certain virtues was necessary for any kind of flourishing human life.[10]

---

[6] See Annas 1993 and Irwin 2007 for comprehensive critical overviews of ancient ethical views by well-known scholars of ancient philosophy. Annas defends ancient virtue ethics in the tradition of Aristotle. Irwin defends a broadly eudaimonistic approach to ethics, also in the tradition of Aristotle. Kraut 2007 is an original "developmental" account of human well-being or flourishing, also in the tradition of Aristotle, by another well-known scholar of ancient philosophy.

[7] Modern natural law theorists include George 1993, Finnis 1980, Grisez and Shaw 1974, Budziszewski 1986, Braybrooke 2001, M. Murphy 2001. Hittenger 1987 is a critique. On the traditional natural law theory of Aquinas, see e.g., O'Connor 1967, Lisska 1996, Bowlin 1999. Copp (1995) defends an original "society-centered moral theory" that also emphasizes universal human needs, and has some affinity to (and differences from) some modern natural law theories. Copp compares his view to Braybrooke's in an insightful essay (2009). Kellenberger (2001) also emphasizes common human traits despite cultural diversity.

[8] Annas ibid. See, e.g., contributors to Crisp and Slote 1997 and Statman 1997, and Sherman 1989, S. Brown 2004, Adams 2006.

[9] Hursthouse 1999: 3; Foot 2001. Others who take this broadly neo-Aristotelian approach to virtue include G. Taylor 2006 and Gottlieb 2009. Taylor's 2006 is an insightful discussion of "vices" from this perspective. Becker 1998 offers a modern Stoic version of virtue ethics.

[10] Annas ibid.: 515–16. Some modern theories of the virtues, including Slote 2001, Driver 2001, Hurka 2001 and Swanton 2003, depart from this classical approach to varying degrees. (Hurka regards his view as a theory of the virtues but not a virtue ethics in the strict sense.) Lovibond (2002), like many of these others, argues that the cultivation of virtues allows us to fulfill needs for certain human goods. Brewer 2009 develops a very original defense of virtue ethics by appeal

I want to make two claims about these natural law and virtue ethical traditions. The first is that we can and should grant a basic assumption that underlies them: Appeals to human nature have much that is essential to teach us about the human good. As a consequence, the search for common human goods, needs and virtues must be an important *part* of any inquiry into ethics – where ethics is conceived broadly (as it was for the ancient thinkers) as the search for the "good life." If, for example, it is a universal human requirement for flourishing and happiness that children be loved and nurtured when young (as it surely is), then societies in which child abuse and neglect are common are going to produce much misery and disorder. Humans ignore such knowledge of human nature at their peril. Such appeals to human needs and to virtues necessary for flourishing lives and communities have already played a role in our discussion of the first three dimensions of value; and I will be returning to them because they are an important, indeed an indispensable, part of any adequate ethical theory.

But the second claim to be made about these venerable traditions in ethics is equally important and it is the one I want to focus on: While appeals to human nature and to common goods and virtues required for a flourishing life must be a *part* of any inquiry into ethics, such appeals will not alone get us to the ethical aspects of the fourth dimension of value, *even if the requirements for happiness or flourishing are universal and apply to all humans.* For, even if it could be shown that one or a few forms of life would best satisfy all human needs and interests (which is itself a controversial matter), it would not necessarily follow that humans ought to care whether all persons besides themselves and their favored circle (family, kin, tribe, culture, race) attain such a life.

### 3. TWO KINDS OF UNIVERSALITY

At issue here is an important distinction, not often emphasized in ethical discussions, between two kinds of *universality*, one in the third dimension of value, the other in the fourth. Suppose it is true (as mentioned earlier) that

(1) <Being loved and nurtured when young> is a good *for all humans* in all human forms of life.

to what he calls "dialectical activities." For critical discussion of modern virtue ethical views, see Solomon 1988, Terzis 1994, Harman 1999, Doris 2002, Copp and Sobel 2004. Sreenivasan 2002 is a response to the influential critique of virtue ethics by appeal to social psychology of Harman and Doris. Stuhr and Wellman 2002 is a useful overview of recent debates.

Then <being loved and nurtured when young> would be a *universal* third-dimensional value for humans because it would be a value common to all human societies, cultures and forms of life; and third-dimensional value is the domain of different societies, cultures and forms of life.

But now consider a different claim. Suppose an unfortunate child in a distant land and culture has been abandoned (as Mary was in the example of Chapter 5); and we want to say

(2) <This abandoned child's being loved and nurtured when found> is a good that should be recognized by *all persons* from *all points of view* as worthy of being realized (whether or not the persons and points of view are of the same culture, society, ethnicity, race, religion or form of life of, or care about, this child).

If this claim is true, then <this abandoned child's being loved and nurtured when found> would be a universal *fourth-dimensional* value, something that should be recognized by everyone from every point of view as a good worthy of being realized.

Claim (2) is a stronger claim, which persons may reject even if they accept (1). That is exactly what is done by those enlightened self-interested persons mentioned earlier who care only about their own group (family, clan, society, race), but not about others outside their group. These persons may acknowledge that being loved and nurtured when young is a universal human need for happiness and flourishing; and so they strive to love and nurture their own children. But they do not acknowledge that the happiness of strangers who are not in their favored group is a good or right *they* must also recognize.

Perhaps these self-interested persons are wrong. Perhaps a condition for their own flourishing or happiness is that they recognize the right of all other persons and groups to be happy or flourish as well. But it is far from obvious why this must be so; and powerful further arguments would be needed to show it to be so. Simply to define human "flourishing" or "happiness" so that the happiness or flourishing of some requires recognizing the right of *all* other persons or groups to be happy or flourish begs too many fundamental questions of ethics.

There remains a gap that needs to be filled between describing what is required *by everyone* for happiness or flourishing, and saying whose happiness or flourishing should be recognized as valuable *by everyone else*, a gap between the third and fourth dimensions of value. Traditional appeals to human nature or to virtues required for a flourishing life will not necessarily bridge this gap, even if they are universal. Suppose that to have a flourishing life for themselves and their communities, all humans must satisfy certain needs (shelter, clothing, love, friendships, approbation by others, and so on). It is very likely that many of these needs are universally required for human flourishing in some measure and toward some persons.[11] If so, and N were a representative need of this kind, claim (1) above could be generalized as follows:

(1') \<Satisfying N\> is a good *for all humans* in all human forms of life.

And this would be a different claim from the corresponding generalization of (2):

(2') \<This individual's (or group's) satisfying N\> is a good that should be recognized by *all persons* from *all points of view* as worthy of being realized.

Though both these claims are universal, they are so in different senses, one in the third dimension, the other in the fourth. With such a difference in mind, fourth-dimensional value may be characterized as follows:

(FD) A fourth-dimensional value is something that should be (is worthy of being) recognized as good or right by everyone, from every point of view.

If \<this abandoned child's being loved and nurtured when found\> is such a value, then anyone from any point of view who recognized it as good or right would have a correct attitude toward it and anyone who denied that it was good or right would have an incorrect attitude toward it. Similarly, a fourth-dimensional *disvalue* should be recognized as *bad* or *wrong* by everyone from every point of view; and anyone who so recognized it would have a correct attitude toward it.

Note that this account of fourth-dimensional value expresses the kind of recognition the retreatants wanted for their *ways of life* (or religions or ideologies). Most of them (excepting the relativists, skeptics and some others) did not believe, or at least did not want to believe, that their ways of life or religions or ideologies were merely (relatively) good or right *for them*. They wanted to believe their ways of life (or religions or ideologies) were worthy of being recognized as good or right by everyone, from every point of view.

Of course, the retreatants had limited success convincing others of their beliefs. The dogmatists who left the retreat were certain their respective ways of life had this absolute rightness and believed those who did not recognize it were fools or willfully ignorant. But those who stayed at the retreat had a more complex attitude. Though many of them also wanted to believe their points of view and ways of life were not merely good or

---

[11] I argue so in Chapter 13.

right for them, they realized how difficult it is to show this from the culturally conditioned (third-dimensional) points of view they necessarily
inhabited. They thereby recognized the gap between the third and fourth
dimensions of value and the difficulty of bridging that gap.

### 4. INCLUSION: PARTICULAR AND UNIVERSAL, RELATIVE AND ABSOLUTE, VALUES

These remarks about two kinds of universality not only throw light on
how fourth-dimensional value (if it existed) would transcend the third
dimension. They also show how the fourth dimension of value may
*include* the third dimension while transcending it. If <this abandoned
child's being loved and nurtured when found> is a fourth-dimensional
value, then the child's being so loved and nurtured is worthy of being
recognized as a good by all persons from all points of view. But the
child's being so loved and nurtured would not be worthy of such recognition, *if* being loved and nurtured was not in the first instance a good *for
this child* (rather than something bad for the child). In sum, the fourth-
dimensional value of the child's being loved and nurtured from *every*
point of view depends upon the third-dimensional value of being loved
and nurtured from the point of view *of the child*. Indeed, the fourth-
dimensional value *consists in* the child's being so loved and nurtured,
since the child's being so loved and nurtured is *what* is worthy of being
recognized as good by all persons.

In a similar way, the fourth dimension may include all three other
dimensions of value while transcending them, as the other dimensions
include, yet transcend, dimensions below them. If an individual's experiencing joy (a first-dimensional good), or fulfilling a practical goal (a
second-dimensional good) or attaining an excellence in some practice
(a third-dimensional good) is worthy of being recognized as a good by
all persons from every point of view, then something that is a value in
one of the other three dimensions (and hence something that is good *for*
some individuals and those who happen to care about those individuals)
is "raised up" to the fourth dimension. It becomes something that should
be recognized as a good from the points of view of all persons whether
they acknowledge it or not. The good so raised up or transfigured would
then have not only *relative* value or worth for some particular being(s) in
some form of life who have the experience or attain the excellence, but
also objective or *non-relative* (absolute) worth that should be recognized
as such from all points of view.

Not all value in lower dimensions need be so raised up to the fourth dimension, even if one accepts the possibility of fourth-dimensional value (a matter that remains an open question at this stage). Some value in lower dimensions may instead be overridden in the fourth dimension. For example, if an ethical theory implies that the joy a torturer takes in torturing his victim should not be recognized as a good by everyone (clearly not by the torture victims and those who care about them), then instead of being raised up as a good to the fourth dimension, the torturer's joy would be excluded or would become bad in the fourth dimension (something worthy of *not* being realized). Any such claims about overriding would have to be justified by ethical argument, to be sure. Indeed, affirming the very existence of a fourth dimension of value would require ethical argument, as noted. The example is merely meant to show how value in lower dimensions might be overridden, as well as included, in the fourth dimension, if fourth-dimensional value is possible at all.

Note also that if some values were so raised up to the fourth dimension, and not overridden, they would be values that are, in different senses, both *particular* and *universal*, and both *relative* and *non-relative* (or absolute). The child's experience of joy when found is a *particular* good for the child and those who care about her. But if raised up to the fourth dimension, it would also be a *universal* good, worthy of being recognized as such by all persons from all points of view. It would be a particular good when viewed from the first dimension (from the child's point of view) or from the second dimension (from the points of view of those who care about the child), but universal when viewed from the fourth dimension. Similarly, when viewed from the first and second dimensions, it would be a *relative* good for the child and those who care about her, whereas, if raised up to the fourth dimension, it would also be a non-relative or absolute good worthy of being recognized as such from every point of view *without ceasing to be a relative good for the child* and those who care about her.

Fourth-dimensional value is thus also related to what was called "all-things-considered" value in Chapter 5. If something is worthy of being recognized as good by all persons from all points of view (and hence is a fourth-dimensional good), then it must be good in *some* dimension of value or other and must not be overridden (becoming bad) in any dimension higher than that dimension (that is, it will be an all-things-considered good). Conversely, if something is good in some dimension of value and is not overridden in any dimension higher than that dimension, then it is worthy of being recognized as good by all persons from all points of view.

What is good in the fourth dimension (hence non-relatively or absolutely good) is thus also all things considered good, and vice versa.

### 5. ABSOLUTENESS AND CERTAINTY

None of this, of course, yet shows that there *is* anything like fourth-dimensional value. We are trying to understand what such value would be like, if it existed. But it is important to try to do this. For one may conclude too hastily that there is no such thing as fourth-dimensional value because one has the wrong idea of what it is.

One has to be cautious, for example, in referring to fourth-dimensional value as "absolute" value, as in the previous section. For, it is not uncommon in ordinary discourse to associate the term *absolute* with what is *certain*: Absolute values are often assumed to be those one knows with certainty. But no such implication attaches to the term "absolute" when used to describe fourth-dimensional value. Fourth-dimensional values are rather "absolute" in the sense of being "not merely relative." Whereas a *merely* relative good would be something that is good "for this or that person, or group, but not for all," an absolute or non-relative good (or truth) is something that is worthy of being recognized as good (or true) "by all persons from all points of view."

Nothing in this distinction implies that absolute values (*or truths*) must be knowable with certainty. If Einstein's general theory of relativity is absolutely true then it is worthy of being recognized as true from all points of view and hence from the points of view of all persons in all societies, whether or not all persons can understand it or agree with it. Those who deny its truth and believe some other theory about the nature of space and time have an incorrect attitude towards it. But from this, it does not follow that Einstein's theory can be known to be true with certainty; and the same may be said about absolute values. If there are such values, they are worthy of being recognized as good from all points of view and hence by all persons in all societies, whether or not they are actually so recognized; and being goods of such kinds does not necessarily imply they are, or can be, known to be so with certainty.

Not recognizing such distinctions may make one susceptible to a simplistic argument for relativism that tempts some persons: Absolute values are those we could know with absolute certainty. But we cannot know anything with absolute certainty. So there cannot be any absolute values; all values must be relative. This is not a good argument. From the fact that we cannot know that something is good with certainty, it does not follow that it cannot be worthy of being recognized as good from all points of view. One can seek to understand what might have value in the fourth dimension without assuming one has certainty about it. What matters in the search for fourth-dimensional value, as in other areas of inquiry, is whether we can have good reasons to believe or assert that at least some things have such value, even if the claims fall short of certainty; and this is a possibility that must be left open.

## 6. ANOTHER LOOK AT RELATIVISM: THE HARD PROBLEM

These remarks return us to the issue of relativism. I suggested in Chapter 7 that *relativism* about values might be defined as the view that there is no fourth dimension of value: The first three dimensions exhaust the dimensions of human value. I further suggested that a relativism of this kind is what troubles most ordinary persons and social theorists. They fear that we may not be able to justify claims that some things are worthy of being recognized as right or wrong by everyone, from every point of view, because there can in principle be no higher (fourth-dimensional) standpoint above all historically and culturally limited (third-dimensional) points of view from which to make such claims.[12]

When I use the term "relativism" hereafter without further qualification, I will mean value relativism in this sense. Viewed in this way, value relativism presents a powerful challenge to modern thought that cannot be answered by simple or facile arguments. This point is worth making because value relativism is often identified with other views that are more easily refuted.[13] One such view was encountered in the previous section on absoluteness and certainty. Another is the doctrine described as a "relativism of indifference" (in Chapter 2 by Bloom and others) that "no point of view (about values) or no form of life is absolutely better than any other." Borrowing an expression from Bernard Williams (1972), we might also refer to such a view as "vulgar relativism." It is a problematic view for reasons noted since ancient times.[14]

---

[12] Bloomfield expresses the problem aptly in the title of his perceptive paper "Is There a Moral Highground?" (2003). Also see Cooper 1978 and Coburn 1982 for insightful discussions of this problem.

[13] The literature on value relativism (including moral relativism) is vast. Useful overviews include Brown 1984, Stewart and Lynn 1991, Cook 1999, Baghramian 2004, Dreier 2006, Gowans 2008. Defenders of the kind of value relativism intended here include Harman 2000. See, e.g., the debate between Harman and Thomson (1996). See Stroud 1998 for a critique of Harman's view. Wong (2006) defends a qualified "pluralistic moral relativism."

[14] A critique appears in Plato's *Theatetus* among other ancient texts.

Ancient philosophers argued that relativists who assert that "no point of view is absolutely better than any other" as if this were *the* true view are in a way contradicting themselves. For in order to say that no one point of view or form of life is absolutely better than any other, one has to jump up to the fourth dimension, so to speak – to an absolute standpoint above all particular (third-dimensional) forms of life – and from that higher standpoint pronounce that no form of life or point of view is better than any other. Yet relativists who claim this also usually argue that all claims about what is good or right are relative to point of view. So they in effect deny that there is such an absolute standpoint from which one could justify the kind of general pronouncement they themselves are making.

To refute such a vulgar relativism, however, is not to refute the stronger kind of relativism just defined that worries most people. For this worrisome relativism is the *denial that one can make absolute judgments at all from the fourth dimension – either* to say that some particular third-dimensional point of view or form of life (your own, for example) is absolutely better than others *or* to say (as vulgar relativists do) that *no* point of view or form of life is any better than any other.

Relativism understood in this way (as the denial that any fourth-dimensional claims can be justified) is not so easily refuted. Refuting it might be called the "hard problem" of relativism. Facile arguments about self-contradiction will not do the job. The only way to fully dispose of worries about this kind of relativism is to ask how one can justify claims about what is good or right for all persons and from all points of view despite the realization that, as finite creatures, we must always see the world from some limited point of view or other. Such a task calls for more than logical sleight of hand. I suspect the difficulty of this task is why relativism never seems to die entirely as a challenge to philosophical inquiry, despite the refutations of various versions of relativism that philosophers have frequently put forward. As Simon Blackburn aptly says near the end of his *Ruling Passions* (1998: 308): "Perhaps we should not want [relativism] to disappear entirely. For it reminds us ... of the difficulty of even beginning to find the One True System of Things, as many moral philosophers seem to try to do."

## 7. GOOD "FOR" AND GOOD "FROM THE POINT OF VIEW OF"

It will be useful to summarize in conclusion the meanings of three expressions that have played a prominent role in the arguments of this chapter and earlier chapters and will play a prominent role in later chapters. They are

(1)  "good *for*"
(2)  (recognized or regarded as) "good *from the point of view of*"
(3)  (worthy of being recognized or regarded as) "good *from all points of view*"

What is "good *for*" beings or groups of certain kinds (humans, persons) in sense (1) is what contributes to their happiness or faring well or flourishing *in the first three dimensions of value*. That includes the accomplishments, virtues and excellences of the third dimension; and it includes goods in the first and second dimensions as well, insofar as the third dimension includes lower dimensions of value (basic value experiences, achieved purposes, satisfying personal relationships) that are not overridden in the third dimension. Goods in sense (1) were thus said to be *relative* goods for the beings who possess them (which, as argued in this chapter, does not preclude their also being non-relative goods, if they are not overridden in the fourth dimension).

But what is "good for" persons in this sense (1) need not be what they recognize or regard as "good from their point of view" in sense (2). For persons may fail to recognize what is actually good for them or what will actually lead to their faring well or flourishing. Thus, I have been careful throughout to distinguish what is good "for" persons (sense (1)) from what is good "from their point of view" (sense (2)), where the latter expression is short for "recognized or regarded as good from their point of view."

Recall from Chapter 1, that "points of view" were defined by persons' "beliefs and other psychological attitudes that together tell us how they experience the world, what they believe about it and what their 'values' are, in the sense of what they *regard* as, or *believe* to be, good and bad, right and wrong." The "values" of persons or groups in this definition are thus to be understood in sense (2); and (as noted in Chapter 1) the values of persons or groups so defined may or may not be the correct or true values, since points of view may be mistaken. One may have false beliefs and wrong ideas about what is good or valuable, even about what is good in sense (1) *for* oneself and one's own happiness or flourishing.

Consider the woman in the example of Chapter 6 who pursued a career in law. She found it unfulfilling and eventually abandoned her career in order to become a teacher, which she did find fulfilling. Before she made this self-discovery, the woman had believed a career in law was a good thing for her and would contribute to her happiness and flourishing. It was thus, at the time, good "from her point of view" (2). But it turned out not to be actually good "for her" (1). Note also that the gap between what she believed to be good "from her point of view" (2) and what was in fact good "for her" (1) was eventually closed *by value experimenting.*

Finally, expression (3) – "(worthy of being recognized or regarded as) good *from all points of view*" – describes *fourth-dimensional* value. As (1) refers to what is (relatively) "good for" persons in the first three dimensions of value, (3) refers to what is (non-relatively) "good from all points of view" in the fourth dimension. And just as something may in fact be "good for" persons in sense (1), *whether or not* it is recognized or regarded as good "from their point of view" in sense (2), so something may be worthy of being recognized as good by all persons from all points of view in sense (3), *whether or not* it is *actually* recognized as good by all persons "from their points of view" in sense (2).

In addition (as further argued in this chapter) being worthy of recognition as good by all humans and persons *from all* points of view in sense (3) does not mean, nor is it entailed by, being good *for all* humans or all persons *in sense* (1).[15] That is to say, universality in the third dimension does not entail universality in the fourth. Nor, as also argued, does being worthy of recognition as good by all persons from all points of view in sense (3) entail, nor is it entailed by, being *actually* recognized as good *in sense* (2) by all persons from all points of view. But then one might justly ask: If fourth-dimensional value cannot be determined by establishing what is good for all humans or all persons *or* by universal agreement among all persons, how then *can* it be determined, if at all? *That* is the "hard problem" of relativism described in the previous section which must be addressed.

---

[15] The converse also does not hold, as we see later: That something is worthy of being recognized as good by all humans and persons from all points of view (3) does not necessarily entail that it is good *for* all humans or persons in the sense that it contributes to their happiness or flourishing (1).

# CHAPTER 9

# *Aspiration*

## I. LOOKING BACK AND LOOKING AHEAD

Let us take stock of where we have come and where we are headed. I said in Chapter 1 that the ethical arguments of Chapters 2–4 would introduce the central themes of the book. But those arguments would be incomplete in a number of ways. Subsequent chapters would attempt to fill the gaps by situating the arguments of Chapters 2–4 in a broader theory of value (Chapters 5–8) and in a theory about the nature of philosophical inquiry (Chapters 9–11). We have undertaken the first of these tasks in the past four chapters. Among the things we have learned is that the arguments of Chapters 2–4 are situated at the divide *between the third dimension of value and the fourth dimension.* The challenge posed by relativism at the end of Chapter 8 was this: How, if at all, might one access the fourth dimension of value from the limited points of view and forms of life of the third dimension in which we necessarily find ourselves?

As it turns out, this was the problem faced by the retreatants of Chapter 3. (Hereafter, as in Chapter 3, I mean by the "retreatants" those who stayed behind to continue the search after others had left.) What did they do? They decided to take an attitude of respect in the sense of openness toward all points of view and forms of life. And what was their purpose in doing this? They did it as a way of limiting narrowness of vision, expanding their minds beyond their own limited points of view and forms of life in order to find out what was true from every point of view (non-relatively true). The attitude of openness they assumed was thereby viewed, not as the final truth about the good and the right, but as a way of searching for that truth under conditions of pluralism and uncertainty.

Looking at their efforts from the perspective of Chapter 8, we may now see the retreatants' reflections as their way of *groping toward the fourth dimension* of value from the different third-dimensional points of view and forms of life they inhabited. Viewed in this way, their reasoning provides clues we must now explore. Pursuing these clues leads to the second of the tasks mentioned in Chapter 1 – situating the arguments of Chapters 2–4 in a theory of the nature of philosophical inquiry, which is the goal of the next three Chapters (9–11).

## 2. WHAT THE RETREATANTS COULD AND COULD NOT SAY

The retreatants reasoned that the traditional way of searching for what is good and right from all points of view, and hence of accessing the fourth dimension, was thwarted by pluralism and uncertainty. That traditional way – positioning oneself in one's own point of view and trying to prove it absolutely right and every other view wrong – led to fruitless bickering. The attitude of openness suggested itself as an alternative, first, because it took pluralism and uncertainty seriously and, second, because it focused on the fact that the good from every point of view was what they were searching for. If you want to find out what should be recognized as good from every point of view, they reasoned, open your mind to every point of view and way of life to the degree that you can and strive to maintain conditions in which everyone acts with similar openness to the degree that they can.

The results thereby arrived at by the retreatants – about the moral sphere, ethical rules and exceptions, and so on – were substantial, as we saw. But many questions about their way of proceeding were left unsettled. Most importantly, how could they be sure their results were universally true for all persons and from all points of view rather than merely from their own points of view? For it was assumed that only a finite number of them chose to remain at the retreat; and it was further assumed that those who stayed could not entirely escape their own points of view. To show that the results of their reflections were universally valid, it seemed that they would have to demonstrate that *anyone* who reasoned correctly about these matters from *any* point of view would come to the same conclusions as they did.

But the retreatants did not claim this; nor could they claim it. For they were aware that there were many persons from whose points of view their conclusions would not follow. Among these persons were the dogmatists who left the retreat: They believed they already had the truth and would not agree with the idea of respecting others' views in the sense of openness when those other views conflicted with their own. Then, there were the relativists, who did not think there was any such thing as non-relative, fourth-dimensional, value to be searching for. Finally, we might add the enlightened egoists of Chapter 8 who accepted some obligations to those they cared about or those in their own group, but not to others outside their group. We can imagine they left the retreat as well.

Are the retreatants claiming that their reasoning demonstrates or proves that these other points of view are wrong? No, they cannot be claiming that either. To claim that would be to undercut the assumptions of pluralism and *uncertainty* with which they began their inquiries. If they could prove these other views wrong by some necessary line of reasoning from undeniable premises, what would be the point of continuing to be open to all other views to the degree possible when it was inconvenient to do so? It is *the belief that they are still searching for the truth, not that they have already found it* that motivates the retreatants in their initial position of openness, even to those who profoundly disagree with them.

What then does the retreatants' reasoning show, if it does not demonstrate that other competing views are wrong? It does show something of importance. It shows that, while the retreatants' ethical conclusions would not be arrived at by anyone from any point of view (or form of life), their conclusions would be arrived at by anyone from any point of view (or in any form of life) *who was willing to start with an attitude of openness* to all other points of view and forms of life. Anyone who, in the interests of limiting narrowness of vision, chooses initially to respect every other point of view and way of life in the sense of openness, and persistently strives to maintain this ideal in the face of obstacles and conflicts, would arrive at the ethical conclusions at which the retreatants arrived.

### 3. WHAT OPENNESS DOES AND DOES NOT IMPLY

So the further question to which the retreatants' reasoning leads is the following: Why should the retreatants (or anyone) take an attitude of openness to begin with? Recall from earlier chapters that openness is a *stance* or attitude one must choose to take, as the retreatants have done. One cannot antecedently prove it is the right stance. One cannot demonstrate, for example, that taking it is an inescapable requirement of practical reasoning or purposive agency or rational action, as some rationalists in ethics have attempted to do.[1] Or, at least nothing described in the retreatants' reasoning (or ours) thus far demonstrates such a thing.

Further, by taking an attitude of openness, the retreatants have not abdicated their finiteness, nor consequently have they disposed of pluralism

---

[1] Prominent examples include Gewirth 1977 and more recently Illies 2003.

and uncertainty. They know their stance of openness is itself one point of view among others that must be chosen; and they can't prove the other views are wrong. They continue to respect other points of view – to the degree possible – even those that do not accept openness, in the hope of finding out what is right *and* wrong. Nor does accepting openness accord *privilege* or *superiority* to the retreatants' own finite points of view. Recall that many of those who stay at the retreat and accept openness continue to hold their traditional religious, cultural, political and personal beliefs. Accepting openness does not require that they renounce their particular views and ways of life, but neither does accepting openness accord any privilege or superiority to their particular views and ways of life. To the contrary, it requires that they disown certain kinds of privilege or superiority, that of claiming absolute certainty for their points of view or the right to impose their points of view on others except as a last resort in order to restore the moral sphere.[2]

Nor does the *practice* or *practical application* of openness in their engagements with others accord special privilege or superiority to the retreatants' points of view. For they are to be treated no differently from an ethical standpoint than others, *including* those who do not accept openness: If the retreatants themselves break the moral sphere, their views also become less worthy of being treated with openness by others. Their belief in openness affords them no special treatment they do not earn by their plans of actions and practical engagements in the world. Indeed, there may be some persons or groups out there in the world who do not believe in openness, yet end up doing more good (relieving suffering, comforting the afflicted, helping the needy) than many of the retreatants who believe in openness do. But, of course, those who do not believe in openness may be capable of doing much evil as well, often in the name of their beliefs.

Nor can the retreatants who choose openness thereby attain a position of complete *neutrality* above all competing points of view or ways of life. Complete neutrality is not possible for finite persons embedded in limited points of view. If the retreatants claimed to possess it, they would be making the same mistake as vulgar relativists, who assume that from a position entirely above the fray, they could look down on all points of view and say with finality that no one is absolutely better than any other. The retreatants may hold their retreat as high up in the Himalayas as they can. But they cannot get that high.

---

[2] They lack such certainty both about the consistency and completeness of their belief systems – whether the belief systems consist of only truths and no falsehoods or include all truths.

Nor can the retreatants assume, like dogmatists, that their own view of openness is absolutely better than all others, as if openness were itself the absolute point of view. Far from it. Openness is a way of searching for the absolute point of view, not that point of view itself. Indeed, the retreatants learn by practicing it that openness is not the final view. For the truth they find is that, in the end, you cannot open your mind to all points of view in an imperfect world. Openness to all ways of life is itself a defeasible good.

In sum, openness is a way of groping toward the fourth dimension from finite forms of life, not a privileged position already in the fourth dimension. It is a path, not the goal. The retreatants must never forget this, lest they lose sight of the fact that they do not possess the whole or final truth about the good, but rather are searching for it. They should recall Augustine's sentiment that the way of seeking wisdom for finite creatures is a manifestation of humility.[3] The whole and final truth is not something one can possess from finite perspectives. Indeed, one might aptly say that the truth in this final and complete sense, the ethical truth, is not something to be *possessed* by finite beings at all, as one might possess a pot of gold, hoarding it from others, as a miser hoards his gold. The retreatants' goal is not to possess this truth in such a fashion, but, as Plato said, to *partake* of it or *participate* in it from finite points of view by the way one lives. If the ethical truth were something that only some persons could in principle possess, hoarding it from others, it would only be *a* truth, not the Truth.

#### 4. ASPIRATION TO WISDOM: KANT'S THREE QUESTIONS

So let us return to the key question. If the attitude of openness is itself a finite stance that one is not compelled to take, but must choose to take, what should motivate anyone to choose it?[4] The retreat again provides clues. Those who stayed and agreed to take an attitude of openness had reasons for doing so that those who departed did not share. Among those reasons, two were paramount. First, the retreatants who stayed took pluralism and uncertainty seriously – enough to wonder about the truth of their own beliefs. At the same time, they were not yet ready to give up

---

[3] In an original study, Grenberg (2005) argues that humility plays a significant role in Kantian moral theory as well, a different role than the one being suggested here, but with some similarities having to do with the "finiteness" of the human condition.

[4] The notion of aspiration developed in these sections was first introduced in Kane 1993 and 1994 (chapter 4).

the search for the objective good and thus to succumb to relativism or skepticism. We may say they were persons who continued to *aspire* to find what is good and right from every point of view despite concerns about pluralism and uncertainty; and this aspiration was motivated not merely by an abstract concern to find out what, if anything, had such worth, but by a desire to attain such worth and to learn whether they and their ways of life possessed it.

This response suggests that the stance of openness is grounded in, or motivated by, two primary attitudes: (1) the belief or recognition that we are finite beings who must see the world from limited points of view, which is the source of pluralism and uncertainty; and what I shall call (2) an *aspiration to wisdom* in an ancient philosophical sense. This aspiration is a desire to find what is true and worth striving for in the nature of things and the willingness to make efforts to search for such truth and worth under finite conditions. These are not neutral or content-less motivations by any means. Yet they can in principle be accepted by persons who otherwise have very different beliefs and forms of life, as did the retreatants.

The first of these motivations, the recognition of pluralism and uncertainty, has been discussed in earlier chapters. It is now time to consider the second motivation, the "aspiration to wisdom in an ancient philosophical sense." As its title suggests, this motivation has much to do with the nature of philosophy, understood in the traditional sense as the love (*philia*) of wisdom (*sophia*). In Chapter 1, I suggested that the nature of philosophy, understood as the love of, and search for, wisdom, would provide clues to answering questions about values and ethics in subsequent chapters. It is now time to explain what was meant by saying this.

Near the end of his *Critique of Pure Reason*, Kant says there are three great philosophical questions humans may ask.[5] (I depart from Kant somewhat in the translation of the second two of these questions for reasons to be explained in a moment.)

> What can I know?
> How should I act or live?
> What should I aspire to?

The second of these questions "How should I act or live?" is the ethical question. Through the centuries, philosophers have tried to answer this second, ethical, question in terms of answers to the first question – to determine how we should act in terms of what we can know. Find the facts

---

[5] Kant 1958: 165 (A805; B833). Thanks to Thomas Seung for this source.

about human nature and the cosmos, it was said, and you would have definitive answers to ethical questions about how to live. But a theme of earlier chapters has been that, given the conditions of modernity, including pluralism and uncertainty, one can no longer assume the ethical question can be fully answered in this simple way. Answers to the second, or ethical, question ("how should I act or live?") must depend to some degree on answers to the first question ("what can I know?"). We must learn about human nature to know what human happiness or fulfillment would require. But such knowledge is not sufficient to fully answer the second or ethical question, as argued in Chapter 8. To do this, I now want to suggest, we must bring in the third question as well: "What should I aspire to?"

"Aspiration" will be viewed as a special term in these chapters from this point onward, having to do with the search for truth. Kant himself, in his third question, uses the term "hope" rather than "aspiration." His actual question is "What can I hope for?" ("*Was kann Ich hoffen?*"). The two terms "hope" and "aspiration" are related, to be sure. But hope is an attitude one could have while sitting in an armchair doing nothing to attain what is hoped for. Whereas aspiration, as viewed here, is a "form of life" involving a patient spiritual or intellectual search or quest for the true and the good – as in the Socratic dictum "the unexamined life is not worth living." It is with this meaning in mind that I have altered the formulation of Kant's third question from "hope" to "aspiration." Likewise, Kant's actual second question is "What should I do?" ("*Was soll Ich tun?*"), which I have altered to "How should I act or live?" in order to emphasize a connection with the broader ancient philosophical quest for a "life worth living."

## 5. SEARCHES IN THE REALM OF ASPIRATION

By phrasing the questions in this way, I mean to emphasize that the move beyond the first two Kantian questions to the third question about aspiration is not a move away from rational inquiry toward "irrational" hope. To the contrary, aspiration as understood here does not preclude rational inquiry, but requires it. What aspiration adds to rational inquiry is a recognition of the radical contingency of such inquiry. Aspiration requires an intelligent search for what is aspired to, but with the recognition that we can never know (in the sense of having certainty) that we have attained the goal even when we have attained it.

To illustrate, consider that there are different kinds of searches. In the simplest kind, we have lost something, such as our keys in the yard, and are looking for them. We know that what we are looking for exists and will know when we find it. Contrast this with the search for something that, for all we know, may not exist. The ancient explorer Pythias went in search of the land of the midnight sun (a place where the sun never sets), though most everyone of his time doubted there was any such place to be found; or physicists look for magnetic monopoles or faster-than-light particles, not knowing whether any such things exist. Still, even in these cases, Pythias and the physicists know what they are looking for and can know they have found it when they have found it.

Now contrast this with yet another kind of search. A knight journeys into a dangerous forest in search of the Holy Grail. He has heard that it is a golden chalice of a certain description and it is somewhere in this forbidding place. But he does not know that this is so. His search requires the skill of Pythias and other explorers and involves as much danger. But there is a new twist to the knight's search that Pythias and other explorers do not face. Even if he should find a golden chalice of the appropriate description in the forest, he cannot know that it *really is the Holy Grail* of legend, rather than a fake or substitute. He cannot know with certainty that he has found what he is looking for *even if he has found it*.

Let us call searches such as the knight's, "searches in the realm of aspiration," which means they have the following characteristics. He (a) aspires to (and therefore desires and seeks) something of great importance (the Holy Grail), (b) which, for all he knows, is attainable, but whose attainment is difficult and not assured. There are (c) actions he can perform, a search he can undertake (to find a golden chalice in the forest), that he has reason to believe may lead to the goal, which (d) will not guarantee its attainment, but are such that (e) the failure to undertake these actions (seeking the golden chalice) would mean for him abandoning hope of attaining the cherished goal (finding the Holy Grail).

Searches in the realm of aspiration, like the search for the Holy Grail, are called "quests" in the language of the great myths and legends of human history, where (for good reason) they play a prominent role. But it would be a mistake to think that searches in the realm of aspiration have their place only in myth and legend.

The searches of scientists for the ultimate truths about the natural world or the fundamental laws of nature also have the characteristics of searches in the realm of aspiration, owing to the fact that the scientists can never know with certainty that they have attained the truths or fundamental laws even if they have in fact attained them. Any explanatory scheme they possess may have some errors, be incomplete or superseded by something better. Scientists who have this lofty goal (and I am not claiming all of them do) (a) aspire to (and therefore desire and seek) something of great importance (the ultimate truths about nature), (b) which, for all they know, is attainable, but whose attainment is difficult and not assured. There are (c) actions they can perform (consider all available evidence, do experiments, criticize existing theories, look for the most precise and comprehensive explanations) that they believe will lead to the goal, (d) not guaranteeing its attainment, but such that (e) failing to undertake these actions (considering all available evidence, doing experiments, etc.) would mean for them abandoning hope of attaining the goal (understanding the ultimate truths about nature).

This example illustrates the way in which aspiration is more than hope, though it involves hope. The point of the Grail legend and other mythical quests is to highlight the difficulty, skill, character, discipline and effort required to persist in the search for cherished goals and high ideals. And so it is also with the skill, discipline and effort of scientific inquiry. It is in this sense that aspiration is not merely an attitude, but a form of life – a form of life that involves patient, disciplined, intelligent searching for cherished goals whose attainment can never be assured. In the words of the pre-Socratic philosopher Xenophanes[6]

> The gods did not reveal from the beginning
> All things to us, but in the course of time
> Through seeking, men find that which is the better
> But as for certain truth, no man has known it,
> Nor will he know it; neither of the gods ...
> And if by chance he were to utter
> The final truth, he would himself not know it.

## 6. ASPIRATION

"Aspiration" is an apt word for this radically contingent seeking. It signifies "an outflowing or going outward of the spirit," from the Latin "*aspirare*," which means "to breathe ('*spirare*') forth," but also "to have a fixed desire or longing for something" and "to seek to attain it." The image suggested by the term is of our spirits reaching beyond the finite points of view we inhabit in order to find out what should be recognized as true or right from every point of view. Aspiration is thus a kind of "self-correction by consciousness of its own initial excess of subjectivity," to use words that Alfred North Whitehead (1978: 22) once employed to describe

---

[6] Kirk and Raven 1960, fragments 189, 191 (Xenophanes). The translation is Popper's 1965: 18.

philosophy. They are words that might well have been used to describe science or any other quest for objective truth that goes beyond one's own subjective understanding.

Indeed, the idea of an "outflowing or going outward of the spirit," reaching beyond its finiteness of point of view, was at work in the movement beyond the first dimension of value to higher dimensions in Chapters 5–8. The initial "excess of subjectivity" in the first experiential dimension of value gives way in the second dimension to purposive action through which humans attempt to give meaning to their lives by making an objective mark upon the world, as Nozick put it.[7] In the third dimension, the human spirit seeks to "correct its own excess of subjectivity" still further by participating in practices, traditions, cultures, communities and forms of life in which various excellences of character and achievement can be pursued with others (these traditions, cultures and forms of life being what Hegel aptly called "objective spirit"). The aspiration to a fourth dimension of value, reaching beyond the particular practices, traditions, cultures of the third dimension, may then be viewed as a continuation of this philosophical quest to overcome the limitations of finite points of view.

Those who stay at the retreat aspire in this manner to find out what is good and right from every point of view, as scientists aspire to find out what is objectively true about the natural world. The retreatants tried openness because they did not know for sure what was right in this sense and wanted to give every view a fair hearing, allowing it to be tested, as scientists allow competing theories to be tested. In such manner, to go beyond the first two Kantian questions to the third question "what should we aspire to?" is not to give up the rational search for the good and the right, but to recognize its *contingency* and *experimental* nature. Kant's third question is thus also a *philosophical* question, as he says, which like all philosophical questions, is inspired by wonder.

But what is the goal that philosophical aspiration seeks? What is this *wisdom*, the love of which gave philosophy its name, and what is its connection to the value questions of this book? This is the topic of the next two chapters.

---

[7] Nozick 1974: 44–45.

# CHAPTER 10

# *Wisdom*

## 1. FIRST PHILOSOPHY: ARISTOTLE

We turn now to the object of the aspiration that inspires the retreatants to try openness, which was said to be "wisdom in an ancient philosophical sense." On this topic, it is useful to get our bearings once again from Aristotle. Ancient commentators placed after Aristotle's treatise on physics a collection of writings that dealt with the deepest philosophical issues about reality that went beyond physics and other sciences. These collected writings consequently came to be known as the "Metaphysics." But Aristotle's own name for their subject matter was simply "wisdom" (*sophia*) or "first philosophy" (*prote philosophia*);[1] and it was the love of this wisdom that gave philosophy its name.

"Wisdom" or "first philosophy," as Aristotle described it, seeks true and comprehensive answers to the questions "what is?" and "why?" It seeks to know the way things really are in the most comprehensive sense ("what is"). But more than that, wisdom or first philosophy seeks to know "why" things are as they are (their causes or first principles) and why it is reasonable to believe or accept any answers that may be offered about the nature of things.[2] In this respect, as Aristotle points out, the lover of wisdom – the *philosophos* (whether scientist or philosopher, he made no distinction) – is more demanding than the lover of myth – the *philomythos* – though they are kindred spirits. For, both the lover of wisdom and the lover of myth seek true explanations of the way things are and why they are, though the lover of myth does so uncritically, the lover of wisdom critically.[3]

A second important feature of wisdom or first philosophy for Aristotle (as for most other ancient thinkers) is that it seeks not only to understand what is true of the nature of things (*objective reality*), but also what is *good*

---

[1] Aristotle 1941: *Metaphysics*, Book 1.    [2] Ibid.    [3] Ibid.

and *worth striving for* in the nature of things (what has *objective value or worth*).[4] Indeed, these two goals tended to converge for Aristotle and other ancient thinkers: To understand what is true about the nature of things would be to understand what is good and worth striving for in the nature of things. In Aristotle's case, the convergence comes about because wisdom not only seeks answers to the question "what is?" but also to the question "why?" But answers to the question "why?" involve knowing the ultimate sources or causes (*archai*) and explanations (*aitiai*) of things, which include knowing their final causes or ends; and these final causes or ends also inform us of what is good for each thing.[5]

## 2. ANCIENT WISDOM AND THE SUNDERINGS OF MODERNITY

As noted in Chapter 1, attitudes toward these two goals of ancient wisdom – understanding what is objectively real and what is objectively good – have changed in the modern age. With the rise of modern science, there has been a tendency to pry apart objective explanations of reality (the ways things are) from considerations of objective value and worth (the way things ought to be). Objective explanation of the cosmos became the province of the new natural sciences, which were supposed to be value neutral, leaving questions about objective value and worth precariously dangling in the winds of intellectual change. The result, noted in Chapter 1, was a series of what Hegel called "sunderings" in modernity of fact from value, scientific explanation from purpose and theoretical inquiry from practical inquiry about the good.

Not only has the relationship of the two ends of ancient wisdom – understanding what is objectively real and what is objectively good – changed in the modern era, but our ability to attain *both* ends has also been questioned. In this case, the additional culprits included the two further conditions of modernity, pluralism and uncertainty. The fact that human inquirers are embedded in historically and culturally limited points of view threatens the goal of understanding objective reality as well as objective worth and for similar reasons. How can we grasp an objective reality in the sense of "the way things really are" in themselves rather than merely how they "appear" to us, it was asked, if all understanding is dependent upon some framework of interpretation – a conceptual scheme or theoretical perspective or form of life?

---

[4] Ibid.    [5] Ibid.

This problem – the scheme-dependence of all understanding – which puts in jeopardy both goals of ancient wisdom, lies behind various postmodernist and other contemporary critiques of traditional metaphysics and philosophy. Jean-Francois Lyotard tellingly defines "the postmodern condition" as the "rejection of all meta-narratives," by which he means the rejection of any theories about reality or value that claim to be true for all persons and all societies at all times.[6] Lyotard's idea is that we all have our particular "narratives" or stories to tell about the nature of reality and value embodied in our different cultures and traditions, myths, religions, philosophies, language-games and forms of life. But none of the particular narratives is, or could be, the one true story of the world – a "meta-" narrative standing above all particular forms of life and true for all of them to which traditional metaphysics (i.e., "wisdom") aspired.

As a result, it has been said (by Richard Rorty, for example[7]) that a postmodernist culture would also be "post-*metaphysical*" and "post-*philosophical*." It would have abandoned the ancient goals of wisdom or first philosophy of understanding objective reality and objective worth (for all persons and from all points of view); and it would therefore reject the possibility of a fourth dimension of value.

Such contemporary critiques of the ancient goals of wisdom or first philosophy give us further insight into the position of the retreatants who remained at the retreat. We may say of those retreatants that they were *reluctant to abandon these ancient goals of wisdom and enter into such a postmodern condition.* That is, they continued to "aspire to wisdom in an ancient philosophical sense." So they stayed at the retreat in order to keep searching for what should be recognized as good and right from all points of view, despite their concerns about pluralism and uncertainty. The problem the retreatants faced, however, was how such a search was to proceed without merely assuming, as the ancients did, that the two goals of understanding objective reality and objective worth will necessarily converge (given the sunderings of modernity) and without assuming that either goal is directly accessible to the searchers (given pluralism and uncertainty). How can the aspiration to wisdom in the ancient philosophical sense survive this postmodern challenge?

In an attempt to respond to this question, I think we must look more closely at both goals of ancient wisdom, focusing first on objective reality and then coming back to objective worth. We can no longer simply assume the two goals of first philosophy will converge as the ancients believed.

[6] Lyotard 1987: Preface.   [7] Rorty 1989: 73.

But understanding one of these goals may nonetheless throw light on the other. That is the strategy I shall pursue in this chapter and the next, considering first the goal of understanding objective reality to see what clues it may reveal about the goal of understanding objective worth.

### 3. THE WAYS THINGS ARE

In the past, the force of the term "objective" in "objective reality" was usually taken to be this: As the subject matter of wisdom or first philosophy ("metaphysics" as it came to be called), reality was to be understood *as it is in itself* and not merely as it is known by us or *appears* to us. We recognize this as the central philosophical problem of "appearance versus reality." The postmodernist critique of first philosophy or metaphysics makes this problem especially troubling. If all understanding is dependent on conceptual scheme or linguistic framework, how can we grasp an objective reality in the sense of the way things are in themselves, rather than merely as they appear to us?

The first thing to note in response to this question is a point that has been made by a number of contemporary philosophers: The central theme of the postmodernist critique – the scheme dependence of all understanding – does not of itself imply that we must relinquish notions of objective truth and reality. Donald Davidson puts this point nicely when he says: "In giving up dependence on the concept of an uninterpreted reality, something outside all schemes and science, we do not relinquish the notion of objective truth."[8] Why not? The answer to be given here is not exactly Davidson's, though it owes something to his work as well as to the work of other recent thinkers, such as Elliott Sober, John Post, Hilary Putnam, Ernest Sosa, Colin McGinn, Simon Blackburn, among others.[9]

When it is said that "if all understanding is scheme dependent, we cannot grasp the way things are in themselves," trouble is already brewing in the expression "the way things are in themselves." The expression presumes that there is such a thing as *the* way things really are, when it is likely that there are different ways things are, described in different vocabularies for different purposes.[10] Think of the history of a city, like New York, over a twenty-four-hour period, as told by a society columnist, an economist, a weatherman, a political reporter, a social historian, the

---

[8] Davidson 1973–4: 6.
[9] Sober 1982, Putnam 1987, Post 1987, McGinn 1999, E.Sosa 1993, Blackburn 2005.
[10] This point is made by a number of the authors cited in the previous note, notably Sober, Putnam, Post and McGinn.

director of sewers and sanitation, and other interested parties. Each of them gives us a different description of the city from his or her limited point of view. But what is the true picture? What is the real New York "in itself"? This question will seem odd and unanswerable, if an answer were to require (as postmodern critics of metaphysics sometimes claim) identifying a neutral perspective from which the city could be described as it is "in itself," but *not* from any particular point of view.

Yet there is an alternative suggested by the authors mentioned. The real New York may be regarded as the *summation* of what is correctly described from all the different points of view and in all the different vocabularies. The real city would be what is correctly described by the weatherman *plus* the social historian *plus* the director of sanitation *plus* the society columnist, and so on. Then it would be true that there is no neutral description of the city; we cannot avoid describing it *from* some point of view, in some vocabulary. But the absolute or (in Putnam's expression) God's-eye point of view of the city would not require such a neutral description. Rather it would be the summation of the true statements about the city from the different finite points of view. Each point of view might tell us something true, not about a phantom New York, but about the real one. Each would fall short, not in failing to describe the real New York, but in not being the whole story about it.

This idea is by no means new. It can be compared to the ancient Buddhist tale of the blind men describing different parts of an elephant. Each man has a different story to tell depending on whether he feels the legs or the trunk or the torso; and each wonders what this "thing" could really be. One point of this tale was that each blind man has it wrong, if he claims to be describing what the elephant "really" is. But one need not thereby conclude that the real elephant is some unknowable thing-in-itself. It may be what is correctly described (if only partially) by each of the blind men and by others from other perspectives. Each goes wrong only in claiming to have the *whole* truth about it.

This theme is importantly related to something that was said in the previous chapter regarding the retreatants' "aspiration" to wisdom, namely, that the *whole* or *final* truth is not something finite creatures can possess entirely. What they can do is partake of or participate in that truth from limited points of view. This is what the weatherman, society columnist and the economist do when they describe New York from their perspectives, or the blind men when they describe that part of the elephant they can touch, but not see. Or think of a small cube described by astronomer Phillip Morrison. A chemist would tell us, says Morrison, that the cube is made up of very thin alternating strips of different metals and he would give us a full physical analysis of it. But the chemist would fail to say that the cube tells the story of Huckleberry Finn (the thin layers of metal form a code). Chemistry lacks the vocabulary to do that. But it does not follow that the chemist is not describing the real cube. He is, but so is the person who says that it tells the story of Huckleberry Finn. Or think of reciting the history of chess to some people who understand English but have never heard of chess.

The point is that "the *ways* the world is" may be accessible to us only with the proper conceptual schemes or language games or forms of life in place. This much (i.e., the "scheme-dependence of all understanding") supports the postmodernist critique of first philosophy or metaphysics. But it does not rule out the possibility of describing an objective reality. For the way the world is may simply be all the different ways the world is, described in the different vocabularies. To fully describe it would require learning and using many vocabularies or language games. To learn about particle physics one has to learn about mathematical objects called vector spaces; and to do this is not only to learn a new vocabulary, but a new way of thinking. Yet human beings can learn new ways of thinking and speaking, adding them to the ones they already have. If some of these ways of thinking or speaking should be irreducible to one another (if they cannot be wholly translated into, or reduced to, some one level of description), so be it. Reality, like value, may come in layers, as Colin McGinn has put it[11]; and objective truth may be the sum of truths from different levels of description.

Note as well that if each person, the weatherman, the sanitation engineer, the social historian, gets his or her description of New York right from his or her perspective, then what each says is true *for* everyone, not just for that person. If the weatherman correctly describes the New York weather, then what he says about the weather is true so far as it goes for everyone, the economist, the sanitation engineer, the social historian, and so on. It would be bizarre to say that the weather as described by the weatherman is true or false only *for* the weatherman and his cohorts, but not true or false for the sanitation engineer or anyone else.[12] The descriptions of the different parties may be relative to point of view, but *not* their truth or falsity. As Davidson says, "in giving up ... the conception of an uninterpreted reality" (something that can be understood outside all conceptual schemes and language games), we need not thereby "relinquish the notion of objective truth." If the blind man clutching the elephant's leg correctly describes his part of the elephant, then what he says about the leg is objectively true

[11] McGinn 1999: 47.    [12] Blackburn (2005) makes this point.

for everyone though he only describes part of the elephant. He only goes wrong if he claims the whole elephant is like a leg.

### 4. STANDARDS OF EVIDENCE: ASPIRATION REVISITED

But one might argue that there is still a problem about whether the persons involved, the weatherman and the rest, are *correctly* describing the city or elephant even from their respective points of view or in their distinctive vocabularies. One must add that for each of them, in their different vocabularies, there must be conformity to standards of evidence and correctness if they claim to state truths about the city. Meteorology is a science and there are standards for collecting and interpreting evidence about the weather within it. The weather is a complex topic and sometimes it is difficult to determine whether meteorologists have got their predictions and explanations right, even by the standards of their own science. We all suffer the consequences when they go wrong. The same is true of the sanitation engineers who are reporting on water flow throughout the city and keeping track of leaks in the system. They also can be right or wrong. But the point is that there is something for them to be right or wrong about; and that something is a part of the real New York.

One might think things are different for the society columnist, a member of a profession where standards of correctness are not so clear. Nonetheless, if the goal is a *true* description of New York society, there are criteria for accurate reporting and collecting of evidence, even if the line between accurate reporting and mere gossip or innuendo may not always be easy to draw. The same is true of financial columnists whose job is to report the news from Wall Street of a given day. When we talk about human beings in New York City, or anywhere else – about their thoughts, emotions, and behavior, the reasons why they do what they do – the evidence is more elusive to be sure. Yet we still think there is something to be right or wrong about, whether it be descriptions of social events or financial markets.

But one might argue that while different professions, areas of expertise or subject matters, may require different vocabularies and standards of correctness and evidence, it is not clear how we know that the standards accepted by any community of inquirers are themselves *correct* in the sense of leading to the objective truth rather than merely cohering with other beliefs they happen to hold. Expressing a favorite theme of postmodernists again, Rorty says we can talk if we wish about what is true or real, so long as we realize that these terms signify only what is "warrantedly assertible" from our point of view, within our language game or tradition or form of life.[13] Thus the weatherman, the sanitation engineers, the social historians may have their standards for what is warrantedly assertible within their communities of inquirers. But how do they know that satisfying these standards will yield the truth from all points of view?

The answer to this question takes us back once again to Chapter 9. The proper answer, I believe, is that they do not *know*, if "know" means know for sure or with *certainty*. This was the point of emphasizing that all inquiry is a matter of *aspiration*, not of certain knowledge. All forms of human inquiry from the most humble to the most profound, whether of physicists, sanitation engineers, meteorologists, social historians – or of each of two lovers trying to find out what the other is really thinking – all are "searches in the realm of aspiration." Like the scientists looking for the final truth about nature or the knight looking for the Holy Grail, inquirers must do what they think they can do within their necessarily limited points of view (collecting as much evidence as possible, questioning sources, doing experiments, testing alternative theories, considering criticisms) which may not guarantee attainment of the goal, but without which they would have to abandon hope of attaining the goal. The possibility that their efforts may fail does not show there is no objective truth from all points of view to be found; it only brings out the radical contingency of any search for such truth by finite beings.

Remember that if the weatherman gets it right about the New York weather despite the fallibility of his claims, then what he says about the New York weather will not just be true for him, or for the community of inquiring meteorologists of which he is a part. It will be true for everyone, the mayor, the social historian, society columnist, and so on, whether they think it is true or not. If it is true, it is true from every point of view, not just his own. If I tell you there is a wombat in your garden, and there is a wombat there, then it is true for you (and not just for me), even if you would vigorously deny it and even if you have no idea what a wombat is and don't understand what I am talking about.

### 5. GLOBAL ILLUSION AND ANCIENT WISDOM: DESCARTES AND OTHERS

But what if the wombat is an illusion we both share? What if your garden is not real? What if New York with its weather and its sewers, its Wall Street moguls and society matrons, is a veil, a movie screen, a

[13] Rorty 1989: 15.

matrix, behind which the reality is utterly different? What if everything we experience is such an illusion? Then the weatherman or the sanitation engineer may have got all their calculations right and yet they would still be wrong. This is the ultimate epistemological worry about "objective reality" that everyone must share (physicist, philosopher, weatherman, and so on) – the possibility raised by Descartes that everything might be a dream or illusion, mere appearance.

In such skeptical reflections lies a final lesson about the goals of ancient "wisdom" or "first philosophy." Descartes' problem of global illusion – which tellingly arose at the beginning of "modern" Western philosophy and played such a crucial role in its development – is in fact the expression of ancient themes about human consciousness that have often appeared in mythical as well as philosophical form. Similar ideas have appeared in many other traditions. In the Hindu Upanishads, the world is said to be *maya* or illusion. The Taoist philosopher Chuang-Tzu asked whether he was a Chinese sage dreaming he was a butterfly or a butterfly dreaming he was a Chinese sage. "Trickster" gods who create illusions are a commonplace of African myths and the myths of other cultures.

What is their message? The ultimate message is of course different in different traditions. But at the very least, all such myths and reflections are a warning against human pride and against assumptions that we can know with certainty what objective reality is really like: Any such knowledge of the really real lies in the realm of aspiration. We think for example that there are three people in the next room. So we go into the room and look to make sure we are not in error. Philosophers and mythmakers tell us that the people in the room might be illusions and the room itself a dream; and they might be right for all we know. But they might be wrong also. And if we are to have any hope of ever knowing what's really in the room, if there is a room, what else can we do but go and look?

What else can scientists and other inquirers do but try their best to eliminate error by careful reasoning, observation and repeated experiments, and then trust that their result is the reality? That was Descartes' solution to his own problem: Do your best to make your ideas and perceptions clear and distinct, and then *trust* that you are not deceived. Descartes put his trust in God. But all inquirers in the realm of aspiration must trust that they are not deceived, whether they invoke God or not. The ancient Greek word for belief, "*pistis*," literally means "trust."[14]

---

[14] Railton (unpublished) also emphasizes this notion of trust in belief in an original account of rationality in belief, desire and action.

This is one lesson to learn from our collective myths and philosophical puzzles about illusion. These myths and puzzles do not invalidate notions of objective truth and reality, but they do show the radical contingency and incompleteness of any search for such reality. (There is also a lesson here, I will eventually argue, regarding "objective value," as well as object- ive reality.) There is always the possibility of learning that one's current vision is wrong or incomplete, that it stands as appearance to some still deeper reality. Many of the ancient myths of illusion also implied this. The possibility of learning that one's current view is wrong or incomplete is in fact tied up with the very meaning of *objective* truth and reality. The idea that no finite conceptual scheme or language game can demonstrate from within itself, or any other, that it has the objective truth is connected to the idea that what accounts for such truth is something – namely, object- ive reality – that cannot be determined solely by linguistic conventions, conditions of evidence, verifiability, or warranted assertibility within any finite language game or community of inquirers.

In other words, objective truth and reality *transcend* finite human texts and ways of knowing them. That is part of what we mean by saying they are *objective*, rather than merely subjective or relative to point of view. That is why objective truth and reality can be aspired to, but not known with certainty; it is why we may partake of, or participate in, the true and the real as through a glass darkly, but not wholly possess them without ceasing to be *us*, with a point of view. The suggestion I want to pursue is that this may also be the case for the *other* goal of wisdom in the ancient philosophical sense – objective worth – to which we now turn.

# CHAPTER II

# Objective worth

## I. ALAN THE ARTIST

The second goal of ancient wisdom is understanding what is objectively valuable and worth striving for in the nature of things. I call this second goal *objective worth* – worth from all points of view, not merely from one or a limited number of points of view. It is another name for fourth-dimensional value. We have some indication from the discussion of fourth-dimensional value in Chapter 8 that this notion of objective worth has more complexity than one might initially assume. But we only touched the surface of the complexity there. The best way to delve more deeply into it is by reflecting on certain kinds of narratives or stories. Here are two such narratives showing different aspects of the notion of objective worth.

Consider, first, a fellow we will call Alan the artist. Alan has been ill and depressed of late, so much so that a rich friend devises a scheme to lift his spirits. The friend arranges to have Alan's oil paintings bought at a local gallery (under assumed names) for substantial prices ($20,000, $30,000, and more). Alan is elated. He had always thought – let us assume mistakenly – that his paintings have great artistic merit. He now assumes they are at last winning the recognition of knowledgeable critics and collectors.

Now imagine two possible worlds. In one world, Alan thinks he is being recognized as a great artist, but in fact is being deceived – the world just described. The other is a world as similar as possible to the first in which Alan has many of the same experiences and thoughts, including thinking he is a great artist. But in this other world he is not deceived.[1] In this second imagined world, Alan's paintings do have artistic merit and

---

[1] This example has similarities to Nozick's "experience machine" (1974: 18), but it brings out some different features of the notion of objective worth that I want to emphasize. See Bernstein 1998 for a critical discussion of Nozick's example and this example of Alan from an earlier work of mine (1994).

are in fact being bought at these prices by knowledgeable experts and collectors, as he believes. Finally, imagine that in *both* worlds Alan dies happily, deceived about the truth in one, but not deceived in the other.

Those who believe there is no objective merit to works of art – who believe that no one such work could be objectively more excellent than another – will not accept all the premises of this story. But that should not surprise or deter us. For the story is meant to tell us what objective worth would be like, if it did exist; and consequently it is meant to tell us something about what those who deny the possibility of such worth are denying. Whether or not objective excellence in art or any other forms of objective worth do exist and how they might be known are issues I will revisit in due time.

Return then to Alan and his two worlds. We begin to understand what objective worth is when we ask whether it would make any difference to Alan which of these worlds he lives in, given that he believes he is a great artist in both and is no less happy subjectively in one world than in the other. For, recall that he dies happily in both worlds, knowing the truth in one, while being deceived in the other. Being aware of how Alan's spirits were lifted by the thought that he was at last receiving recognition, we expect he would answer the question "Which of the possible worlds would you rather live in?" by opting for the world in which he is not deceived.

But for Alan to acknowledge a difference in importance of the two worlds in this way, even though he would feel equally happy in both, is for him to endorse a notion of *objective* worth. One of the consequences of such an endorsement is that a person's subjective (or felt) happiness cannot be the final measure of value for him, since Alan *feels* equally happy in both worlds. To understand what objective worth means for him, we have to tell him the story of the two worlds and ask him which he would rather live in; and if he answers, as we might expect, that he would prefer to live in the second (undeceived) world, this will show that the objective worth of his accomplishments rather than merely subjective happiness means something to him. Like most of us, Alan would find it demeaning to be told "Your painting (or music, or scientific work or whatever) is objectively worthless, but so what? You feel happy doing it, and that is all that counts."

Of course, we can imagine a third world in which Alan is deceived by his friend as in the first world, but finds out he is being deceived before he dies; and this third world is clearly the worst of the three, since in it Alan is terribly deflated and more depressed than ever. But the fact that the third imagined world is the worst of the three for Alan in no way changes his judgment that the first world where he is deceived (and never knows it) is worse than the second where he is not deceived. And this shows that objective worth means something to Alan. Subjective happiness without objective worth (as in the deceived world) is deficient even though the two together would be best of all.

## 2. THE OBJECTIVE VIEWPOINT: NAGEL, RILKE

It is important to notice that for Alan to make judgments about the comparative worth of these worlds, he must step back from his immersion in them and view them objectively, from outside both. From *inside* the first and second worlds (that is, from his subjective point of view), things look pretty much the same to him, since he believes he is a great artist in both worlds and dies happily believing this in both. It is only when Alan takes what Thomas Nagel (1986) calls an "objective viewpoint," imagining himself standing outside the worlds, viewing them as a whole and knowing that he was deceived in one but not the other that he can judge their comparative worth. This is what gives point to the expression "objective worth."

Now modern skeptics about such worth will surely respond that there is something odd and problematic about the choice we have given Alan, precisely because in order to make the judgment that one of the worlds is better, he must stand outside both, viewing them objectively. These skeptics might argue that the subjective view from inside the worlds is the only one Alan, or any of us, can ever *really* have. In reality, he must live subjectively in one or another of the worlds. It is therefore irrational for him to worry about how things would look from outside both. What does it matter to Alan, they might say, if he never knows he was deceived, so long as he dies as happily in the one world as the other? What difference can other merely imagined worlds make to him if they are never realized? But I suggest that it is an important fact about human beings that other imagined worlds do "strangely concern us" as the poet Rainer Maria Rilke has said.[2] We are creatures of fantasy and myth and storytelling for a reason; and it is an important fact about us that we can step back and take the objective view of such imagined worlds, for therein we come to recognize the objective worth of things.

These modern skeptics are trying to tell us that subjective experience is the only and final measure of value, and it might be so if we were like

[2] Rilke 1963: 73.

beasts, thoroughly immersed in our own immediate experiences and not capable of taking the objective view outside our experienced world. But it is not true that the subjective view from inside the worlds is the only one Alan, or any of us, can really take. We are capable of taking the objective view as well; and we can perfectly well understand how Alan could be right to say "the undeceived world would be better for me, even if in the other world I would never know I had been deceived." This is to acknowledge the importance of objective worth.

### 3. *SOLARIS*: LEM, HOPKINS

The story of Alan tells us something about objective worth, but not all we need to know. Here is a second narrative, adapted from a science-fiction novel by the Polish writer, Stanislaw Lem (1971), that shows another side of this complex notion. Lem writes about a planet called *Solaris* (the book's title) that is covered by an ocean with astonishing powers. Readers may be familiar with one or both of two films made from Lem's novel. Both take a few liberties with the plot and I will do so as well, though in a different direction. But it is Lem's original work, not the films, that inspires these reflections.

The living ocean with astonishing powers that covers the planet Solaris can conjure up what seem to be real people – people from the past of humans who have come to the planet. The story involves one of these visitors, a scientist studying the swirling ocean from laboratories on a space station hovering over it. The ocean conjures up the figure of his long-dead ex-wife. He believes she is resurrected. They renew their affair, trying to change some of the traits that pushed them apart; they make love, converse and review the past. But a strange thought begins to dawn on the scientist. The wife-image is not a real person. It is a simulacrum reconstructed by the planet's mysterious ocean out of his unconscious mind and memories. It is a more elaborate phantom than he could conjure in his own dreams, because the ocean has greater access to his unconscious memories than he does; but it is a phantom nonetheless.

What interests us here is the point where this shocking revelation occurs to the scientist. Let us assume that he greatly loved his ex-wife, loved her even more than the man in Lem's novel (here I depart from Lem a little for a purpose). Let us say the man deeply regretted the events that had pushed them apart before his wife had died. It is not difficult to imagine how devastating would be his realization that this phantom wife was not the real one, that the real wife had not been resurrected, as he believed, and their affair not renewed. He would grieve; and the loss he would feel would be more than that described by Kierkegaard, when he says that despair over the loss of something is often despair over the loss of oneself.[3] The scientist would grieve most profoundly because loving this woman as he did, he wanted it to be the case that she was resurrected for *her* sake, not merely for his.

A favored theme of Augustine's was that to love anything (as God loved us on his view) is to want it to *be*.[4] I have always thought this to be one of the most profound of metaphysical insights because it connects objective reality and objective worth (the two goals of wisdom or first philosophy): To love something, anything (whether it be a cherished keepsake or another person), is to want it to be – *real*. But that is not quite the whole story either. If what one loves is a person or any living thing and not merely a keepsake, to love it for its own sake is not only to want it to be and not to perish, but to want its being to go well rather than poorly, to want the being to be happy and flourish.

If the scientist did not care about the objective reality and worth of what he loved in this way – if he cared only about his own pleasures – he might find the phantom wife just as good a companion as the real wife. In every observable way the phantom wife was a simulacrum of the real one – same voice, same features, traits of character, ways of acting, an equally satisfying sex partner. In some respects, it would have been better if he had gone on being deceived. But this would have been to look at the situation from a selfish point of view. Since he truly cared about the woman, he cared about more than that; he cared about whether she was real and was grieved to find she was not. *Like Alan*, he could not say it was just as good to be deceived, because he was having just as much "fun" with the phantom wife and "this was all that mattered." As with Alan, he cared about more than his subjective satisfaction. But unlike Alan, it was not the objective worth of his paintings that concerned him, but the objective reality of something he cared about; and this is another aspect of objective worth.

This *Solaris*-inspired story shows something else of importance. It shows how objective worth is connected to the "inner life," as we might call it, of consciousness and feeling. The phantom figure conjured up by the ocean is not the real wife, though in every outward aspect it is like the real wife. What is missing is something on the inside. The phantom lacks the inner life of consciousness and feeling of the real wife, experiencing

---

[3] Kierkegaard 1954: 196ff.    [4] Augustine 1948: 521–82.

*him* from *her* point of view. When we care about another in the sense illustrated by this story, what we want to be real and flourish is not just the outer appearance, the public self, but the inner self, the subjectivity of the other – "what it is like to be" that person from the inside, as Nagel puts it. Poet Gerard Manley Hopkins wonderfully calls this the person's "inscape."[5] Without that, what we have is not the person, but a simulacrum.

### 4. TWO ASPECTS OF OBJECTIVE WORTH

These two stories illustrate two aspects of the notion of objective worth. One is the worthiness for *clear recognition with praise* for one's *deeds* and *accomplishments*, the other the worthiness for *concern* or *care* for the faring *of one's inscape for its own sake*. The first of these aspects of objective worth represents the worth of one's public self, so to speak, the contributions one makes to the wider world; the second represents the worth of one's private self, the course of one's inner life. The two aspects of objective worth are related, of course, because the *life* of a person has both public and private aspects. But the relation between these aspects of the life of a person has important implications for ethical theory, as we shall see. Alan's story demonstrates the first of these aspects of objective worth; the adapted *Solaris* story demonstrates the second. By favoring the world in which he is not deceived about the real worth of his paintings, Alan demonstrates the desire that his accomplishments be objectively worthy or deserving of "clear recognition with praise" from others.

The expression "clear recognition with praise" is borrowed from Thomas Aquinas, who uses it to define a more ancient name for the first of these aspects of objective worth, namely, "glory." Following his teacher Ambrose, Aquinas offered the following simple but elegant definition of "glory" in his *Summa Theologiae*: "*gloria est clara notitia cum laude*" ("Glory is clear recognition with praise").[6] To say that the worthiness or desert for such recognition with praise is *objective* is to say that anyone from any point of view who accords such recognition is right to do so, while anyone who refuses to accord it is wrong to do so.

Such worth or desert does not mean that Alan actually gets the recognition he deserves from all others. Actual recognition from others is a more complicated matter because it depends on *their* worthiness to render such recognition as well as one's own worthiness to receive it. As Whitehead put

---

[5] Hopkins 1953.  [6] Aquinas 1950: *Prima Secundae*, Question 2, article 3, p. 11.

it, the problem with honor and esteem by others is that it requires an "audience fit to render it."[7] Actual recognition or esteem by others is a good. But, like Alan, we show our concern for objective worth when we favor the recognition of those who understand or are sensitive enough (about painting in Alan's case) to be "fit to render it." They provide us the more reliable evidence of the objective worthiness of our accomplishments.

The *Solaris* story, by contrast, illustrates the second aspect of objective worth – the worthiness for concern or care for one's inscape or inner life. The desire for objective worth in this sense is the desire to be worthy of the kind of concern for one's existence bestowed on the ex-wife by the scientist in our version of the *Solaris* story. The idea is that our existence and how things go for us be the object of concern to others for ourselves alone (for our own sakes) and not merely for what we have achieved or what we can do for them (reciprocal altruism), not merely as the phantom wife might be cared about as a sex object or conversational partner, but as the real wife was cared about. This is a kind of "love." But it is the kind of love (often called *agape* in the Western tradition) that may be accorded even to those we may not know or have personal relations to, such as that abandoned child, whose faring well we may care about without admixture of personal gain.

One must add, however, that it is the *worthiness* for such concern or care from others that constitutes this second aspect of objective worth, just as it is the *worthiness* for clear recognition with praise for accomplishments that constitutes the first aspect of objective worth. *Actual* care or concern from others (like actual recognition and esteem for deeds or accomplishments) depends on the worthiness of others to render such care (an "audience fit to render it") as well as on one's own worthiness to receive it. In the case of this second aspect of objective worth, the audience fit to render such care or concern are those who are themselves objectively worthy of such care and concern from others. Actual care or concern from others is a good, but the failure to receive it from all other persons does not necessarily entail that one is not worthy of receiving it from all persons and all points of view.

One can see, in the light of these remarks, why these two aspects of objective worth are instances of fourth-dimensional value. In Chapter 8, I noted that if <this abandoned child's being loved and nurtured when found> was worthy of being recognized as a good by all persons from all points of view, then it was a fourth-dimensional value. The same is true

---

[7] Whitehead 1955: 271.

of Alan's paintings if they are worthy of recognition with praise from all points of view. What this means is that anyone from any point of view who accords such recognition (for the paintings) or concern or care (for the abandoned child) is right to do so, while anyone who, knowing the thing in question, refuses to accord it is wrong not to do so. What we see in such a notion is that fourth-dimensional or absolute value does not have to be actually recognized in every point of view in order to be good from every point of view. And, in this respect, absolute value is like absolute truth, as noted in Chapter 8. If it is absolutely true that the planets of the Solar System revolve around the Sun, then this is true for everyone from every point of view. If some primitive tribesmen or modern flat earthers believe otherwise, they are simply mistaken.

### 5. IF THE BEASTS HAD NO EARS

This point is important enough to dwell on. Some people despair of finding absolute value because they think it requires finding something on which everyone from every point of view can be brought to agree. And they despair of ever finding such a thing, especially about the good, since so much valuing is personal and particular. But if one views absolute value as a kind of objective worth, one sees that actual universal consensus is not what one is looking for. It is no argument against the absolute value of Mozart's music that tone deaf persons cannot appreciate it, any more than it is an argument against the truth of $13 + 21 = 34$ that it cannot be appreciated by people who cannot count higher than 10.

A poem about the Greek myth of Orpheus by Jack Gilbert (1962) illustrates this well. The mythical Orpheus went down into hell to rescue his beloved Eurydice from the beasts who were holding her captive, planning to distract them with his beautiful music. In the original myth, Orpheus succeeds in his mission of rescuing Eurydice, but the poem offers a different scenario. What if Orpheus should descend into the depths of hell, "out of the clean light down," it asks, and there "surrounded by the closing beasts" and preparing his lyre, he should "notice, suddenly, they had no ears"? What if, indeed? If the beasts had no ears this would certainly be a blow to Orpheus' plan to save his beloved Eurydice from them. But would it tell against the objective beauty of his music that these earless beasts were not swayed by it? No more than it tells against the truth of $13 + 21 = 34$ that numbers cannot be appreciated by mathematical illiterates; and no more than it would tell against the worth of Alan's paintings that eyeless beings could not appreciate them.

The same is true of worthiness for concern or care from others. Your worthiness for concern or care from others does not depend on whether everyone accords such concern or care to you, or upon whether everyone *can* accord it. It surely does not depend on whether a Hitler or Stalin or Jack the Ripper or Vlad the Impaler might or could have accorded it to you. Failure to receive their care or concern has more to do with them than you, more to do with their fitness to render it than your worthiness for it, just as Orpheus' problem of winning the praise of the beasts had more to do with their fitness to hear it than the worth of his music.[8]

But, if we acknowledge this, the important and pressing question that naturally arises is the following: How *does* one determine that something has objective worth in either of the two aspects discussed in this chapter, if it is not by universal consensus?[9] This question will be the subject matter of the next three chapters, which will also relate the question to the arguments of Chapters 2–4, thereby completing the ethical arguments of those chapters.

[8] A somewhat different but valuable account of desert or worth is Sher 1987.
[9] Bernstein 1998 includes a critical discussion of an earlier version of some ideas of this chapter to which I am much indebted.

# CHAPTER 12

# The Bach crystals

## I. TWO ASPECTS OF THE SELF

I said in Chapter 1 that the discussion of the nature of philosophical inquiry in Chapters 9–11 would allow us to fill out and complete the ethical argument of Chapters 2–4. I now undertake this task in several stages in the next three chapters (12–14), beginning with some further reflections on the themes of Chapter 11.

As noted in Chapter 11, the two dimensions of objective worth are connected to two aspects of the self. Worthiness for glory, or clear recognition with praise for deeds and accomplishments, is associated with the outer or public self – the roles, accomplishments, projects and achievements that (like Alan and his paintings) we identify as ours and want to be worthy of recognition by others, whether or not we receive such recognition. Worthiness for concern or care, by contrast (as in the *Solaris* story), is connected to the inner or private self – the inner life of consciousness and feeling that Hopkins called the "inscape." In reality, each of us is only one self, as noted, with inner and outer aspects; and we must use our imagination, as in the *Solaris* story, to think of the inner and outer aspects separately. But it is important to use our imagination in this way, if we are to understand why such worth for *self-conscious* beings has these two aspects.

To illustrate, consider the case of Johann Sebastian Bach, who worked as an organist through much of his life, while composing the music that made him famous. Suppose that during Bach's lifetime, the officials and nobles who supported his music discovered a set of amazing crystals made of an unknown substance that spontaneously produced polyphonic music like Bach's. The most knowledgeable musicians and critics could not distinguish the productions of these Bach crystals from Bach's own music. We might further imagine that the officials and aristocrats who supported Bach were a callous lot who then lost all concern for Bach the man. The crystals produced all the beautiful music they could desire and they did not have to feed and clothe the crystals as they did Bach and his large family. For these nobles, Bach would have been valuable only for what he produced. Music of the kind he created was worthy of recognition with praise, but it was not important that *Bach* produced it. It could just as well have been produced by someone named Miller or Herrmann, or even by some organic crystals, so long as it was beautiful music.

Glory, or clear recognition with praise for accomplishments, can be impersonal in this way, but concern or care for the inscapes of others cannot. The accomplishments of the public self can be imagined to be the achievements and accomplishments of someone or something else; they are interchangeable. Not so for the inner self. The phantom wife may be a praiseworthy conversationalist and partner, and in this sense her deeds are interchangeable with those of the real wife, but she herself is not. Concern or care in the sense intended by the second aspect of objective worth (wanting the inscape of another to fare well or flourish for its own sake) is directed at the inscape and not merely the public self; and inscapes are unique. They cannot be interchanged with one another without loss. If Bach lost his employment because of the miraculous crystals, he might say "the officials and nobles seemed to care about me, but all they really cared about was what I could do for them." And this is not usually how we want to be conceived by others, as mere instruments of their satisfaction or servants who are expendable if an equivalent could be found.

Of relevance here is Kant's claim that anything for which there is no equivalent in value has not only value, but also *dignity*.[1] This statement shows how the notion of dignity is related to uniqueness and individuality, and how both are related to the worthiness for concern or care in the sense intended here. The dignity Kant has in mind signifies that one is irreplaceable, as the real wife was irreplaceable by a phantom wife, even if the latter could do all the same things; or as a beloved and faithful servant is not merely to be treated as a commodity to be replaced as soon as he or she becomes less efficient.

Kant learned to appreciate such a notion of dignity or worth from his parents. His father was a humble workingman, a harness-maker. Once in Kant's youth there was a bitter labor dispute between the harness-maker's guild and the saddle-maker's guild. Even though a young boy, Kant marveled at the honorableness and forbearance of his parents throughout this dispute. Though the dispute became bitter at times, his parents never spoke of, or treated, their opponents as mere adversaries or enemies, but

[1] Kant 1959: 53.

as individuals with a right to a resolution of the conflict that preserved their dignity.[2] The incident had a profound effect upon Kant's thinking about dignity and worth in later life.

To sum up, glory attaches to what is universal, but concern or care to the particular. In desiring to do things of significance to others, and yet not be a mere tool or instrument in their service, we desire to be worthy of both clear recognition with praise for the outer self and of concern or care for the inner self. In the officials' callous behavior, Bach sees that they would have cared about the accomplishments of Bach, but not that these were the accomplishments *of Bach*. This is one way in which the two aspects of objective worth are related, but not the only way, as we shall see.

## 2. ASPIRATION AND WISDOM REVISITED

How does one determine what has objective worth in each of these aspects? This question, posed at the end of Chapter 11, is a formidable one and we need some direction even to begin to answer it. The direction we need, I suggest, is to be found in the notions of *aspiration* and the quest for *wisdom* of Chapters 9 and 10. Consider the worthiness for concern or care for one's inscape first. How can one know one is objectively worthy of such concern from every point of view, whether or not that worth is recognized in every point of view? The question overwhelms us with a numbing sense of inadequacy if we think the only possible answer has to be a certain and final one. That is why we must first acknowledge that we cannot *know* anything has an objective worth of this kind in the sense of having the certain and final truth about it, any more than the scientists can know they have found the final truth of nature or the knight can know he has found the Holy Grail.

What we can do rather is *aspire* to possess such worth, which means that while we cannot guarantee attainment, there is something we can do to seek it. Scientists cannot be assured that if they do all the right experiments and subject their theories to all the available evidence, they will have found the final truth about nature. But they have every reason to believe that if they do *not* do these things, they will not have found the final truth; and so it is with the knight and the search for the Holy Grail. (These are the characteristics of "searches or quests in the realm of aspiration" as described in Chapter 9.)

So it is also, I would argue, with most of the important things in life, and that includes the objective worthiness for concern or care for the

---

[2] Scharfstein 1980: 146.

faring well of one's inscape. They are matters of aspiration. It is beyond our human capacity to do something that will guarantee we are worthy of such concern from every point of view. Yet there is something we can do, if we aspire to such value – something which, if we do not do it, we will not be worthy of such concern from all points of view. We can ourselves show such concern for others; and if we cannot perfectly attain this goal, we can strive for it. This striving will not guarantee the worthiness of our inscapes to be objects of concern by all, but it is that-without-which our worthiness for such concern cannot be more than mere relative worth.

Why not? Recall that in Chapter 8, when considering how fourth-dimensional value transcended the other three dimensions, the example was given of persons who agreed with us about the nature of human needs, but cared only about whether they, or the groups to which they belonged, fulfilled these needs; they did not *care* whether other persons or groups out-side their favored ones did so. Their society attained high degrees of happi-ness or flourishing for their own members while marginalizing or exploiting other groups, some of which were the object of ethnic cleansing.

Now anyone who acts in this way cannot be unqualifiedly worthy of concern or care for the flourishing of their inscapes from *all* points of view because there is no good reason why the persons or groups they exploit should regard them as worthy of such concern. That is, there is no good reason why the exploited persons should think that the flourishing of the exploiters' inscapes is worthy of being realized – not if the persons being exploited care about their *own* existence and flourishing. For their own flourishing is inconsistent with the flourishing of the exploiters. If one group enslaves or exploits another then the enslaving group is not worthy of concern in this sense from the point of view of the enslaved, and thus the enslavers are not worthy of concern for their flourishing from *all* points of view.

To say there is no "good reason" for exploited persons to care about the flourishing of their exploiters, is not to say the exploited must lack a reason or motive of any kind. Some people have strong motives of attach-ment to those who exploit them, a devotion they cannot escape. Cases of domestic violence, of abused and battered spouses, are familiar examples. But while some battered spouses may have powerful motives inclining them to stay with their abusers, it does not follow that they have good reasons to do so, *if* they care about their own happiness and well-being.[3] If

---

[3] For an understanding of the notion of a "good reason" assumed here I am much indebted to work of, and discussions with, Jonathan Dancy (2000, 2004).

counselors in cases of domestic violence are right in thinking the attachment of abused spouses to their abusers is pathological and destructive, it is for this reason.

Two claims are thus involved in answering the question "Why is there no good reason for exploited persons to have unqualified care for the flourishing of those who exploit them?" First, it is reasonable to desire one's own happiness – to desire that one's inscape "fare well" or flourish. Second, to have concern for the inscapes of others in the intended sense is to want *them* to be happy and to flourish in their purposes and goals, in their way of life. But these two things are at odds in the case of exploiters and exploited. The exploiters can only flourish in their purposes and goals at the expense of the happiness of the exploited. So if the exploited have good reasons to desire their own happiness, they do not have a good reason to desire that the exploiters flourish in every aspect of their way of life. (One should note the connection here to the notion of moral sphere breakdown of Chapters 2–4, to which I shall return in a moment.)

The argument assumes that we have good reasons to desire our own happiness. One might deny this premise on the grounds that desiring one's own happiness leads to selfishness. But it need not, as philosophers from Butler onward, have reminded us: Desiring one's own happiness is compatible with desiring the happiness of others.[4] Moreover, in the present context, desiring one's own happiness *is an important premise of an argument* that leads to the conclusion that one should *not* selfishly exploit others. Another premise is required, to be sure: that we do not merely desire our own happiness, but also aspire to be objectively *worthy* of concern for our happiness by others. In other words, it is the combination of (1) desiring one's own happiness and (2) aspiring to be objectively *deserving of the happiness one desires* that leads to the conclusion that one should not be selfish and exploit others. But desiring one's own happiness is an essential part of the inference.

Insofar as we live in the first three dimensions of value – having experiences, pursuing purposes and seeking excellences – we naturally desire our own happiness and flourishing. But insofar as we also aspire to transcend these ordinary dimensions of value and to access the fourth dimension, we desire to be deserving of the happiness so attained from all points of view; and this latter step requires caring about (having concern for) how things go for others.

[4] Butler 1983.

### 3. SELF-REFLECTION AND THE OBJECTS
### OF CONCERN OR CARE

There is thus a connection, as suggested three paragraphs earlier, between the preceding argument and the ethical arguments of Chapters 2–4. To spell out that connection, one further distinction is needed. Concern or care for the inscapes of others may be manifested in different ways, depending on the kinds of beings involved. Of special importance is whether or not those other beings are capable of *self-reflection* – of rising above their natural desires and instincts and assessing and choosing for themselves which purposes they will pursue.

Consider the relation of parents to children. In the earliest stages of infancy, caring for one's children is a matter of caring that their basic needs are satisfied and their inscapes experience joy and not suffering (the first dimension of value). As children develop, however, continued interest in their happiness or the flourishing of their inscapes (the "outflowing" of their spirits) entails that parents relinquish a merely protective love in favor of enabling and assisting them in the pursuit of more complex purposes and goals in the second and third dimensions of value. The ultimate test of parental concern is allowing adult children to make their own choices about what purposes or goals they will pursue even when parents think the choices may be wrong and think they know better. At a certain stage, one may try to persuade, but no longer coerce.

This parental "letting-go" is a requirement of caring for children *for their own sakes* to the extent that they are capable of ascending to higher dimensions of value and choosing for themselves more complex forms of life. Note how pluralism and uncertainty enter into this picture. If there was one way for humans to be happy and we could know with certainty what that way was, concern for the flourishing of the inscapes of others for their own sakes, including children, might take a different form. But as beings ascend to higher dimensions of value, the ways of pursuing the good become more varied and plural, and one size does not fit all.

Comedian Lily Tomlin once made a list of "things my mother told me that aren't true." At the top of her list was the statement "Whatever will make you happy, will make me happy." Her point is more than merely humorous and goes well beyond the relation of parents to children. A woman may love gardening. Doing it well increases her feelings of self-worth. But her husband sees no value in it; and he puts every obstacle in her way until she finally gives it up and feels miserable. The wife's gardening does indeed conflict to some degree with the husband's wants, but he is not willing to compromise. Since gardening has no value from *his* point of view, he thinks it should have no value from hers. Does he care about her flourishing or the "flowering" of her inscape? Not really – if this is his normal way of behaving – not *for her own sake* anyway, but only for his sake.

What this implies is that concern or care for the inscapes of others must be differently manifested depending on the beings involved and their capacities. For beings capable of self-reflection and choosing their own purposes, concern for the flourishing of their inscapes involves allowing them to exercise their powers of self-reflection to pursue happiness in ways of their own choosing. By contrast, for beings not capable of self-reflection, such as very young children and non-human animals, concern for their inscapes is a matter of caring that their basic needs and desires are satisfied, that they do not suffer, and doing what one can to enable these outcomes. Only self-reflective beings can reach the third (and eventually the fourth) dimension of value. This fact does not make them the sole objects of care or concern, but it does mean that care or concern for their happiness must take a different form.

### 4. THE MORAL SPHERE REVISITED: THEORETICAL AND PRACTICAL INQUIRY ABOUT THE GOOD

Return now to the arguments of Chapters 2–4 with this distinction in mind. The retreatants were trying to find out which *ways of life* among the many conflicting ones gathered at the retreat were worthy of being *treated with openness* from all points of view and which were not. The question of this chapter has been how one determines what has objective worth in the sense of *worthiness for concern* for the flourishing of one's *inscape* from all points of view.

Though framed in different terms, the questions are connected for beings capable of self-reflection and choosing their own purposes. In the case of such beings, as just argued, concern for the flourishing of their inscapes involves allowing them to exercise their powers of self-reflection to pursue happiness in ways of their own choosing. But that is just what the attitude of *respect in the sense of openness* (taken by the retreatants) toward other persons and their ways of life amounted to in Chapters 2–4.

To *treat persons with respect in the sense of openness* (or equivalently, to *treat them as ends*) is to treat them with openness – i.e., to allow persons to pursue their ways of life and realize their desired ends ("to live and pursue happiness as they choose") without interference – to the degree that one can do so while maintaining a moral sphere in which all persons can be treated with similar openness by all others.

Respect in this sense of openness toward other *ways of life* in the argument of Chapters 2–4 is thus what *concern for the flourishing* of the *inscapes* of others as described in this chapter would initially require *when* those others are self-reflective beings capable of choosing their own purposes and ways of life.

The retreatants learned that the openness required by such an attitude of respect has limits at the point where the moral sphere breaks down; and we should thus expect that these limits of openness to ways of life would also be the limits of worthiness for concern for the flourishing of self-reflective beings as well. Insofar as such beings pursue moral sphere-breaking ways of life, they would not be *objectively worthy of care or concern* for the flourishing of their inscapes because other persons could not have care or concern for their flourishing *and* for the flourishing of all other inscapes as well, *including* the inscapes of those they would be treating as mere means.

This argument sheds further light on the role of openness for the retreatants. Openness was said to be their way of expanding their minds beyond their own limited points of view to find out what should be recognized as good from every point of view, not merely from their own. But the preceding argument suggests that there is a deeper motivation for taking such an attitude of openness, if one aspires to objective worth for one's point of view, as the retreatants did.

That deeper motive is not merely to *find out* which ways of life should be recognized as good by all persons from all points of view, but to *attain* such a status for *one's own* way of life. And it turns out that these two tasks converge: *The way one finds out which points of view and ways of life should be recognized as good by all persons from all points of view is the same way one goes about showing one's own point of view and way of life should be recognized as good by all persons from all points of view.* One does it by living one's life in a certain way (striving to avoid breaking the moral sphere to the degree possible) that we commonly designate as "ethical" or "moral." One thereby seeks to attain objective worth in the form of worthiness for concern for one's inscape and flourishing from others, by striving to have concern for the inscapes and points of view of others.

There is thus a sense in which *theory* and *practice* converge in the retreatants' search for wisdom about the good. They were engaged in a *theoretical* task of trying to find out which ways of life were worthy of being recognized as good by all persons from all points of view. But they had a *practical* goal as well. For they wanted to learn whether their own way of life or some other had such worth in order to live such a life and to attain such worth (or to continue to do so if they were already doing so); and these tasks were convergent. One seeks to answer the theoretical question of which ways of life have objective worth in the same way one attains such worth for oneself – in practice, by living in a certain way in one's engagements with others.

### 5. POSTSCRIPT ON OBLIGATIONS TO NON-HUMAN ANIMALS AND OTHER NON-SELF-REFLECTIVE BEINGS

It also follows from the arguments of this chapter that if one does not show care or concern for the inscapes of beings without capacities for self-reflection, such as young children, those with mental disabilities and non-human animals, one is also not worthy of unqualified concern for the flourishing of one's own inscape (and hence not worthy of being treated with openness by others). Those who treat beings without such capacities cruelly, including non-human animals, are also not worthy of being allowed to pursue their plans of action without interference. The moral theory of Chapters 2–4 focused on obligations to other persons or rational agents capable of reciprocating as moral agents. But, as noted at the beginning of Chapter 5, the theory of Chapters 2–4 was not meant to be a complete ethical theory, much less a complete theory of the good. Our ethical obligations extend to all beings with *inscapes* capable of suffering, not merely to persons or *rational* agents, though, as the arguments of this chapter show, the obligations take different forms toward rational beings capable of self-reflection and toward beings with inscapes not so capable.[5]

---

[5] Cf. Mayerfeld (1999) on the moral significance of suffering and Bernstein (1998) on "moral considerability."

# CHAPTER 13

# *Human flourishing*

## I. WORTHINESS FOR GLORY: THE THIRD DIMENSION REVISITED

At the beginning of the previous chapter, I said that the discussion of philosophical inquiry of Chapters 9–11 would allow us to complete the ethical arguments of Chapters 2–4. The argument of Chapter 12 represents the first stage in this process. Further stages are added in this chapter and the next.

The argument of Chapter 12 addressed the question of how one determines what has objective worth in the sense of worthiness for concern from all points of view. We must now address a similar question about the other aspect of objective worth: How does one determine what has objective worth in the sense of glory, or worthiness for clear recognition with praise for deeds and accomplishments (such as Alan and his paintings)? This is a complex question that leads to a different set of issues that must be considered to give a full account of objective worth; and it will turn out that how one deals with these further issues also has an important bearing on the ethical arguments of Chapters 2–4. I will argue that the question of how one determines what has objective worth in this second aspect of glory must be dealt with in two stages. The first is the subject of this chapter, the second the subject of Chapter 14, where the arguments of Chapters 12 and 13 will be brought together and completed.

One reason for the complexity of the question about objective worth in the aspect of glory is that this second aspect of objective worth is related in a special way to the third dimension of value. The pursuit of clear recognition with praise for deeds and accomplishments takes place in practices, traditions, cultures and forms of life that give specific content to the human quest for the good by conferring meaning on activities and endeavors. We must begin therefore with some reminders about the third dimension of value from Chapter 7.

The hunter in a primitive tribe does not merely hunt for food, but takes pride in his skill because of what it says about his standing as a human being. The activity signifies he is an excellent archer, a loyal member of his tribe, and the like, and thus defines what he is and his status in the world and the community of which he is a part. Third-dimensional value was related in this manner to (i) the expression of meaning (of one's life), to (ii) competence or mastery (of some activity for which one might be deserving of clear recognition with praise), to (iii) contribution and commitment (to one's community or form of life) and to (iv) virtues and excellences that define the highest achievements in forms of life that are also deserving of clear recognition with praise.

The third dimension of value is thus, among other things, the home of the *virtues* (being a loyal employee, a caring parent, a courageous soldier, etc.) for which one may be worthy of clear recognition with praise; and it is the home of MacIntyre's "practices" and "traditions" – socially established human activities through which persons strive to achieve excellences of varying kinds: architecture, medicine, law, physics, and so on. As a result, third-dimensional value may be realized in different ways. There are many practices, traditions and forms of life through which humans may pursue meaningful expression, mastery, contribution, virtue and excellence. Diverse practices and traditions have different standards of excellence. To fully appreciate the excellences of each, one has to know something about the practices and traditions of which they are a part; and the practices and traditions in turn provide the contexts in which excellences of achievement have significance.

These thoughts throw light on a feature of third-dimensional value not emphasized in Chapter 7, but important for this chapter: That feature is the profound desire of humans for *roots* in the sense of an historically defined sense of belonging to groups, communities or ways of life with which they identify – the sense of belonging to a tribe or ethnic group, a religion or culture, a people or nation. There is ample evidence that this concern for roots is more than a desire; it is a genuine human need.[1] But it is also worth noting that it is a complex need. Having roots in this historically defined sense is not just a matter of security and solidarity with one's community and past, though this is surely part of it.

The desire for roots also has to do with the *meaning* we give to our accomplishments and is thereby related to the pursuit of glory. Humans must pursue objective worth in this second aspect as beings embedded

---

[1] See Pugh 1977, Kolakowski 1989, Taylor 1989, Deveaux 2000.

in cultural contexts of some kind (cf. Harré 1980, MacIntyre 1981, Raz 2003). Excellence in literature, for example, must be pursued in a particular language. There is no neutral language, no neutral medium, in which to pursue it; and the same is true for other practices such as physics, sculpture and music. Novices must learn to use and appreciate the media and techniques through which they are pursued.[2] Such rootedness is the soil in which to plant the seeds of glory and excellence. The human desire for roots is for more than security and solidarity; it is interwoven with the desire to find meaning in life that can only be pursued in the rich milieu of particular activities and forms of life.

## 2. ROOTS, VIRTUES AND FORMS OF LIFE: RELATIVISM AGAIN

But this need for roots poses a familiar problem. If the pursuit of excellence and other third-dimensional values requires roots in practices and forms of life that give it specific content, would not the excellences and other goods so achieved be merely *relative* goods for those who participate in the practices and forms of life or who benefit from them or who can appreciate the excellences? This is the problem of relativism in the guise of glory: Different cultures and traditions have different ideals and standards of excellence. How can one establish which are objectively right (worthy of clear recognition with praise) from all points of view, when one must always judge from some particular point of view in terms of values and standards of excellence or virtue that one holds, but others may not?

The first thing to note in response to this question is a further observation about third-dimensional value made in Chapters 7 and 8: Showing that accomplishments, virtues and excellences of the third dimension contribute to the flourishing of persons who participate in practices and forms of life, though it may not be sufficient, is nonetheless necessary, for showing they are worthy of being recognized as good by all persons from all points of view. For, as argued in Chapters 7 and 8, if something that purports to be a third-dimensional value does not contribute to the flourishing of *anyone* in *any* form of life, there is no reason why it should be recognized as good by everyone from every point of view.

So the initial step in showing that the virtues and excellences of the third dimension are objectively worthy of clear recognition with praise

---

[2] MacIntyre (1981), Raz (2003) emphasize this point.

from all points of view – the step to be taken in this chapter – is to show that they contribute to the flourishing of persons who participate in the practices and forms of life in question. And, as further argued in Chapters 5–7, human nature being what it is, the fact that various activities, accomplishments, virtues and excellences tend to contribute to flourishing human lives in the first three dimensions of value is not a merely subjective or arbitrary matter.

Consider, for example, the virtues mentioned above as examples of third-dimensional value: Being a good provider for one's family, a loyal employee, a caring parent, a courageous soldier, and so on. They involve playing valued roles within human communities and forms of life and doing them well; and it is not a merely arbitrary or subjective matter whether these roles are well or poorly played. Nor is it a merely arbitrary or subjective matter whether playing such roles well contributes to the flourishing of human communities and forms of life. Good providers provide for basic human needs, such as food, clothing and shelter, necessary for a flourishing life; courageous soldiers protect their communities from outside threats, thereby providing safety and security, two other requirements for a flourishing human existence; caring parents provide the love and attention so necessary for children to mature into confident and competent adults – and so on for other third-dimensional virtues discussed in Chapter 7. By contributing to the fulfillment of basic human needs and interests, these virtues contribute to the flourishing of individuals and communities.

Annette Baier (1986) has argued, for example, that human societies cannot exist and be perpetuated without the relation of trust and trustworthiness that occurs between parents and their children.[3] Nor are the children as likely to flourish if they do not cultivate these virtues of trust and others, such as caring and sharing, in their relationships with friends. Human nature being what it is, there is every reason to believe such claims are true; and in any case, there is an objective fact of the matter about whether, and to what degree, they are true. Similarly, persons are not good providers for their families or caring parents or courageous soldiers merely because they think they are, or because other people may believe they are. They and others may be deceived about how caring or courageous or loyal they are – which means there is something to be objectively right or wrong about in making such judgments.

---

[3] Cf. Crisp and Slote 1997: Introduction.

One might object that there is often disagreement about the standards for judging virtues and valued roles both within and between cultures and forms of life. True enough. People often disagree about what counts as honesty or loyalty or fairness or who counts as a caring parent or a courageous soldier, or what basic human needs such as protection or nurturing actually require. There may, for example, be different expectations and standards about how children should be raised in different cultures or among different individuals (and hence what a caring parent should be) or about honesty in exchanges of goods (and hence what an honest merchant should be) or about what is required of a courageous soldier or loyal employee or friend.

Yet, when it comes to certain virtues, such as honesty, courage, loyalty and others, differences across cultures are not as great as one might think, as many authors who defend various versions of virtue ethics have noted.[4] Insofar as different cultures and forms of life are *human* cultures and forms of life, they share the goal of human flourishing; and that includes satisfying common needs, purposes and interests.[5] Human infants need to be loved and nurtured when young; there must be a division of labor in which persons play different roles effectively, human societies must be protected from outside aggression, and so on. If the virtues involve playing these valued roles well, we can see why virtues like courage, honesty, trustworthiness, loyalty, care and responsibility would be commonly valued as worthy of clear recognition with praise, even if the exact standards for them might vary in different communities and cultures. The value of the virtues is rooted in needs and purposes required for the flourishing of individuals and communities, which remains an objective standard, even if it can be realized in different ways.

### 3. PRACTICES AND EXCELLENCE

What has been said about the virtues can be extended to other examples of third-dimensional value, such as MacIntyre's practices and traditions: physics, medicine, farming, carpentry, ship-building, and many more. Excellence in these practices is also not merely a subjective or arbitrary matter, for the practices have distinct goals that are also related to

[4] E.g., Foot 2001, Slote 1992, Hursthouse 1999.
[5] Cf. Pugh 1977, Griffin 1986, Nussbaum 1988, Hurka 1993, Copp 1995, Sumner 1996, Sher 1997, Braybrooke 2001, Pettit 2001, Kraut 2007.

human flourishing and can be well or poorly realized. Given the goals of physics, identifying great physicists such as Galileo or Newton is not an arbitrary or subjective matter; and the same can be said of the discovery of a polio vaccine or of the structure of the DNA molecule – discoveries in their respective practices of medicine and biology worthy of clear recognition with praise.

In some cases, it may take experts in the practice to judge what is excellent, but they are not judging by merely arbitrary or subjective standards. There may be disagreements about standards of excellence in practices, just as there are disagreements about what constitutes a caring parent or loyal employee. But that would be expected to the degree that human purposes and expectations (in a carpenter, surgeon or engineer, for example) may differ – just as purposes and expectations in parenting or in an employee may differ. One carpenter may be excellent for one task, another for another task. One surgeon may be better for one kind of surgery, another for another kind. In such cases, we might engage in fruitless and irresolvable arguments about who is the better carpenter or surgeon; and yet, for all that, each carpenter or surgeon might be objectively excellent at what he or she does.

One may object that one is stacking the deck by focusing on practices, such as physics, medicine, carpentry or engineering, where objective judgments of excellence are easier to acknowledge because the practices serve practical human needs and have well-defined goals. This fact is not as obviously the case for many other practices mentioned by MacIntyre, most notably the arts and aesthetic practices among others: architecture, painting, sculpture, music, literature, drama, dance, and many more. Do we have objectivity here or is excellence in the arts or aesthetic value merely a matter of subjective taste, as many people believe? (Recall that this question arose when the example of Alan and his paintings was first introduced; and I said we would return to it.)

### 4. ARTISTIC EXCELLENCE AND AESTHETIC VALUE: HUME

Artistic practices and aesthetic value present the greatest challenges to claims about the objectivity of third-dimensional value; and it is important therefore to consider them in the light of the above arguments. Subjectivist and relativist attitudes toward the arts and aesthetic value are supported by pervasive disagreements about what is good and bad art, by the historical and cultural variability of tastes and styles, and by other considerations suggesting that aesthetic value is merely a "matter of taste."[6]

Opposed to these considerations, however, is a point forcefully made in the eighteenth century by Hume and supported by some contemporary philosophers.[7] Hume observed that those who understand and appreciate musical styles or painting, sculpture, poetry and other arts more often than not agree about who are the great or excellent musicians, painters, sculptors and poets. Persons knowledgeable about art are as confident that Raphael is a great painter as those knowledgeable about physics are confident that Newton is a great physicist. How could this be, Hume opined, unless there is some source of commonality and objectivity in human standards of taste?

This was one of Hume's ways of attempting to overcome to a degree the "gap" between "fact" and "value" that he himself had brought to the attention of philosophers. It may be true that in his eighteenth-century world Hume experienced less variability and disagreement in artistic taste and judgment (not to say ethical beliefs) than we experience today. So he could speak with more confidence than we can about common human sentiments in such matters. The pluralism and uncertainty of modern experience have made it more difficult for us to share Hume's Enlightenment confidence in common human "sentiments" (in aesthetics *or* ethics) just as it has made it more difficult to share Kant's Enlightenment confidence in a common human "reason." Nonetheless, I think Hume was on to something of importance regarding artistic excellence and aesthetic value that needs to be further explored.[8]

How, if at all, can we account for the variability and disagreement about what is good art in different cultures and historical periods while making sense of Hume's point that those who understand and appreciate different styles and forms of art frequently agree on who are the great or excellent practitioners of the style or art form? Here is a suggested response to this question that requires a little background.

---

[6] See Dickie and Sclafani eds. 1977, Eaton 1988, Danto 1981 for discussion of these issues.

[7] Hume 1882. See Railton (2003 and unpublished), who pursues this Humean theme at some length. I am much indebted to his insightful work on this topic.

[8] Hume's appeal to common human sentiments (sentimentalism) has also undergone something of a revival in recent ethical theory. See D'Arms and Jacobson 2006 and Slote 2006. Recent work in moral psychology also provides support. See Sinnott-Armstrong 2008, 2008a, 2008b. Nichols (2004) makes a strong case from modern empirical research that moral judgment arises from an interaction of normative considerations and "affective reactions." Prinz (2008) appeals to empirical data from anthropology and evolutionary psychology to defend a "constructive sentimentalism" that is Humean in inspiration.

## 5. NEUROSCIENCE AND NEUROCHARMS:
### DAMASIO, TURNER

Contemporary neuroscientists, such as Antonio Damasio, among many others, have argued that higher reasoning capacities in human beings are never entirely divorced from those areas of the brain that are the seat of feelings and emotions.[9] As a consequence, human reasoning and perception of the world are invariably suffused with feeling and emotion. Damasio, along with other neuroscientists and psychologists, distinguishes "primary" human feelings, such as anger and fear, joy and sadness, pleasure and pain, which go further back in our evolutionary history and reside in the older parts of the brain, from "secondary" feelings and emotions, such as indignation, guilt, pride, love, humiliation, and many more, that could not exist without the higher cortical regions of the brain engaged in reasoning.[10] The development of this rich spectrum of emotional experience, Damasio argues, is necessary for a fully human form of life. For example, lesions in the brain studied by neuroscientists that disrupt these natural cycles of primary and secondary emotions with higher brain functions lead to serious psychological pathologies – and hence to diminished capacities for happiness or flourishing. Sometimes they lead to no *human* life at all.

Let us now add to this neuroscientific evidence a second theme. Poet and literary critic Frederick Turner has argued that the human sense of beauty and aesthetic value evolved bio-culturally out of traditional ritual and other practices (e.g., myth-making, ritual dance, facial markings, dress, cave painting, and the like) through which humans attempted to give meaning to their existence (1991: 1–9). But giving "meaning to one's existence," as the neuroscientific evidence suggests, is not merely a matter of coming up with an intellectual theory or explanation. It involves integrating the newly evolved higher rational or intellectual capacities of humans with their emotional and sensory life of instinct and feeling.

To bring about this integration, new neurobiological capacities have evolved to deal with a more complex human form of life. And since the resulting neural structures are common to human brains, as Damasio and Turner both note, it is reasonable to suppose that the resulting neurological capacities for integrating reason and emotion would be common to human beings as well. One might suggest therefore that one of the

---

[9] Damasio 1994 passim; see also Nauta and Feirtag 1986: 130.
[10] Damasio, ibid.: chapter 6.

goals of the arts would be to effect this integration between emotion, thought and sensory experience which is so necessary for a flourishing human existence.

Turner (p. 79) gives a name to these integrative neural capacities. He calls them *neurocharms*. Some (though not all) of the neurocharms Turner identifies from research of others on the brain and behavior have to do with language. This should not surprise us, given the importance of language for human forms of life. The linguistic neurocharms involve the capacities to understand syntactical organization and reference in language. They also involve abilities to appreciate trope, metaphor and analogy by which linguistic meaning expands, as well as to appreciate meter and rhyme. The poetic and ritualistic features of language (meter and rhyme) as well as its theoretical features (meaning and reference) are both involved in the exercise of the linguistic neurocharms – as one would expect if the neurocharms are concerned with integrating the rational, emotional and sensory sides of human experience.

Another neurocharm is the evolved capacity in humans for what Turner calls "dramatic mimesis," the ability to engage in interpersonal and intra-personal reflection. Such dramatic mimesis includes the ability to model other persons' inner lives and imagine what it is like to see the world from their point of view, also a capacity necessary for an evolved human form of social life. This capacity is significantly diminished, as is well-known, in cases of autism. Further neurocharms mentioned by Turner are auditory and visual in nature. These include, among others, the appreciation of musical meter, tempo and rhythm, tone, melody and harmony and the recognition of patterns and combinations of colors. The ancient Pythagorean philosophers were the first to discover the four-fold correspondence among (i) the numerical ratios of arithmetic (2:1, 3:2, etc.), (ii) the spatial ratios of geometry, (iii) the vibratory properties of strings of different lengths and (iv) harmonic preferences of the human ear – suggesting a connection between the auditory neurocharms and the external world.[11]

This connection is supported by a series of interesting experiments performed by psychophysicist Ingo Rentschler and associates. By showing visual images to subjects consisting of rows of converging and diverging lines, Rentschler showed that the human eye craves a certain complexity of visual structure. But the complexity cannot be too great and uniform or the eye reduces it to a simple texture that produces fatigue and

---

[11] Turner, ibid.: 83.

boredom.[12] Still other neurocharms involve touch, taste and physical motion – including, among others, dance, gymnastics, martial arts, and so on. Turner sees these as mediating between the visual, auditory and motor structures of the brain.

### 6. THE HUMAN SENSORIUM

Let us introduce the expression *human sensorium* to refer to the combination of Damasio's primary and secondary emotions (representing the first dimension of value) together with Turner's neurocharms. My suggestion is that, whatever else it requires, human flourishing requires the development or "attunement" of this human sensorium so that it attains an integration of higher reasoning capacities with the emotional, sensory and motor capacities by which we interact with the world around us. The goal of this integration or attunement of the human sensorium would be a kind of harmony within the self (a notion anticipated by Plato), an integration of cognitive, emotional and sensory experience with an active life.

Viewed in this way, art and artistic practices would be among the primary vehicles through which this attunement of the human sensorium to higher cortical functions and to the world around it takes place. Different arts focus on different aspects of the sensorium and hence different combinations of neurocharms (visual, auditory, linguistic, kinesthetic). But appreciation of fine art and artistic practices in general contributes to this integration; and excellence in art contributes to it at the highest levels of complexity and organization. As Turner notes, humans have a deep desire to exercise the neurocharms and to do so with mastery and autonomy. Human infants take great delight in babbling even before they speak. The sounds and tones of language fascinate them; and they cannot wait to exercise the linguistic neurocharms on their own.

In the light of Chapters 5–8, I would further suggest that so exercising any of the neurocharms is a matter of "out-flowing" of the spirit (the literal meaning of "aspiration" noted in Chapter 9), which takes us from merely passive experiences of the first dimension of value to active engagements of higher dimensions. Such an out-flowing of the

---

[12] Ibid.: 86ff. Michael Benedikt (unpublished) also discusses Rentschler's work and many other empirical studies in a highly original work supporting the general idea that human flourishing requires a balance of complexity and organization in experience. On a number of topics of this chapter and others of the book, I have benefitted greatly from discussions with Benedikt and his wife, Amelie Benedikt.

spirit is an essential feature of "flowering" or flourishing in distinctively human ways. Aristotle, as is well known, held that human beings are rational animals. But he sometimes went beyond this claim, going so far as to say at certain points that "Reason" above all *is* man and controversially suggesting that the best and highest form of human flourishing (*eudaimonia*) would involve the cultivation and exercise of reason in pure thought or contemplation. Whether this was Aristotle's whole or final view is much debated.[13] But, if Damasio and other neuroscientists are right, the flourishing of human beings, qua human, is not likely to involve the cultivation of reason alone detached from the feelings, emotions and physical activity, but the cultivation of the entire human sensorium.

Living extraterrestrial beings very different from us humans might have different sensoria than ours – different feelings and emotions and different neurocharms. If so, flourishing for these different creatures would be very different from *human* flourishing; and their artistic tastes and aesthetic values might be very different from ours.[14] In general, the flourishing of any kind of creature with a sensorium would involve the cultivation of its distinctive sensorium. (This point is crucial, as we shall see in the next chapter, for ethical theory as well as for the value theory in general.)

Therein also lies a clue to the variability and disagreement in artistic tastes and aesthetic evaluation. For just as there might be alien beings with sensoria different from our human ones, with correspondingly different tastes and aesthetic values, so the human sensorium itself is not the same in all humans. If the neurocharms as described by Turner are common to all humans, this is because they are described in very general terms as capacities to appreciate linguistic organization, metaphor, trope, analogy, other inscapes (dramatic mimesis), and so on.

But such capacities can be developed or cultivated in different ways; and they *are* developed and cultivated in different ways by different human cultures and forms of life. Human language (the exercise of the linguistic neurocharms) is only the most obvious example. The general capacity for language is universal in humans given normal experience and development. Yet humans learn to speak different languages; and the languages

---

[13] Kraut 1989 and Lear 2004 are the most extended and subtle recent defenses of the so-called "dominant" interpretation of Aristotle's view, according to which *eudaimonia* consists dominantly in a life of contemplation. Many others argue, however, for an "inclusive" view in which *eudaimonia* consists as importantly in the exercise of both moral and intellectual virtues.

[14] Cf. Griffin 1986.

they speak may "tune" their sensoria to the world in different ways, not only in describing things differently, but in feeling them differently.

The same is true of the other neurocharms, including the musical and visual ones. Westerners may have difficulty appreciating the classical music of India or, say, Chinese calligraphy. Our neural networks have not been trained to the task. We can learn, but it is difficult, like trying to learn a second language later in life. By contrast, those who have grown up with the music and the calligraphy from childhood have no difficulty with them, for their sensoria have been trained differently. What is interesting, however, is that there is considerable agreement among those who do understand the music or calligraphy about which examples and practitioners of them are excellent and worthy of clear recognition with praise. Much the same sort of agreement is seen among classical Western musicians when they agree on the excellence of Beethoven or Mozart, or among jazz musicians agreeing about the excellence of Duke Ellington, Louis Armstrong or Charlie Parker.

In all such judgments of aesthetic excellence, we should therefore grant that there *is* an ineliminable degree of subjectivity and relativity, since excellence is a function of responses to the music or art by a *suitably cultivated sensorium*. But subjectivity of this kind is consistent with objectivity in judgments of taste. For it is consistent with saying that if one's sensorium is cultivated in a certain way, one will feel a distinctive kind of enjoyment in the experience of or creation of certain works of music or painting; and this experience will be objectively valuable for anyone whose sensorium is so cultivated. It will be valuable because it allows one to experience the world in new and more complex ways without devolving into chaos and meaninglessness, thus promoting a harmony within the self between reason, emotion and sensory experience that is a condition of human flourishing. (As noted earlier, this idea is reminiscent of Plato's notion of justice as a *harmonia* of parts of the soul, though there are also differences from Plato and other ancient thinkers noted in the next and final section.)

In late-nineteenth-century France, a skeptical art critic attended an exhibit of new works by impressionist painters such as Renoir and Monet. At first, the critic was appalled by the exhibit. The works were alien to anything he had previously experienced as art. But on the way home he noticed the mist gathering around a streetlight in a way he had never noticed before; and he realized that the impressionist painters were teaching us to see and experience the world in new ways. His sensorium had been expanded in a satisfying way.

## 7. A CAUTION: ANCIENT VERSUS MODERN VIEWS OF FLOURISHING

The theme of this chapter has been that third-dimensional excellences and virtues worthy of clear recognition with praise – in artistic practices and other aspects of everyday life – might be objective, even if they are also to some degree subjective and relative to human individuals, cultures, practices and forms of life. This objectivity is rooted in the satisfaction of human needs, interests and purposes. Prominent among these needs, interests and purposes is the cultivation of the human sensorium, which is necessary for human flourishing, though it may be cultivated differently in different practices and forms of life.

It is worth repeating, however, that these observations do not by themselves solve the problem of relativism regarding objective worth in the form of glory. The values involved may still only be (relatively) good for those who share the forms of life in question or who can appreciate the excellences and whose needs, interests and purposes are thereby satisfied. The argument of this chapter therefore represents only a step in a longer argument, as noted. But it is a necessary step if, as argued in Chapters 7 and 8, virtues, excellences and other third-dimensional values must first be objectively good for *someone* in *some* form of life, to be worthy of being recognized as good by everyone from every point of view.

Finally, it is worth noting that (in part because it is only a step in a longer argument) the account of flourishing in this chapter falls short of notions of human flourishing of ancient philosophers, such as Plato and Aristotle (as those knowledgeable about ancient philosophy will no doubt have observed). These ancient thinkers saw the cultivation of virtues and excellences as something making a human life objectively valuable in the nature of things in a *fourth-dimensional* sense and not merely relatively valuable for those who cultivate the virtues or attain the excellences in certain forms of life. The fact that the discussion of human flourishing in this chapter falls short of such ancient views of flourishing carries an important lesson: To solve the problem of relativism regarding objective worth in the form of glory, one must move beyond the third and lower dimensions of value to the fourth dimension. The argument of this chapter is only a necessary step in that direction.

# CHAPTER 14

# *The Faust legend and the mosaic*

## I. EXCELLENCE AND RELATIVISM

It is one thing to argue that something (such as a work of art) may be excellent or worthy of clear recognition with praise from those who participate in a practice or form of life or those who have a suitably cultivated sensorium or can appreciate the excellence because it contributes to *their* flourishing. It is quite another thing to say that the same object should be recognized as objectively excellent and worthy of clear recognition with praise by all persons from all points of view – whether or not they participate in the practice or share the form of life or can themselves appreciate the excellence. This difference is the difference between what has merely relative worth for some persons or groups and what has non-relative worth for all (between the third and fourth dimensions of value). How do we know that the excellences recognized in our practices and form of life – even if they should contribute to our flourishing in ways described in Chapter 13 – are worthy of clear recognition with praise by all persons from all points of view, whether or not those other persons can appreciate or even understand the practices or excellences?

To answer this question we must return again to themes about the search for wisdom of Chapters 9 and 10: We cannot *know* that excellences achieved in our practices and traditions are objectively worthy of clear recognition with praise in this sense, if "know" means having the certain and final truth about it. Objective worthiness for glory, like objective worthiness for concern from others *and* like the search for objective reality, is an object of *aspiration* rather than certain knowledge, which means that nothing can assure us of its attainment. But seeking those excellences available to us in our practices and traditions is that-without-which we cannot hope to attain such worth. Like the scientists who cannot be assured they have found the final truth of nature, but do what they can to attain it by looking for the best possible theories, we do that-without-which we could not hope to attain objective worth. On the side of worthiness for concern from others, we do it by seeking to manifest concern for others; and, on the side of glory, we do it by seeking those excellences available to us in the cultural traditions in which we are rooted.

But, as with all "searches in the realm of aspiration," though one cannot be assured of the outcome, there are better and worse ways to go about searching. So questions remain about *which* excellences and *which* practices, traditions and forms of life are worth pursuing and are more likely than others to have objective worth from all points of view and how one might determine this.

The answers to such questions, as noted in Chapters 11 and 12, cannot be given merely in terms of the ability of beings from all points of view to recognize or appreciate excellences of particular practices or forms of life. As noted there, it would not count against the excellence of Orpheus' music that beasts in Hades, who had no ears, could not appreciate it, any more than it would count against the truth of $34 + 47 = 81$ that mathematical illiterates could not appreciate it. With objective *worth* as with objective *truth*, there is the issue of an "audience fit to recognize it." But if worthiness for clear recognition with praise from all points of view does not depend upon the ability of persons from all points of view to render such recognition, on what does it depend?

## 2. FAUST AND THE TWO ASPECTS OF OBJECTIVE WORTH

I now want to argue that the answer to this question has something to do with the relation between the two aspects of objective worth, worthiness for glory and worthiness for concern from others. Could we pry these two aspects apart and seek objective worth by way of glory alone, or concern alone? This question is particularly important for ethics. For if one sought glory alone, one might do it immorally, since the ethical requirements embodied in traditional moral rules, such as the central Mosaic commandments, the Golden Rule, and the like, come from the concern side of objective worth, as argued in Chapter 12. For this reason among others, fear about the dangers of seeking glory alone has been at work in many of the wisdom and religious traditions of human history. These traditions often downplay the pursuit of worldly glory as a human goal at the expense of other persons, even though it also seems that the desire to excel and to be recognized for one's deeds and achievements is as deeply embedded in human nature as is the desire for love or concern from others.

There are many stories of famous people who pursued their own paths to glory and excellence while neglecting their families or cruelly exploiting others along the way. The case of the French painter Paul Gauguin, who left his family in poverty in order to pursue his art in the South Sea Islands, has been a staple of philosophical discussion.[1] But perhaps the most famous example of the pursuit of glory at the expense of concern for others is the legendary case of Faust, who sold his soul to the devil in order to become the great knower of all secrets and who cruelly treated others, including a young maiden, along the way. The Faust legend is one of those myths that has had a profound and lasting influence because it probes deeply into the human psyche and the human condition. In this case, the myth touches upon the basic relation of the two aspects of objective worth, glory and concern for others.

To see how the Faust legend does this, we must first return to the point made at the end of the previous section. Just as Orpheus' music could not be appreciated by the earless beasts, so the music of Bach and the paintings of Michelangelo could not be appreciated by extraterrestrials whose auditory and visual capacities turned the music into meaningless noise or the paintings into random squiggles. On what grounds, then, might the music of Bach or the painting of Michelangelo be deserving of clear recognition with praise from all points of view, even from the points of view of these very different beings?

The answer I now want to suggest is that beings in different forms of life or with different capacities can fittingly acknowledge the objective worth of something they cannot directly appreciate, if they are able to acknowledge the objective worth of *beings* different from themselves *who can appreciate it.* In other words, the extraterrestrial beings just mentioned must be able to say something like the following. "We earless or sightless beings cannot appreciate Bach and Michelangelo, so we cannot *directly* see how their excellence adds to the overall good of the Universe. But indirectly we can see how it adds to the overall good of the Universe, if we acknowledge the objective worth of you human beings and other beings who *can* appreciate such excellence and to whose flourishing it does contribute. We would then acknowledge that what we can directly appreciate from our point of view is not all that counts towards the overall good. Human beings have worth too and some of the objective worth of the Universe (some absolute value) flows through them, even if we cannot directly appreciate it."

Such acknowledgement that other points of view add to the overall good of the Universe provides a clue about the relation of the two aspects

---

[1] Williams 1972, Slote 1983.

of objective worth. To say of other beings that what is good *for them* adds to the overall good of the Universe (even if we cannot appreciate it because we do not share their experiences and sensibilities) is to express what worthiness for concern for other inscapes is about. It is to say of others that you want them to be and flourish, not because you benefit from their existence or can appreciate what they can do, but because their being and their experiences are an essential part of the value of the Universe, which would be diminished without them.

### 3. COUNTING IN THE NATURE OF THINGS: NOZICK'S SUPERIOR ALIENS

Consider what it would be like to take an opposite attitude. Robert Nozick has imagined a race of alien beings far superior to us in intelligence and accomplishments.[2] They look down upon us humans as inferior. To them, any accomplishments the human race can boast of, including those of Bach or Michelangelo, are insignificant and negligible in the larger scheme of things. These superior beings acknowledge that certain experiences and achievements are regarded as good or excellent by us humans or *from* a human point of view. But since they believe humans are inferior and insignificant beings, they do not think that anything valued from the human point of view is really valuable in the nature of things (i.e., objectively valuable).

We do not have to go to science fiction in order to find examples of such attitudes. Ordinary human beings for centuries have reasoned similarly about people of different tribes, races, nations and cultures from their own. The ancient Greeks would have said of the Scythians who lived in the regions north of Greece that the Scythians valued a different kind of pottery and dress than the Greeks. But the Scythians were barbarians with an inferior culture, according to the Greeks, and so what these Scythians regarded as beautiful or virtuous did not count as *real* beauty or virtue in the nature of things. The Chinese felt the same about the barbarians who surrounded their Middle Kingdom, as did all other advanced civilizations of the past (and most other civilizations no matter how advanced they were). More than a century ago, many Americans could see no value in "Negro" spirituals and the first beginnings of jazz as an art form. They knew that American blacks created and valued this music. But these white Americans regarded the black race as inferior, so

---

[2] 1981: chapter 5.

what blacks may have valued wasn't really valuable and was not worth taking account of.

In other words, *if you or your kind do not count in the nature of things, then what you value and what is valuable for you does not count in the nature of things.* Or, putting it another way, if something is only valuable and can only be appreciated by some beings from their perspective, and they and their perspective do not matter in the larger scheme of things, then what they value does not matter either. And note that "counting or mattering in the larger scheme of things" in this context means "being raised up from the *third* dimension of value to the *fourth*." It means that what is good for some particular beings and from their point of view is not merely (relatively) good for them, but is worthy of being recognized as objectively good by everyone, whether others in fact recognize it or not.

It is worthiness for concern from others that allows one to make this transition. For such concern is directed at the inscape or inner self. Worthiness for concern from all points of view means that the inscapes of the beings so worthy, their experiences, and ultimately their points of view, matter in the nature of things. There would be less value in the Universe if they were not included. This point is what the earless or sightless beings acknowledged when they said that even though they could not themselves appreciate the excellence of the works of Bach or Michelangelo, they could recognize its objective worth if they acknowledged the objective worth of beings like us who could appreciate such excellence.

The thinking of these earless and sightless beings was the opposite of Nozick's superior beings who thought humans were of no value. Nozick's beings reasoned that since humans have no significance in the nature of things, what they value is also of no ultimate significance. The two groups come to different conclusions because they have different views of human worth. But their reasoning was based on a common assumption. Both assumed that if what you or I or anyone values is to count in the nature of things, we ourselves have to count; and if we don't count, then what we value doesn't count either, unless there is some other reason to value it from some other point of view which does count. This assumption, which is shared even by Nozick's superior beings, is the one on which the present argument depends.

So in this unique way, worthiness for glory from all points of view depends upon the worthiness for care or concern from all points of view. But the dependence is indirect. We cannot say that because of Gauguin's callous treatment of his family, his paintings were less worthy of clear recognition with praise *by those who could appreciate them*. It would be a mistake to make artistic merit depend on ethics or moral worth in this direct way. The connection is more subtle. Gauguin's paintings could be appreciated by normally sighted human beings as excellent by the standards of his art, quite independently of his personal life. But it would be different for sightless beings, like our imagined aliens, or others with different sensibilities than ours, who could not directly appreciate the aesthetic value of Gauguin's paintings. They would have no reason to appreciate that value unless they recognized the objective worthiness of some other beings like us who could appreciate it.

So the value of Gauguin's work *to us*, and others like us, is assured by its artistic merit. But this is only relative worth. If the work is to additionally be objectively worthy to all, it will be because some of those who can appreciate it and for whom it has artistic worth are worthy of concern by all. By the worthiness of their inscapes to be and to flourish, these beings would "raise up" something that is valuable to them from mere relative value to something of objective worth in the Universe.

## 4. THE FAUST LEGEND: GLORY AND CONCERN

Viewed in this way, the relation of the two aspects of objective worth also has importance for individuals, as we can see by returning to the Faust legend. Faust wanted to attain his full measure of glory and was prepared to do so by forsaking objective worthiness for the concern of others. He would forsake commitments to others and even to the whole human community, if need be, to fulfill his dream of glory.

This is one way of reading Faust's pact with the devil. According to older versions of the legend, Faust accomplished much, yet lost all in the end and was destroyed. Because glory attaches to deeds or accomplishments, it is always in principle "detachable," as we saw in the story of the Bach crystals. So, like Faust, we might accomplish much and yet lose ourselves (our souls, as the legend implies). In such manner, the city officials and aristocrats cared about the accomplishments of Bach, but not that they were the accomplishments of Bach. Miraculous crystals would have done as well. Likewise, our accomplishments might survive in the final picture if we are not objectively worthy of concern. But like Faust, in the older legends, *we* will be lost – like the people of Orwell's *1984*, whose names were expunged from all records as if they had never existed.

Some of the original Faust legends were supposed to show that the desire for glory (or "greatness" of some sort) was ultimately destructive and motivated by a ruinous pride or *hubris*. Whatever we accomplish, and however great it may seem from our limited human perspective, we are invited by the legend to see how little it comes to in the overall scheme of things. We are little and the Universe is great. The lesson is worth learning. Yet, it would be hard to eliminate the desire for glory in human beings without taking away much of what we call their human nature and the motivation for great and good achievements.[3]

Such thoughts about glory seem to have been on the mind of Goethe in his famous later version of the Faust legend.[4] Goethe seemed well aware that there is a perpetual tension in human endeavor between the desires to be worthy of love and concern from others, on the one hand, and for glory, on the other – as exemplified in conflicts that arise between the pursuit of artistic excellence and morality, or in ethical conflicts involved in the unlimited pursuit of power or knowledge. But while Goethe was aware of this perpetual tension, he seems also to have been convinced that there is something deeply wrong with the idea that the desire for glory should be completely expunged from human life or entirely overridden by moral concerns. If the demands of duty should erase all "Faustian" desires to excel and to achieve great things, human life would become hollow and empty, even if it is also true that, if the pursuit of glory should overwhelm all love and concern, life would be nasty and cruel.

The proper ethical response to this tension, I would argue, is not to deny the importance of the desire for glory, but to put it in perspective: To show how, though lives and achievements may indeed be little in the broader scheme of things, they can have objective worth; they can be indispensable parts of the greater good. We might gain this broader perspective, first, by focusing on the worthiness for clear recognition with praise rather than merely on actual recognition; and second, by seeking to be worthy of concern from others as well as of glory.

### 5. THE TWO GOALS OF ANCIENT WISDOM REVISITED AND THE FOURTH DIMENSION

These reflections provide further insights into the fourth dimension of value, which was described in Chapter 8 as a higher standpoint above and beyond all third-dimensional points of view and forms of life. It was emphasized, however, that "above and beyond" did not mean the fourth dimension abstracts from the particulars of dimensions of value below it. The fourth

---

[3] Cf. the pervasive myths of heroic quests in all human cultures, as described in Campbell 1956.
[4] Goethe 1960.

dimension was more accurately viewed as the *summation* of all that is good and excellent in different third-dimensional forms of life, which include goods of the first and second dimensions as well. The fact that glory and excellence must be pursued within particular practices, traditions and forms of life would therefore not mean that activities and achievements could not also have objective (i.e., fourth-dimensional) worth.

This idea of a "summation" of value returns us to a central theme of Chapter 10 to which I said we would eventually return. Of the two goals of "wisdom in the ancient philosophical sense" that were distinguished in Chapter 10, it was suggested that reflection on the first of these goals, understanding *objective reality*, would throw light on the second, understanding *objective worth*. The connection intended was this: Just as there need be no way to grasp the real city of New York "in itself" from some neutral perspective *outside all language games* (as argued in Chapter 10), so there need be no way to appreciate objective excellence, or worthiness for clear recognition with praise, from some neutral perspective *outside all practices, traditions and forms of life*. Bach is excellent in one way, Einstein in another, Michelangelo and Shakespeare in yet other ways. To appreciate the different ways in which they are excellent requires different modes of understanding and initiation into different practices and traditions. But this is no more an argument against their absolute goodness, or objective worth, than is the claim that because descriptions of New York are always made in some conceptual scheme or language game, they cannot be descriptions of an objectively real city.

In sum, absolute good (or fourth-dimensional value) may be conceived as the *summation* of all that is excellent in different practices, traditions and forms of life (music, physics, painting, and the like), just as the absolute truth about the city may be the summation of all that is correctly said about it in the different vocabularies of the social historian, the weatherman, the economist, and so on. As with the descriptions of the city, we would not necessarily go wrong in saying the achievements of Bach or Michelangelo or Shakespeare are absolutely good, but rather in saying that any one of them represents the whole of the absolute good. For the good in that sense would be the sum of all the finite goods that arise out of different points of view and in different forms of life. If grasping the absolute good is elusive, that would be because there may always be more ways to be excellent than we have yet explored. Absolute good or fourth-dimensional value transcends our finite grasp not because we are getting no glimpses of it in small and large examples of human good, but because there is always more to grasp.

### 6. THE MOSAIC OF VALUE

There is an image that nicely captures this idea of the objective good as the summation of particular goods – the image of a mosaic of value. A mosaic, as commonly defined, is a picture or design made by inlaying small bits of colored stone, glass, or other substances in mortar; or by extension, it is any complex picture or design made up of distinct parts put together to form a whole. Let us imagine a complete mosaic as the absolute good (the fourth dimension of value) and the inlaid pieces or parts comprising it as various virtues and excellences attained in different practices and forms of life. The excellences of particular practices and forms of life are different in kind, like the colored pieces of the mosaic. But in the well-made mosaic, each part makes an essential contribution to the whole. Remove any piece and the mosaic is less good. Similarly, to remove particular examples of virtue or excellence in certain particular forms of life would be to diminish the absolute good, the total sum of the good of the Universe, just as removing one of the descriptions would give us an incomplete picture of New York.

According to this image, your importance and mine, insofar as we seek objective worth through glory, is to be a piece of the larger mosaic of value. We have to do it in our own way, with our own talents, rooted as we must be in particular traditions and forms of life. But if we do it well, we may add however small a piece to the overall good. To seek objective worth is not to try to encompass the whole of that good, but to be a piece of it (however great or small), whose removal would make the whole less valuable.

This mosaic image also provides a further perspective on the openness practiced by the retreatants of Chapter 3. By choosing to be open to the degree possible to other points of view, the retreatants were ultimately seeking fourth-dimensional value or objective worth *by letting the value in each objectively worthy point of view come forth* and take its place in the mosaic, thereby contributing to the overall good. Considered in this way, there is no contradiction in saying, as noted in Chapter 8, that goods can be both particular and relative with respect to persons and concrete forms of life, yet universal and absolute as part of the larger mosaic of value.

### 7. THE FOURTH DIMENSION AND EVIL PRACTICES

But one must add that not every relative good in the first three dimensions of value would necessarily be raised up to the fourth dimension and become part of this larger mosaic. Some values in lower dimensions may be overridden in the fourth dimension, as lower dimensions may override values below them. The joy of the abandoned child when she is found may be so raised up to the fourth dimension, but not the joy the torturer takes in torturing his victim.

The possibility of such overriding is related to a problem that concerned MacIntyre (1981: 179) about his account of virtues and excellences in practices, traditions and forms of life. He was concerned about "evil" practices or traditions – terrorism, torture, slavery, mind-control, genocide, drug trafficking, murder for hire, swindling, seduction, dictatorships, and the like. These practices also seemed to have distinctive virtues and excellences (in his senses of the terms) required for their success. A successful terrorist must be patient, self-disciplined, loyal, cool under pressure, courageous, ready to give his life if called upon to die for the cause, and so on. MacIntyre thought that such virtues when exercised within evil practices were not objectively worthy. But he was aware that one could not say why they should be excluded, if the only relevant criteria were *internal* to practices and traditions, as his view suggested they should be.

I do not think this problem *can* be solved if the only criteria to which one can appeal are internal to practices or traditions. One has to also consider the objective worth of the practices and traditions themselves from points of view external to them. But "external" to practices and traditions does not have to mean how they look from *outside any point of view whatsoever*; rather it may mean how they look from *other* points of view. Though virtues of patience, loyalty and courage may be good traits for the successful practices of terrorists or hired assassins or evil dictators, these practices themselves and those who engage in them are not worthy of concern for their flourishing from *other* points of view (those they exploit) and hence not worthy of concern from all points of view. The virtues that make such exploitation effective are not therefore objectively worthy of clear recognition with praise from all points of view.

To get this result, however, one must be concerned with the objective good (the mosaic), not merely with the good from within one or another particular point of view; and to be so concerned, one must be concerned with the external effects of the practice *on others* and not merely with the internal effects on its own practitioners. The beauty of a well-made mosaic not only depends upon the beauty of each stone, but also on how the stones cohere with one another.

## 8. POSTSCRIPT ON MORAL REALISM

On this theory, there can be *objective* (distinctively) *moral* facts, as moral realists require. They would be facts to the effect that persons are treating others with respect in the sense of openness (i.e., as ends) and thus maintaining a moral sphere to the degree possible; and such facts would explain why goods *in the other three dimensions of value* that are realized by persons (who are so treating others as ends) are *objectively worthy* of being realized.

So understood, moral facts, qua moral (as distinguished from the natural facts on which they may supervene) would not so much explain why other facts exist or have objective *reality*, but rather why other facts do (or do not) have objective *worth*. In doing this, however, moral facts would be playing an important explanatory *metaphysical* role. They would be doing so because (from Chapters 10 and 11) metaphysics in the ancient Aristotelian sense – which is equivalent to *wisdom* (*sophia*) or "first philosophy" – has two goals: explaining what and why things have *objective reality* and explaining what and why things have *objective worth*. Moral facts, qua moral, would be doing the latter and thus they would be facts that those seeking wisdom in the broader ancient sense would want to know. Those who deny that moral facts have an explanatory role (e.g., Harman 1977) usually have in mind explanation in the modern scientific sense of explaining why things come to be objectively real in the causal order. I am suggesting that in order to understand the explanatory role of moral facts (as distinguished from the natural facts on which they supervene), we need to take a broader ancient (metaphysical) view of explanation according to which *wisdom* (i.e., metaphysics) demands an explanation of why things have objective worth as well as why they have objective reality.[5]

---

[5] It would be instructive to contrast this account of moral facts, not only with prominent anti-realist and quasi-realist views, such as those of Gibbard (1990) or Blackburn (1993), but with other moral realist views as well, such as those of Sturgeon (1985), Boyd (1988), Brink (1989), Mi. Smith (1994), Railton (2003), Shafer-Landau (2003), Cuneo (2007), and others. But that is another task I must leave for a later occasion. (For overviews on the moral realism debate, see the essays in Sayre-McCord 1988, as well as A. Miller 2003, Sayre-McCord 2005 and Rosati 2006.) In the remaining chapters, I concentrate on comparing the present theory to other prominent *normative* ethical theories, a task that is challenging enough.

# CHAPTER 15

# The good and the right (I): intuitionism, Kantianism

## I. TRANSITION AND REVIEW: THE MST FORMULA

In the next three chapters, I compare the merits of the theory developed in the preceding chapters to some alternative contemporary normative ethical theories. This chapter considers *intuitionist* and *Kantian* approaches to ethics, Chapter 16, *utilitarian* and *consequentialist* theories, and Chapter 17, *contractualist* theories. Other approaches to ethics, including *virtue ethics* and *feminist views*, will be more briefly considered in the final chapter, which deals with the implications of the moral theory for social and applied ethics, political philosophy, law and moral education. This chapter begins with a brief review of the theory.

The ethical view developed in the preceding fourteen chapters may be described as a "moral sphere theory" of the *right* (or right action) supported by a "dimensional theory" of the *good* (or value). Since a convenient name is needed for the entire view, I will refer to it hereafter as the *"moral sphere theory"* of the good and the right (or MST). This designation will be used more regularly from this point onward. One might express the view in a formula that oversimplifies a bit and requires fleshing out, but captures its spirit:

(The MST Formula) "Strive to lead a good life that is objectively worthy of being lived and strive thereby to realize goods by virtue of the living of such a life that are objectively worthy of being realized."

The notion of a "good life" in this formula is to be understood initially in terms of the first three dimensions of value. "Good lives" will tend to have a greater balance of basic value experiences over disvalue experiences in the first dimension of value; and the basic value experiences of such lives (that are not overridden in higher dimensions) will be first-dimensional "goods" realized in those lives. Good lives will also include personal projects and fulfilling personal relations and associations that contribute to faring well in the second dimension of value – meaningful work, friendships, special relations to children, spouses, parents, extended family, communities, associations, and so on. The existence of these personal relations and the success of personal projects will be second-dimensional goods realized in those lives when not overridden in higher dimensions.

Good lives in the third dimension will in addition include playing valued roles in forms of life with which one identifies and exemplifying various ideals through which persons define what they are (their "practical identity," as some call it) – being a caring parent, loyal employee, courageous soldier, grateful friend, generous donor, fair judge, responsible citizen, and so on. Playing such roles and exemplifying such ideals involve exhibiting virtues that define what we are and our place in the world and in the communities in which we live. In addition, good lives in the third dimension will include pursuing diverse forms of excellence in practices and traditions in those forms of life – physics, medicine, law, violin-making, painting, architecture, and many more – practices and traditions through which humans go about achieving diverse kinds of goods. The virtues and excellences thus achieved that are not overridden are third-dimensional goods realized in the forms of life in question.

In general, humans pursue the good in the first three dimensions, not in the abstract, but *rooted* (as they necessarily are) in webs of relationships and in practices, traditions and forms of life through which they seek to express the meaning of their lives, exercise their rational and creative abilities, engage in satisfying personal relations and associations, play valued roles that exhibit virtues and seek various forms of excellence of achievement. In all these ways, they seek to exercise their natural human capabilities.[1] Doing so involves the exercise of distinctively rational capacities in theoretical and practical reasoning, as ancient thinkers emphasized. But human beings are more than merely rational beings, as argued in Chapter 13. They also have inscapes with distinctively human sensoria. So the fulfillment of their nature also involves an integration of the rational aspects of their nature with other aspects, emotional, active and sensory or experiential.

## 2. OBJECTIVELY WORTHY LIVES

Such in summary is the "theory of the good" in the first three dimensions of value supporting the MST formula just given:

---

[1] A "capabilities approach" to human welfare and development consonant with these claims has been defended in well-known works by Sen (e.g. 1999) and is applied to women's affairs by Nussbaum (2000). The novel "developmental" account of human flourishing or well-being developed in Kraut 2007 also has much in common with the view presented here.

"Strive to lead a *good life* that is objectively worthy of being lived and strive thereby to realize *goods* by virtue of the living of such a life that are objectively worthy of being realized."

The theory of the good represented by this formula, however, cannot be defined in the first three dimensions of value alone. The fourth dimension must also be factored in; and that is where the qualifying phrases of the formula come into play: Good lives must also be "objectively worthy of being lived," if the goods realized by those lives in the first three dimensions of value are to be "objectively worthy of being realized." Thus, good lives in the first three dimensions are qualified by an account of what ways of living and acting are *objectively worthy* or unworthy in the fourth dimension.

The basics of this account of objectively worthy ways of living in the fourth dimension are as follows. Ways of life (and plans of action generally) fail to be "objectively worthy of being lived" (or pursued) if they are *moral sphere-breaking* by nature; and goods realized by such moral sphere-breaking ways of life and plans of action are not "objectively worthy of being realized." Plans of action and ways of life that are moral sphere-breaking (as defined in Chapter 4) are those that "(i) require or license agents acting on them to impose their wills on others, or make others do or undergo what they want, whatever the desires, interests or purposes of those others might be in the matter (ii) in situations in which the agents are not doing what they can do to maintain a moral sphere in which all persons can be treated with openness by all others."

The plans of action of the assailant ("to assault and rob someone") and con man ("to cheat someone of their life savings") are moral sphere-breaking in this sense. Such moral sphere-breaking plans of action are not "objectively worthy" of being pursued, according to the MST formula; and the goods realized by them (the money and benefits gained by the assailant and con man from their schemes) are not "objectively worthy of being realized."

Alternatively, one can say that those who pursue moral sphere-breaking plans of action violate the *Ends Principle* (*EP*): "Treat all persons as ends in every situation and no one as means only (or as mere means)." To treat persons *as ends* or, equivalently, with *respect in the sense of openness* (as also defined in Chapter 4) is to "treat them with openness (to allow them to pursue their ways of life without interference) to the degree that one can do so while maintaining a moral sphere in which all persons can be treated with openness by all others." Those who pursue moral sphere-breaking plans of action fail to treat some persons as ends, or with respect, in this sense (i) by imposing their wills on those others *and* (ii) by *not* doing so in an effort to maintain (i.e., restore or preserve) the moral sphere. They thereby "treat some persons as means only" or as "mere means" – which (as defined in Chapter 4) is equivalent to "engaging in moral sphere-breaking plans of action" or "breaking the moral sphere."

Why are plans of action and ways of life that are moral sphere-breaking in this sense not "objectively worthy" of being pursued? Objective worth, as defined in Chapter 11, has two aspects – objective worthiness for clear recognition with praise for deeds and accomplishments from all points of view and objective worthiness for concern for the flourishing of one's inscape from all points of view. In Chapter 12, it was argued that a necessary condition for being objectively worthy of concern for the flourishing of one's inscape from all points of view is that one show such concern for the inscapes of others. To show such concern specifically in the case of beings capable of self-reflection and choosing their own ends (i.e., persons) is to allow them to pursue their ways of life and realize ends of their own choosing ("to pursue happiness as they choose") to the degree that one can do so while showing similar concern for all others. Those who engage in moral sphere-breaking ways of life fail this test. By their plans of action, they make it impossible for others to treat them with openness (allowing them to pursue their plans and realize their desired ends), while at the same time treating all other persons with openness as well, including those they are treating as mere means.

One may reason similarly with regard to one's *own* way of life. If it is moral sphere-breaking, it will also not be objectively worthy of being allowed to be pursued by all persons from all points of view. Thus, as argued in Chapter 12, the way one goes about *finding out* which ways of life are objectively worthy of being allowed to be pursued from all points of view is *the same way one goes about showing that one's own way of life is objectively worthy of being allowed to be pursued from all points of view.* One does it by striving to avoid breaking the moral sphere to the degree possible in one's plans of action and by doing what one can do to maintain a moral sphere in which all persons can be treated with openness by all others. This sphere is an ideal that may never be perfectly realizable in an imperfect world. But it is the degree to which one is aspiring to it and striving for it that is the measure of the objective worthiness of the life one is leading.

### 3. SUMMARY: MORAL RULES

Such, in summary, is the ("dimensional") *theory of the good* and the ("moral sphere") *theory of the right* – with the fourth dimension added – that underlie the (MST) formula:

"Strive to lead a good life that is objectively worthy of being lived and strive thereby to realize goods by virtue of the living of such a life that are objectively worthy of being realized."

Strictly speaking, the second half of the formula could have been left out, as perceptive readers will have noticed, since to lead "a good life that is objectively worthy of being lived" *is* "thereby" to "realize goods ... that are objectively worthy of being realized." But I have included the second half of the formula in order to emphasize this important fact which is relevant to subsequent arguments.

The general idea of the "theory of the right" expressed by the formula is to maintain to the degree possible a sphere of life in which all persons can pursue plans of action and ways of life, subject to the constraint that their plans of action and ways of life are not moral sphere-breaking. Such a constraint, as argued in Chapters 2–4, immediately yields a host of common moral rules widely recognized in different cultures and traditions: "Don't kill," "Don't lie," "Don't steal," "Don't cheat," "Don't injure or harm others," "Don't coerce or use violence," "Don't manipulate others for your own gain," and so on.[2]

What do these rules have in common? All of them forbid *moral sphere-breaking plans of action and ways of life*. The actions forbidden by these rules all normally involve some persons imposing their wills or plans (i.e., intentions, purposes) on some others, whatever the interests, desires or concerns of the others may be in the matter. Moreover, these common moral rules turn out, according to the theory, to be merely *prima facie* or *defeasible* rules. They have exceptions; and the exceptions to them arise *where the moral sphere breaks down* (where one cannot treat all persons with openness, no matter what one does). Moreover, the allowable exceptions follow from the same principle from which the prima facie rules themselves follow, namely, the Ends Principle ("Treat all persons as ends in every situation and never as means only"), which requires that one depart as little as possible from the ideal of a moral sphere in which all

---

[2] These rules also track fairly closely the first eight of the ten "moral rules" that Bernard Gert has argued are central to our common-sense view of morality in many works (1970, 1998, 2004), though Gert defends these rules in a different way than I do here.

persons can be treated with openness by all others when one must depart from that ideal to some degree.


### 4. ETHICAL INTUITIONISM: W. D. ROSS AND OTHERS

Since this moral sphere theory (or MST) captures many rules of common-sense morality, while regarding them as prima facie or defeasible, it would seem to have much in common with *intuitionist* theories in ethics of the kind associated with W. D. Ross, H. A. Pritchard, A. C. Ewing and others.[3] Yet the moral sphere theory just described is not an intuitionist moral theory. It is instructive, therefore, to ask how it differs from intuitionist theories and what advantages it may have with respect to them.

Ethical intuitionism, especially in the tradition of Ross, has been making a comeback in contemporary moral theory, after being marginalized through the middle and late twentieth century; and versions of Rossian intuitionism are now ably defended by a number of philosophers, including Robert Audi, David McNaughton and Piers Rawling, Philip Stratton-Lake, among others.[4] Rossian intuitionist views generally involve two basic claims: They claim first that there is an irreducible plurality of basic common-sense moral principles with no explicit priority rules for resolving conflicts between them. Second, these moral principles are self-evident in the sense that they can be known directly by intuition on the basis of an adequate understanding of them.[5] The basic moral principles in question may be rules of common-sense morality, like those listed above ("don't kill," "don't lie," "don't injure," etc.). Or more commonly, as in Ross's version, the basic self-evident principles may be *prima facie duties*, such as duties of non-injury, justice and beneficence, from which one can infer common rules of morality, such as "don't kill," "don't lie," "don't harm others," and so on.

---

[3] Ross 1930; Pritchard 1912; Ewing 1953. Excellent overviews of intuitionist views include Audi 2004 (chapter 1) and Stratton-Lake 2002. Many moral *particularists*, of whom Dancy (2000, 2004) is the most well-known, are also influenced by Ross and Rossian intuitionism. See Hooker and Little 2000 on moral particularism.

[4] Audi 2001, 2004; McNaughton 1996, 2000; McNaughton and Rawling 1998, 2006; Stratton-Lake 2002: Introduction. Other recent defenders of ethical intuitionism include Huemer (2005) and Bonevac (2004), both of whom offer original accounts, the latter in response to Rawls' critique of intuitionism. Stratton-Lake (1997), A. Thomas (2000) and Montague (2000) criticize Hooker's rule-consequentialism from a Rossian intuitionist perspective. Bedke (2008) criticizes some familiar interpretations of intuitions and offers his own account of how they justify. See also Nelson 1999 and Baldwin 1990 for relevant discussions.

[5] Stratton-Lake 2002: 2, Audi 2004: 21.

As Stratton-Lake notes, even critics of intuitionism generally agree that certain forms of intuitionist ethics

best reflect common-sense morality. One would have thought therefore that intuitionism has a certain default plausibility. But during the 1950s and 1960s intuitionism was rejected out of hand as an utterly implausible theory. How could a theory that aims to stick so closely to common sense come to be thought of as so implausible?[6]

Many reasons have been offered. Intuitionism has been said by its critics to be dogmatic since it regards common-sense moral intuitions as self-evident and not in need of further proof (Nowell-Smith 1954: 67; Frankena 1973: 103). It has been argued that all intuitionists can do in the face of disbelief is insist that what they are saying is true (Korsgaard 1996: 38). Intuitionism has also been charged with merely codifying biases or prejudices of common sense. As Hare says (1981: 83), "claiming self-evidence for moral convictions is simply an illegitimate way of parading subjective convictions as objective, rational truths."[7] Intuitionism has also been called vacuous since it seems to tell us no more than we already knew about common-sense morality (Warnock 1967: 12–13).

In addition to such objections, intuitionism has been frequently charged with being unsystematic, presenting us with an "unconnected heap" of common-sense duties with no underlying theory that would provide a rationale for the moral convictions we have.[8] And it has been charged with offering little help in resolving conflicts of duties. For it denies the existence of explicit priority rules for prima facie duties, or any overriding general principles, such as a utilitarian principle of utility or the Kantian categorical imperative, from which prima facie duties might be derived.[9]

Contemporary defenders of intuitionism have rebutted some of these familiar objections, at least in their harshest and crudest forms. Yet there are many lingering worries about intuitionist ethics among philosophers. I will focus on three classes of such worries that have a special bearing on the relation of intuitionist theories to the moral sphere theory or MST, which endorses similar common-sense rules, but on different grounds. The problems in question for intuitionism are about self-evidence, systematization and conflicts of duties.

---

[6] Stratton-Lake ibid.: 1.     [7] Cf. MacIntyre 1988: 17.
[8] McNaughton 1996 discusses and tries to rebut this objection.
[9] McNaughton 2000 provides an overview of such criticisms.

## 5. SELF-EVIDENCE: MORAL INTUITIONS
## AND FORMS OF LIFE

Contemporary intuitionists deny that self-evident propositions must be *obvious* to anyone who considers them.[10] They note that Ross clearly insisted that moral intuitions were evident only to those with sufficient mental abilities who had reflected properly upon them. Ross drew an analogy to mathematical truths, many of which may not seem obviously true until we come to understand their meaning. Similarly, principles of duty become known to us only upon reflection and on the basis of an adequate understanding of them.[11] Audi offers a further example of a proposition that is not immediately obvious, but is self-evident: "If there had never been any siblings, there would never have been any first cousins."[12]

If self-evident moral propositions need not be obvious, these intuitionists argue, that fact may go some way toward answering another common objection to intuitionism – that it cannot explain disagreements in moral intuitions. Audi and other intuitionists also insist that one need not hold that self-evident moral propositions are certain in the sense that one could not be mistaken about them.[13] Further reflection about them could lead one to change one's mind, as Ross did about several of his earlier claims concerning what did and did not count as a basic prima facie duty.

These responses go some way toward answering criticisms that intuitionism must be dogmatic or that it merely codifies unreflected prejudices of common sense, or that it rests on infallible and therefore unarguable moral intuitions. But it is far from clear that such responses really put to rest deeper worries about self-evidence that have spawned such criticisms. Ross's analogy with mathematical propositions, for example, is not persuasive to many. As Thomas Carson has said: "In the case of self-evident mathematical propositions, there is a consensus among expert mathematicians ... We find no comparable consensus among 'moral experts'"; and this lack of consensus is not surprising, he implies, given the essentially contestable nature of moral claims.[14] Carson cites Berys Gaut on the same issue, who writes:

[10] Audi 2004, McNaughton 2000, Stratton-Lake (ed.) 2002, Huemer 2005. See DePaul 1993, Timmons 1999, McMahan 2000, for views which, recognizing this point, discuss the role of moral intuitions in relation to broader issues of coherence and reflective equilibrium in moral epistemology. For further discussion of these issues in moral epistemology, see the essays in Sinnott-Armstrong and Timmons 1996. Tiberius 2008 contains an original account of the role of coherence in the development of what she calls "reflective wisdom" about values and the good life.
[11] Ross 1930: chapter 2.    [12] Audi 2004: 86.
[13] Audi ibid.; McNaughton 2000: 282–83.
[14] 2004: 176. For similar criticisms see J. Gert 2006, Sinnott-Armstrong 2006 and Crisp in Timmons, Greco and Mele 2007. Sinnott-Armstrong employs a variety of arguments, including

On a broadly Rossian account of self-evidence ... those who deny that some moral duties are self-evident have failed adequately to understand the propositions ... or lack sufficient mental maturity or have paid insufficient attention to the propositions ....But such failures ... are scarcely explanations of why many philosophers have denied the self-evidence of these propositions. Moore, for example, ... appears to have given morality at least as close scrutiny as Ross. So [Moore's] failure to grasp the purported self-evidence of moral duties is not plausibly traced to any failure of understanding or attention on his part. (2002: 144)

Carson adds that "the problem for Ross is even worse than Gaut suggests. Not only does Moore not find Ross's views to be self-evident, Moore claims that contrary views are self-evident; he claims that it is self-evident that we should always do whatever would have the best consequences."[15] Concerning Audi's proposition "If there had never been any siblings, there would never have been any first cousins," Gaut adds that it is indeed self-evident. But that is because when we understand the meanings of its key terms, such as "sibling" and "cousin," we come to see it is true.[16] But Gaut insists that this is not what we find in the case of propositions about moral duties. People can understand the meanings of such propositions quite well and "nonetheless deny that they are self-evident." Denying that moral propositions are self-evident, of course, does not necessarily mean denying they are correct or true. It rather amounts to insisting that they are in need of further grounding or theoretical justification than merely asserting their self-evidence.

I believe there is a deeper problem lying behind all such persisting objections to intuitionism about self-evidence. The problem is nicely expressed by Owen Anderson in a review of Audi's influential defense of intuitionism, *The Good in the Right* (2004):

The intuitions of any given person are part of a world-view that must be critically examined before the intuitions can be relied upon. The major world-views that have developed the civilizations of world history have significant long-term differences of intuition that cannot be ignored and that give differing answers to questions such as "what is it to be harmed" or "what is the good." The need to take into account the variety of world-views does not necessarily entail relativism, but nor can they be ignored when the meaning of key terms such as "good" vary among them ....What exactly does it mean to harm another? Western secularism may have one answer, while the Hindu ... system will have another and Buddhism still another. (2005: 874)

---

empirical evidence from recent work in psychology, to argue that ethical intuitions cannot be trusted without further justification.

[15] Carson 2004: 176.     [16] Ibid.

The general point here is that our moral intuitions are shaped by upbringing and enculturation in various *forms of life*; and these forms of life themselves are in need of justification. For most of the human race, moral intuitions have been parts of complex webs of belief, involving world-views, often with a religious foundation; and this is still true for most of the world's population. When differences arise among these world-views – for example, about whether duties of veracity or beneficence should apply only to one's own group or to all humans impartially, or about whether women should have an inferior social position to men, or whether sexual relations between those of the same sex should be allowed – it will not suffice to settle such differences by asking persons merely to scrutinize their moral intuitions more carefully to see if they turn out to be true upon reflection. For that reflection itself will be shaped by the person's culture, point of view and form of life.

## 6. SYSTEMATIZATION AND CONFLICTS OF DUTY

I believe that general concerns of this sort lie behind persistent worries about self-evidence voiced by critics of intuitionism from Frankena, Hare and Warnock to Korsgaard, Carson, Gaut, and many others. The worry is that by claiming self-evidence for our moral intuitions, even upon careful reflection and consideration of their meaning, we beg the question about whether *our* intuitions are not merely the result of our upbringing and enculturation and therefore only right "from our point of view" or "for persons who were brought up as we were." The question then becomes: How can we show that common-sense moral rules and exceptions we may recognize as right upon reflection are not merely culturally and historically "right as we see it," but right in a way that should be recognized as right by everyone from every point of view, whether others in fact agree with our intuitions or not?

Stated in this way, it is not difficult to see that this question concerns the very problems of pluralism and relativism with which this book began. To answer the question, we need a further test beyond claiming our common-sense moral beliefs seem correct *to us* upon careful reflection. What form, however, should such a further test take? The answer suggested by the moral sphere theory or MST is that the further test for the objective truth of our moral beliefs should take the form of a search or *quest for wisdom* "in the ancient philosophical sense," of the kind the retreatants undertook.

We may begin this quest by believing our moral intuitions are correct, as many of the retreatants did. But in order to put those intuitions to the test, we need to find out if the form of life of which the intuitions are a part is objectively worthy of being lived – that is, worthy of being lived, not just from our own point of view, but from every point of view. To find this out, we have to expand our minds beyond our own limited points of view and forms of life and take into account other points of view and forms of life – thereby overcoming to the degree possible narrowness of vision, as the philosophical quest for wisdom demands. We do this by initially opening our minds to other points of view or forms of life, allowing them to be lived without interference "to the degree that we can do so while maintaining a moral sphere in which all persons can be treated with such openness by all others"; and we do this in order to "allow persons to show by how they plan to live in relation to others that they are worthy of being treated with openness by all others (i.e., objectively worthy)." (Note that these quoted expressions define what it means to "treat persons as ends" or "with respect in the sense of openness," as defined in Chapters 3 and 4.) Those forms of life that are moral sphere-breaking turn out not to be objectively worthy in the required sense.

The interesting point about this procedure with regard to ethical intuitionism is this: By proceeding in this manner, as did the retreatants, *we arrive at many of the common-sense moral rules or duties we may have believed on the basis of intuition* all along: "Don't kill," "Don't lie," "Don't steal," "Keep your promises," "Don't injure or harm others," "Don't coerce or use violence," "Don't manipulate others for your own gain," and so on. We also arrive at commonly recognized exceptions to common-sense moral rules or duties, showing they are merely prima facie or defeasible. But the rules or duties and the exceptions are now no longer justified on the basis of intuition. Rather, living in accordance with them is a precondition for showing that our form of life, or any form of life, is "objectively worthy of being lived" – that it should be recognized as so worthy from all points of view, not merely from our own.

In other words, living in accord with these common moral rules turns out to be a precondition of the search for wisdom in the ancient philosophical sense, *insofar* as that search includes (as it did for the ancients) not only a search for what is "objectively worth believing" about the nature of things, but also a search for what is "objectively worth striving for" in the nature of things (the two aspects of objective worth of Chapter 11). Of special importance is the fact that we do not have to claim *to have already arrived at such philosophical wisdom to affirm these moral rules*. For, following the rules is a condition of the *search* for such wisdom. It is a condition of *aspiring* to wisdom in the form of objective worth – where aspiration entails not merely hoping to attain such worth, but engaging in a persistent and demanding search for it, as scientists engage in a persistent and demanding search for the truth about the natural world.

When viewed in this way, common-sense moral rules and duties are no longer an "unconnected heap" with no underlying rationale. Problems with intuitionism about the systematization of common-sense moral intuitions are thereby addressed. In addition, a pattern for addressing "conflicts of duties" emerges as well. Consider again Kant's case of the murderer at the door. It could be described in Rossian terms as a conflict between the prima facie duty of veracity or truth-telling (to the murderer at the door) and a prima facie duty of beneficence (to the intended victim in the house, who is assumed to be innocent). These prima facie duties must be weighed against one another to decide what the agent's actual, all-things-considered, duty is in the situation. But no explicit higher-order rules will tell us this from a Rossian perspective. One must rely on common-sense intuitions about particular cases. Relying on common sense, one might guess that most Rossians would likely reject Kant's solution to the example in his essay on lying, according to which the duty not to lie, being a "perfect duty," must always trump beneficence and so one should tell the truth to the murderer. But there need be no general rule on which to base this judgment. We must intuit it in the particular case.

Consider, by comparison, how this example would be dealt with in the MST. We do not have to ask which of these moral duties "outweighs" the other in the particular case. Instead, we ask a different question: Of the two parties who will be affected by our action (the man at the door and the one hiding in the house), *which of them has the moral sphere-breaking plan of action* in the present situation? Assuming again the innocence of the man hiding in the house, that would be the man at the door whose intention (purpose or plan) is to murder someone.[17] His plan of action by its nature requires him to "impose his will on some other person, whatever the desires or interests of that other person may be in the matter, etc." He is the one therefore who should not be "treated as an end" in the situation, i.e., who should not be "allowed to pursue his plans or purposes without hindrance or interference." One should lie, thereby thwarting his plan.

---

[17] If the man hiding in the house had committed a previous wrong against the man at the door (something the Kantian example does not assume), the case would be more complicated. But "maintaining the moral sphere to the degree possible" would still require lying to avert a present act of vengeance and to allow the dispute between the two men to be resolved in a way that respected both to the degree possible – e.g., by a subsequent jury trial rather than an act of vengeance in the heat of passion. The case would then be analogous to that of Chapter 4 in which there is more than one guilty party (e.g., opposing factions in a civil war). Maintaining the moral

This result is in line with common-sense intuitions about the case that intuitionists would likely insist upon. But the result is arrived at not by treating common-sense duties of truth-telling and beneficence merely as intuited duties to be weighed against one another. Rather we look to a rationale behind them. That rationale involves trying to sustain a moral sphere of life in which everyone is treating everyone else as an end and departing from that ideal as little as possible when one must. Common-sense moral rules have their force to the degree that following them contributes to sustaining such a sphere to the degree possible and violating them leads to its breakdown. The common-sense moral rules are not an unconnected heap when viewed from this perspective.

## 7. KANTIAN INTUITIONISM: AUDI

Some contemporary intuitionists have attempted in their own ways to address charges that Rossian intuitionism is unsystematic and that it fails to provide an underlying rationale for common-sense moral duties. The most ambitious attempts to address such charges by recent intuitionists are those of Robert Audi and Philip Stratton-Lake, who attempt to systematize Rossian prima facie duties in terms of Kantian-like notions, such as respect for persons and human dignity.[18] Audi's project is especially interesting from the point of view of the MST because of the way that it sheds further light on the relation of that theory to both intuitionism *and* Kantianism. I will therefore focus on it. Audi says that

Rossian principles of duty (though perhaps not exactly Ross's list of them) may be argued to be just the moral principles one would derive – even if not strictly deduce – from a careful application of the categorical imperative to everyday life. For instance, if one is to avoid treating people merely as means – and so to realize the negative standard expressed by the categorical imperative – one must recognize (prima facie) duties of non-injury (including avoidance of murder, brutality and theft), of reparation, and of fidelity and veracity; and if one is to treat people positively as ends – and so to realize the positive standard it expresses – one must recognize duties of beneficence, gratitude, self-improvement and justice.[19]

Audi proceeds to develop a "Kantian intuitionism" along these lines, systematizing common-sense moral duties in terms of the idea of respect for persons (interpreted as treating persons as ends and not as mere means).

---

sphere to the degree possible in such cases implied cooling emotions of the warring parties and getting them to put away their guns and come to the negotiating table.
[18] Audi 2001, 2004; Stratton-Lake 2000. Stratton-Lake's view, it should be noted, is closer to Kant's view in a number of important respects than is Audi's.
[19] Audi 2004: 102.

Before going further, it is worth noting that other contemporary intuitionists have been understandably suspicious of Audi's "Kantian intuitionism." After all, a major motivation for the development of intuitionism in modern ethics has been a distrust of all attempts to derive principles of common-sense morality from a single overriding principle, such as the Kantian categorical imperative or the utilitarian principle of utility.[20] Intuitionism presented itself as a pluralistic alternative to monistic moral theories of a Kantian or utilitarian kind; and intuitionists have been especially suspicious of Kantian (and all rationalist) derivations of the categorical imperative or other principles of morality. Thus, David McNaughton, in a discussion and defense of Rossian intuitionism, says of Audi's view "I am more skeptical than Audi about the possibility of any other theory providing independent support for a list of duties of Ross's kind. Kantianism, for example, appears to hold that some principles are exceptionless and not *prima facie*."[21]

Audi responds to such criticisms by insisting that he is not necessarily interpreting Kant's categorical imperative (CI) as Kant would have interpreted it. Rather Audi is qualifying the CI in certain ways in the light of common-sense intuitions.[22] Even less is he trying to deduce or derive the CI in some a priori fashion from practical reason. Audi is as suspicious as other intuitionists of Kantian or rationalist deductions of the CI. His project is rather one of "reconciliation" or finding a "reflective equilibrium" between Rossian common-sense moral intuitions, on the one hand, and Kantian ideas of respect for persons embodied in (the Formula of Humanity version of) the CI, on the other.[23] Rossian prima facie duties do not have to be derived in a Kantian top-down fashion on such an account since the Rossian duties have independent self-evident support in the sense that understanding them upon reflection is sufficient for being justified in believing them. The theory therefore remains fundamentally intuitionist. What is accomplished by appeals to Kantian notions of respect and dignity is that such appeals give a greater coherence and unifying rationale to common-sense intuitions, thereby providing them further support.

I think Audi effectively shows that many of our common moral intuitions, including those involving Rossian prima facie duties, *can* be understood in terms of a notion of respect for persons. I do not fault him on that score. But I would argue for a different interpretation of his results: I

---

[20] Stratton-Lake 2002: Introduction.     [21] McNaughton 2000: 283.
[22] Audi 2004: 105–13.     [23] Audi 2004, ibid.; 2001: 617–28.

would argue that the results arrived at by his attempt to reconcile com-mon-sense Rossian intuitions with the principle of treating persons as ends are better accommodated by viewing that attempt as a reconciliation of these common-sense intuitions with something like *the moral sphere theory* or MST of this book rather than with Kantian versions of the CI.

The reason for believing this is that, in the MST, the principle cor-responding to the CI – namely, the Ends Principle or EP – though itself a universal principle, nonetheless explicitly entails that common moral rules, "Don't lie," "Don't injure," etc., are prima facie and have excep-tions. It does so because to "treat persons as ends," according to the EP, is "to treat them with openness to the degree that one can do so while maintaining a moral sphere" in which all persons are similarly treated; and maintaining such a sphere often requires treating some persons as means in order to restore and preserve it. Exceptions arise because the requirement of the EP to treat persons with openness (the *initial* step in treating them "as ends") is not the *last* word on moral worth, but is rather a *test* for whether persons are *worthy* of being so treated by oneself and all others (hence, "objectively worthy").

Audi himself qualifies the CI to bring it in line with common moral intuitions whenever it seems to conflict with those intuitions, as in the case of the murderer at the door; and in doing so he arrives at many of the same exceptions to common moral rules that are arrived at by appealing to the EP. But the exceptions are arrived at by appealing to moral intui-tions. They are not derived from the CI itself. Indeed, moral intuitions are needed to supplement and sometimes correct the CI, on Audi's view, while it provides only a very general rationale. That is what gives point to the suggestion that the results arrived at by his attempt to reconcile common-sense Rossian intuitions with the principle of treating persons as ends might be better accommodated by viewing them as a reconciliation of common-sense intuitions with the EP and hence with the MST. One would then not have to qualify the Kantian CI by recognizing exceptions piecemeal to bring it in line with common-sense moral intuitions. Rather the exceptions would follow from the principle of "treating persons as ends" itself.

As a result, when common-sense moral rules and duties are challenged by those in other cultures whose intuitions are very different from our own, we would not merely have to fall back on claims that the rules and duties seem self-evident to us upon reflection. We can say that following such rules is how we go about finding which ways of living, including our own, are objectively worthy of being lived. The rules and duties are justified by the roles they play in the search for the objective good from all points of view and not merely because their appearing good on reflection from our point of view is sufficient to justify them.

## 8. KANTIANISM AND THE FORMULA OF HUMANITY

The upshot of these remarks is that the MST provides an alternative way of supporting and unifying common-sense moral rules and duties that is neither strictly speaking *intuitionist* nor *Kantian*. Objections to intuitionism about justification, self-evidence, systematization, and the like, are dealt with by appealing to a more general (Kantian-like) principle of treating persons as ends and not as mere means. But, this principle in the MST, the EP, allows for exceptions to common moral rules; and it is not derived in an a priori fashion or on rationalist grounds. Thus, concerns of intuitionists and other philosophers about the cogency of Kantian derivations of the CI in its various formulations, the Formula of Universal Law, the Formula of Humanity, etc., are also avoided.

Regarding Kantian derivations of the Categorical Imperative or CI, let me say straightforwardly that I share the reservations of intuitionists and other philosophers about their cogency. I do not believe Kant's attempted derivations of the CI in its various formulations ultimately succeed.[24] (More will be said about the reasons in a moment.) Nonetheless, I also believe Kant's attempted derivations of the CI contain many insights and important clues about morality. And, like many philosophers, I have always been attracted to some of the results at which Kant arrives, especially to his Formula of Humanity. The problem for me in ethical theory was to arrive at what was attractive about the Formula of Humanity without claiming that it could be derived on a priori or rationalist grounds (and, of course, without claiming that it was merely self-evident). The MST is an attempt to do this. It is thus important to also say more about how the MST differs from Kantian accounts of, and arguments for, the CI and what its comparative merits may be.

---

[24] Recent works of note on these derivations, both supportive and critical, include O'Neill 1989; Hill 1992, 2006; Herman 1993; Korsgaard 1996; Wood 1999; Guyer 2000; Cicovacki 2002; A. W. Moore 2003; Dean 2006. Collections include Guyer 1992 and Guyer 1998. A detailed recent study of the derivations of UL and FH, which finds shortcomings in them is Kerstein 2002. Darwall (2006) and Velleman (2006) also express doubts about Kantian and rationalist derivations of the CI; and these doubts inspire them in part to develop original alternative moral theories in which kinds of respect for persons play a significant role. It would be instructive to compare and contrast their theories with the MST, but that is one of many tasks I must leave for a future occasion. Modern attempts to provide rationalist and transcendental arguments for morality continue to be made. A recent ingenious example is Illies 2003.

First, to briefly summarize what has already been said in this chapter and earlier ones about the relation of the MST to Kantianism: The central principle of the MST, the EP, plays a different role in the moral sphere theory than the corresponding version of the CI (the Formula of Humanity) plays in Kantian ethics. The EP posits an *initial* attitude or stance toward persons (treating them with openness to the degree that one can) as a way of determining who is and who is not objectively worthy of being so treated. Taking this initial attitude does not require that we know with certainty (in some a priori fashion or by some rational argument) who is or is not objectively worthy of being treated with unqualified respect in the sense of openness. The initial attitude of openness is part of a search to find this out.

Second, as a consequence, the EP provides a rationale for exceptions to common moral rules as well as for the rules themselves; and it yields in a natural way a distinction between *ideal* and *non-ideal* theory in ethics (at the point where the moral sphere breaks down). It was noted in Chapter 4 that such a distinction was cited by Korsgaard from Rawls' work as a remedy for the fact that the Formula of Humanity on Kant's account seemed to allow no exceptions; and the ideal/non-ideal distinction was proposed as an emendation to Kant's theory in order to "deal with evil." The MST accommodates such a distinction, by contrast, as a necessary feature of the theory.

Third, these differences have a bearing on the Kantian derivation of the Formula of Humanity from the underlying value of humanity or rational nature. Korsgaard and other Kantians plausibly argue that the basic theory of value underlying Kant's Formula of Humanity and perhaps all his formulations of the CI is that "your rational nature is the source of justifying power of your reasons and so of the goodness of your ends."[25] This is a central and important theme of many new Kantians and interpreters of Kant, including not only Korsgaard, but Barbara Herman, Thomas Hill, Allen Wood, Marcia Baron, Paul Guyer, among others.[26] Persons are to be treated as "ends in themselves" because, as autonomous (*auto-nomos*) beings, they are the sources of their own ends.

But, as noted in Chapter 4, even if we grant that "one's rational nature is the source ... of the goodness of one's ends," so that good ends are so

---

[25] Korsgaard 1998: 283.

[26] Herman 1993; Hill 1992, 2006; Wood 1999; Baron 1995; Guyer 2000; Ameriks 2000. Also Donagan 1977 and Banham 2003. Herman's astute studies (1993), attempt to deal with exceptions and non-ideal circumstances by appealing to "rules of salience" governing the application of the CI. A detailed comparison between her approach to Kant and the MST would also I think be revealing though I do not have the space to undertake it here.

because they are the chosen ends of a rational being, the converse does not follow, as these commentators would agree. It would not follow that every chosen end of a rational agent is thereby a *good* end. Persons can exercise their rational nature and autonomy to choose bad ends as well as good ends. So it would not follow that we must treat persons unqualifiedly as ends in themselves by virtue of their rational nature and capacity for choice *irrespective of the plans of action and purposes* they actually choose to pursue.[27] To tell the truth to the murderer at the door out of respect for his humanity or rational nature, even though he has used that rational nature to choose an evil end, is grotesque, as Korsgaard and other Kantians concede. She thus suggests that qualifications must be made to the Kantian Formula of Humanity to "deal with evil." By contrast, such qualifications to "deal with evil," which have to do *with the kinds of plans of action and purposes agents actually choose to pursue*, are integral to the EP and do not have to be added to it.

### 9. THE UNIVERSAL LAW FORMULAS: HILL AND OTHERS

A fourth and most important difference between the MST and Kantian theories, which has not thus far been discussed, is that the MST makes no reference to Kant's Universal Law (UL) formulation of the CI: "Act only on that maxim by which you can at the same time will that it should become a universal law."[28] UL drops out of the picture in the MST and is not needed. The same is true of Kant's related formula of universal law of nature (ULN) "Act as though the maxim of your action were to become by your will a universal law of nature."[29] The avoidance of these formulas by the moral sphere theory is a distinct advantage, in my view, given the persistent problems that have surrounded Universal Law formulations of the CI. Thomas Hill, a noted Kantian who (along with a number of other contemporary Kantians cited in the previous section) has doubts about the sufficiency of the UL formulations, unsupported by other formulations of the CI, nicely summarizes these problems:

The most persistent worries about Kant's universal law formulas is that they often seem to lead to intuitively unacceptable conclusions. They apparently condemn some maxims that we regard as innocent and fail to condemn maxims that we regard as immoral. Frequently, revising the description of the maxim leads to more acceptable results, but there seems no principled way to tell before

---

[27] Dean (2006) tries to accommodate this point directly by arguing (in opposition to most standard interpretations of Kant) that "humanity" in the FH is to be identified with the "good will."
[28] Kant 1964: 222.   [29] Ibid.

applying the test what the "correct" description should be ….Defenders of Kant's universal law formulas have devised many subtle arguments to these … maxim testing procedures, but arguably the proposals are merely ad hoc devices to patch up a flawed procedure or else they amount to an admission that the universal law formulas alone are not sufficient for determining particular moral requirements. (2006: 488)

This is not the place to get into the tangled debates and subtle arguments by which Kantians have tried to defend the Universal Law formulas against these charges.[30] I don't think we have to get into these debates because in my view the second objection Hill offers against the UL formulas is even more telling and is the objection I want to pursue. He says:

Another recurrent concern about treating the universal law formulas as the sole, or primary, moral action-guide is that the recommended test procedure by itself, seems not to reflect what is most central to moral deliberation. As many Kantians now admit, even if the universal law formulas can flag certain maxims as morally wrong, or at least suspect, they do not adequately explain *why* acting on those maxims is wrong. What is wrong with slavery for example is not adequately explained by saying that it is impossible for everyone to act on the maxim of a would-be slave-owner. It may be that those who rob banks and commit murder cannot consistently will both their maxim and that everyone act on that maxim, but this inconsistency seems at best only part of the story why such acts are wrong. (ibid.)

Hill, like some other Kantians, goes on to argue that the Universal Law formulations must be supplemented by other formulations of the CI, especially the Formula of Humanity, to provide an adequate explanation of why acts are wrong. Thus, the reason why holding slaves, robbing banks and committing murder are wrong is because they involve treating others persons as mere means. Such actions would not *become* right if maxims allowing them *under some description* could be consistently willed to be universal laws.

But, one might ask, if the UL formulations of the CI must be supplemented by other formulations to explain why actions are wrong, why not consider giving up the UL formulations altogether and relying entirely on other formulas, such as the Formula of Humanity? Most Kantians, Hill included, are reluctant to do that, even when they may admit (as some do) that other formulations of the CI, such as the Formula of Humanity, are more intuitively satisfying and perhaps even more central to the Kantian project.[31] Moreover, the reason for not wanting to abandon the UL formulations from a Kantian perspective seems clear enough: Moral principles,

---

[30] See, e.g., O'Neill 1989, Herman 1993, Korsgaard 1996: 77–105, Baron 1995.
[31] Herman 1993, Korsgaard 1996 are again good examples.

to be valid, must be *universal*, binding on all persons. So it seems natural to require that morally acceptable maxims should be universalizable – capable of being willed as universal laws that all persons could follow.

My response to this line of reasoning from the point of view of the MST would be to grant that universality in some form or another is necessary for the moral enterprise. Universality in some form is required to establish the objective worth of our plans of actions and ways of life from all points of view rather than merely their relative worth from our own point of view. But I believe that the UL formulations of the CI take us in a wrong direction in the attempt to spell out this basically sound idea (i.e., the need for universalization of some sort); and the UL formulations thereby lead to proliferating sets of puzzles and problems.

There is, moreover, another way to capture the required universality, I would argue, that avoids the problems of the UL formulas, a way suggested by the MST. On this other way, one does not ask: "Could one consistently will that *everyone* act on this maxim (or 'plan of action,' as I would put it)?" Rather one asks: "Can one consistently pursue this plan of action or way of life and *at the same time* allow *everyone else* to pursue their chosen plans of action and ways of life without interference?" If the plan of action or way of life in question is moral sphere-breaking, the answer is no. For the plan of action or way of life would "require or license the agent to impose his or her will on some other persons, whatever the desires or purposes of the other persons may be in the matter"; and then the plan of action willed by the agent would not be consistent with the willings *of other agents*.

By taking this line, one acknowledges that the universality of moral requirements does have something to do with *consistency of willing*. But the consistency is not that of the UL formulas. It is rather a consistency *between one's will and the wills of other agents*, if one should act on a maxim or plan of action. The consistency is represented by the idea of maintaining a moral sphere to the degree possible in which all agents can be treated with openness by all others. A consistency of this kind is violated by moral sphere-breaking plans of action, which make it impossible for everyone to treat the agent so acting with openness and, at the same time, to treat all others with openness as well. Such a focus explains the wrongness of the maxim or plan of action in a direct way: It is wrong because of the effects upon others of acting on it.

The retreat of Chapter 3 further illustrates how universality is arrived at in this different way in the MST. In order to ensure that the results of their inquiries would have universal significance, the retreatants chose to take an initial attitude of openness to all ways of life, including the ways of life of those who had left the retreat and did not agree with them. They did this in order to ensure that the results of their inquiries would not merely have significance for themselves *or* merely for those who stayed behind at the retreat and agreed with them, but for everyone. Such a procedure acknowledges, as Kantians would insist, that universality is a necessary condition for objective worth as for objective truth. But the required universality is arrived at, not by self-legislating maxims for everyone to follow, but by respecting the maxims self-legislated by everyone (for themselves) to follow – until some persons make it impossible to respect their self-legislating and everyone else's self-legislating as well. Self-legislation is important, as Kantians rightly emphasize, but it enters the theory in a different way.

From the point of view of the MST, therefore, one might suggest to Kantians that they drop the UL formulas altogether and focus on the other formulations of the CI, such as the Formula of Humanity. The UL formulas, one might suggest, are not needed and by ridding themselves of them Kantians would rid themselves of a lot of difficulties. I am well aware that Kant himself would almost certainly reject this advice, as would most contemporary Kantians, despite their admiration for the Formula of Humanity. The reason in Kant's case, as I see it, is that he was torn between his firm belief that *laws* and *universal* (i.e., exceptionless) *legislation* were the basis of morality and his equally firm belief that the *love* of *humanity* was the basis of morality. One result of holding firmly to both these beliefs was Kant's persistent assumption that all of the formulations of his CI must amount to the same principle – an assumption that many philosophers have found difficult to believe. Perhaps the relation between Kant's two beliefs about the bases of morality should be reconsidered. A number of influential contemporary Kantians tend to favor the Formula of Humanity over UL anyway. But could they give up the UL formulations altogether and still be Kantians? I must leave it for others to decide that question.[32]

## IO. SPECIAL OBLIGATIONS

To conclude this chapter, I want to make one final point about the MST formula, with which the chapter began:

---

[32] Another route Kantians might take is represented by Cummiskey's original and challenging 1996. Cummiskey aims for a reconciliation of Kantianism, not with intuitionism, but with

"Strive to lead a good life that is objectively worthy of being lived and strive thereby to realize goods by virtue of the living of such a life that are objectively worthy of being realized."

A key feature of this formula, noted throughout the chapter, is that good human lives that are objectively worthy of being lived must first of all be lived *in the first three dimensions of value*. This means that such lives will normally involve (in the second and third dimensions) *special obligations* to particular other persons over and above the *impartialist* demands of the fourth dimension. Such obligations arise in the second and third dimensions of value by virtue of (1) the existence of special relations to others, to children, parents, spouses, friends, (2) particular social and professional roles in communities, practices and forms of life and (3) special commitments to others through promises, agreements or contracts.[33]

To consider obvious examples, we have special obligations to love and nurture children by virtue of having borne them (or adopted them); and the child has a right to expect such special concern and care from parents. On friendship and loyalty between friends, David McNaughton and Piers Rawling aptly note that "it is not just that friends spend time with each other, support each other, and so on. In addition, a friend has the right to expect *your* loyalty and support because she is *your* friend. If you betray her, she has a moral complaint against you that no one else has. Moreover, the (tacit) acknowledgement of a moral tie between friends appears essential to friendship."[34] Similarly, social roles in practices require special obligations to particular others that are not required impartially to all persons. Physicians have such obligations to their patients, lawyers to their clients, priests to those who enter the confessional, and so on. Finally, those who make promises or agreements or contracts involving particular others have special obligations to those others, not owed impartially to everyone.

---

consequentialism. Though many would regard this an unlikely prospect in view of the opposition between the two views, he makes an interesting case for it.

[33] Writings on this topic from which I have benefitted include Blum 1980, 1994; Parfit 1984; B. Williams 1981; Cottingham 1983, 1991; Conly 1983; Friedman 1989, 1991; Piper 1991; Baron 1991; Scheffler 1992; Don Adams 1993; Harris 1997, 1999; Sommers 1986; Stocker 1990; Kekes 1989; Kapur 1991; Grunebaum 1993; Double 1999; Mendus 2002; Stroud 2006; Crary 2007. Fairbanks 2000 is an extended argument that Kantian ethics can accommodate these special obligations as well. Herman 1993, Baron 1995 and Louden 2000 also make this case for Kantian ethics in differing ways. Broome 1991, Scheffler 1992 and Portmore (2001) suggest ways in which special obligations can be accommodated within a consequentialist perspective. Buss 2006 offers a subtle interpretation of how special relations account for reasons for action.

[34] McNaughton and Rawling 2006: 442. Blum (1980) and Helm (2001) also make this case, as do Stroud (2006) and Jeske (2008), who argue that special relations are themselves sources of fundamental moral reasons.

In sum, special obligations to particular others are *constitutive* features of good human lives *insofar as those lives are lived in the first three dimensions of value*. This fact does not mean that the impartialist requirements of the fourth dimension are thereby abrogated. One cannot kill, cheat, steal, injure or otherwise use other persons as mere means to one's own ends out of loyalty to friends or to benefit one's children or to fulfill a promise. The impartialist demands of the fourth dimension must have their say, if good lives in the first three dimensions are also to be objectively worthy of being lived in the fourth. But neither can the impartialist demands of the fourth dimension eradicate the partialist commitments and obligations of the first three dimensions of value, or good lives that are objectively worthy of being lived would lose much of their valuable content.[35]

It is worth recalling that the fourth dimension is not an abstract realm distinct from the first three dimensions of value. Rather, fourth-dimensional value *includes* all the non-overridden value realized in the first three dimensions, as lower dimensions of value include non-overridden value in dimensions below them. *Impartialist* human good of the fourth dimension (understood as what is good from all points of view) is thus the summation of various *partialist* goods realized by the concrete value experiments of different humans in different forms of life in the first three dimensions of value that are not moral sphere-breaking. If these concrete experiments and forms of life involve special obligations to others that are constitutive of their value, then the impartialist demands of the fourth dimension must not entirely override, but must allow a place for, partialist commitments and obligations of the first three dimensions of value.[36]

Thus, the man in an earlier example who misses his daughter's graduation to go on a fishing trip violates an obligation to his daughter that is not owed impartially to others. We may assume that going on this fishing trip, had it not been for the daughter's graduation, would not have violated any impartial obligation the man may have had to other persons. But going on the trip at this time did violate an obligation to his daughter. She would have had a moral complaint against him by virtue of their special relation that others would not have had. We might say that treating *her* as an end required more of him than treating other arbitrary

---

[35] Of the authors cited in note 30, Blum, Helm, Cottingham, Friedman, Piper, Baron and Harris argue persuasively for this point.

[36] See, e.g., Friedman 1991: 830–31. Railton 1984 and Scheffler 1992 are classic defenses of this line of thought.

persons as ends because her purposes and concerns (her *ends*) involved her relationship with him in a special way. In this manner, the general requirement of treating others as ends and not mere means is not abrogated, but rather takes on a thicker meaning and additional stringency where special relations and obligations are involved.

Consider the much-discussed case of two drowning persons, one of whom is one's spouse, the other a stranger. If you can only save one of them, it would be grotesque, as Bernard Williams and others have argued, to save the stranger *or* to flip a coin to decide which of them to save, thereby treating them impartially.[37] One has special reasons to save the spouse by virtue of one's relation to her (or him) that one does not have impartially to all others.

What is noteworthy about such hypothetical examples from the point of view of the MST is that one can only save one of the drowning persons. This fact means that the *moral sphere has broken down* because both parties cannot be allowed to realize their chosen ends, *no matter what one does* (the assumption being that they both want to live). No impartialist norm is thereby violated by saving the spouse in such circumstances, since it is permitted to save either one, and there are overwhelming partialist reasons to save one's spouse. By contrast, if one *could* save both without great cost or danger to oneself, thereby restoring the moral sphere, it would violate impartialist norms to save only one's spouse and allow the stranger to drown.

In summary, the MST formula "Strive to lead a good life that is objectively worthy of being lived …" makes room for special obligations and partialist commitments to particular others since they are essential to "leading a good life" in the first three dimensions of value. Having said this, one must acknowledge that it is not always easy to resolve conflicts between the partialist demands of the first three dimensions and the impartialist demands of the fourth. Some of the deepest problems of ethical theory revolve around the conflict between partialist and impartialist demands, as students of contemporary ethics are well aware; and we will be considering some of these problems in the next few chapters.[38]

What the arguments of this section have shown, however, is that a place must be made for *both* partialist and impartialist concerns in the moral life, according to the MST (and I think for any viable ethical theory). If

---

[37] Williams 1981.

[38] Especially in the final two sections of Chapter 16. I am much indebted to discussions with Robert Audi and Jeffrey Tlumak regarding the themes of this chapter.

impartialist concerns always trumped partialist ones, good lives in the first three dimensions of value would be immeasurably impoverished. But if partialist concerns always trumped impartialist ones, we would have the lives of what Kai Nielsen (1984) calls "classist amoralists" – those persons described in Chapter 8 who always selfishly act in favor of their own group (family, class, tribe, etc.) and do not care about the good of others outside their favored group.

# CHAPTER 16

# The good and the right (II): utilitarianism, consequentialism

## I. DEONTOLOGICAL AND TELEOLOGICAL THEORIES

Is the moral sphere theory (MST) a deontological or consequentialist ethical theory? Many things said in the previous chapter suggest that it lies on the deontological side of this divide, even if it is not strictly either a Kantian or intuitionist theory. But we should not jump to conclusions, since the deontological/consequentialist distinction can be drawn in different ways.

A common way of understanding the distinction is in terms of the relative priority given to the good and the right. Quoting Rawls, "the two main concepts of ethics are the right and the good ....The structure of an ethical theory is, then, largely determined by how it defines and connects these two basic notions" (1971: 24). Consequentialist ethical theories are teleological theories in Rawls' sense. They give priority to the good over the right, defining the rightness of actions (principles, motives, etc.) in terms of their promotion of the good. Deontological theories, by contrast, give priority to the right over the good, defining right actions (principles, motives, etc.) independently of their promotion of the good.

Viewed in this way, the MST might seem to be a teleological theory in one respect. For priority is given in the MST to the promotion of an ultimate good or value, namely objective worth or fourth-dimensional value. Right actions and principles are thus defined with respect to the promotion of the good, albeit a certain kind of good: Fourth-dimensional value includes all the value realized by different beings in the first three dimensions of value that is objectively worthy of being realized. But the appearance is deceptive because, for value in the first three dimensions to be objectively worthy of being realized, it must be realized through plans of action and ways of life that are objectively worthy of being pursued; and the pursuit of the ultimate good in the form of fourth-dimensional value is thus constrained by moral rules that forbid seeking the good in certain ways. These constraints make the MST a deontological theory rather than a teleological theory of one of the paradigmatic kinds Rawls has in mind, such as utilitarianism and other forms of consequentialism.[1]

## 2. UTILITARIAN AND CONSEQUENTIALIST THEORIES

One way to clarify the situation is to note that, while both the MST and teleological theories of Rawls' kinds are concerned with the promotion of the good of a kind, they differ about the kind of good to be promoted. In the MST, that good is *fourth-dimensional value*; and right action is a precondition for promoting this kind of good. By contrast, teleological theories of the kinds Rawls has in mind, such as utilitarianism and other forms of consequentialism, define the good initially in terms of *the first three dimensions of value* independently of the right.

Utilitarian theories, for example, characteristically define the good in terms of the *happiness* or *welfare* or *well-being* of individuals spelled out in terms of various aspects of the first three dimensions of value (pleasure, fulfillment of purposes, desire-satisfaction, etc.).[2] Right actions (principles, motives, etc.) are then defined as those that promote the most good or best consequences so understood, considered *universally* and *impartially* – i.e., taking into account the happiness, welfare or well-being of all individuals affected (universality) and weighting the happiness, welfare or well-being of all equally (impartiality).[3] These latter two requirements are summed up in Bentham's familiar slogan that "everyone is to count for one, no one to count for more than one" in determining what produces the greatest good.

There are variations on this general theme, depending on how value in the first three dimensions is conceived. In the classical utilitarianism of Bentham and Mill, the good is defined hedonistically in terms of

---

[1] Mixing teleological and deontological elements is not unprecedented. Herman (1993), e.g., argues that Kant's moral theory, usually considered deontological, actually is a teleological theory based on the underlying value of humanity as an end. Cf. Guyer 2000, Korsgaard 1996, Wood 1999, Banham 2003. Aristotle's theory is often considered paradigmatically teleological. Yet the final or ultimate good (*eudaimonia*), on most interpretations of his view, cannot be attained without right action of a sort (i.e., virtuous action). Cf. Cooper 1975, Broadie 1991, Actenberg 2002, among many others.

[2] See Lyons 1965, 1994, Parfit 1984, Kagan 1989, 1998, Brink 1989, 2006, N. Barry 1990, Goodin 1995, Shaw 1999, Frey and Morris 1993. Notable recent theories of well-being to which I'm indebted include Griffin 1986, Broome 1991, Sumner 1996, Kraut 2007, Haybron 2008 and Tiberius 2008. The latter two discuss recent psychological research on the nature of happiness or well-being.

[3] See references in note 2 and Hare 1981, Quinton 1989, Pettit 1991, Barrow 1991, D. Sosa 1993, Scheffler 1982, Scarre 1996, Bailey 1997, Frey 2000, Hooker 2000. Valuable anthologies on consequentialist and utilitarian theories include Bayles 1968, Sen and Williams 1982, H. Miller and W. Williams 1982, Scheffler 1988, Glover 1990.

pleasures and absence of pain (i.e., in the first dimension of value), though Mill muddies the waters by talking about higher and lower pleasures.[4] In later versions of utilitarianism, the good in the form of welfare or well-being is defined more broadly in terms of desire-satisfaction or preference-satisfaction, which includes goods in the second and third dimensions as well. Some modern consequentialists go farther, including in their accounts various "objectivist" or "perfectionist" values of the third dimension, such as knowledge, beauty, achievement, virtues and excellences.[5] The good is thus conceived more broadly as some kind of "flourishing" in the third dimension of value. But, while utilitarian and consequentialist accounts of value differ in such ways, their accounts of the right normally proceed in a common fashion: Right actions (principles or motives) are those that promote the greatest amount of good or best consequences so defined, taking into account the well-being or flourishing of all individuals and weighting the well-being or flourishing of all equally.

It is noteworthy that utilitarian and consequentialist theories that proceed in this way have three things in common with the MST. They all agree, as noted, that (i) right actions or principles are those that promote the good of a certain kind; and they agree that moral rightness requires (ii) *universality* and (iii) *impartiality* of some kind. But the theories differ in their interpretations of all three requirements – not only about the kind of good to be promoted, as just described, but also in their interpretations of universality and impartiality.

In utilitarian and consequentialist theories, universality and impartiality are introduced by defining the right as what promotes the most aggregate (or average) good in the form of well-being or well-faring in the first three dimensions of value of all parties involved and weighting the good of each equally. By contrast, in the MST, universality and impartiality are derived from the requirement that the kind of good to be promoted by right actions must be worthy of being recognized as good from all points of view (i.e., fourth-dimensional good). As a result, the MST *does not require that we promote the greatest overall amount of good in the first three dimensions of value*, since some third- and lower-dimensional goods may be overridden in the fourth dimension. The MST requires rather that we strive to ensure that whatever good *is* promoted in the first three dimensions of value *will also be good in the fourth dimension*.

---

[4] Feldman (1986, 1997, 2004) defends a hedonistic version of utilitarianism. On Mill's utilitarianism see Crisp 1997, Ryan 1970, Berger 1984, Riley 1988, Lyons 1994, Shaw 1999, West 2003 and Heydt 2006.

[5] E.g., Brink 1989, Hurka 2001.

### 3. THE ILL-GOTTEN GOODS RESTRICTION (IGG):
### SLAVERY, TORTURE

These differences account, I believe, for many of the reasons why utilitarian and consequentialist accounts of rightness so often seem, in the words of T. M. Scanlon, to be "wildly at variance with firmly held moral convictions," or with common-sense moral intuitions.[6] It is instructive in this regard to compare how various familiar objections to act-utilitarian and act-consequentialist accounts of right action relating to these supposed variances from common sense would be dealt with by the MST. (I will return to rule-utilitarian and other consequentialist alternatives later in the chapter.)

The first thing to note is that if the good in terms of which the right is defined must be good that is objectively worthy of being realized (as in the MST), one cannot simply sum the goods realized by potential actions in terms of the pleasure or welfare of all parties affected. One must also consider how the goods were brought about. As the MST formula states, goods that are objectively worthy of being realized must be brought about by *objectively worthy ways of living*. Goods brought about by moral sphere-breaking plans of action and ways of life are not objectively worthy of being realized in the required sense.

This result, which is central to the MST, may be generalized: *In determining whether or not actions (principles or motives) promote the good and how much good they promote, consequences realized by moral sphere-breaking plans of action or ways of life are not to be counted as relevant goods.* Call this requirement the *Ill-gotten Goods* or *Ill-gotten Gains* (IGG) restriction. According to this restriction, the goods realized by the con man from bilking the old couple out of their savings are not objectively worthy of being realized and should not count in judging whether actions, principles, etc. are right in terms of whether they produce the best consequences for all involved. I believe such an Ill-gotten Gains restriction, which is entailed by the MST, is deeply embedded in common-sense moral intuitions; and it helps to account for many of the reasons why act-utilitarian and act-consequentialist conclusions often seem at variance with common-sense moral intuitions.

To illustrate, consider some common examples cited in standard objections to act-utilitarianism, such as slavery. If the total well-being of 90 percent of the population of a society realized by enslaving the other 10

[6] Scanlon 1982: 103.

percent was so great as to outweigh the misery of the enslaved, so the objection goes, then slavery should be judged right in such circumstances by act-utilitarian standards. In response, act-utilitarians, such as R. M. Hare, argue that such hypothetical possibilities are irrelevant.[7] In real-world circumstances, they argue, it would most likely be the case that the enhanced well-being realized by freeing those who are enslaved would outweigh the reduced well-being of the enslavers. Free societies would generally produce more aggregate well-being for all parties concerned. This latter claim may be so in many cases. But it is far from clear that it *must* be so in all cases; and many philosophers have felt that the mere possibility that slavery might in some circumstances lead to the greatest aggregate (or average) good of the greatest number – and therefore might be right in some cases, however rare – shows that something is wrong with the act-utilitarian criterion.

In the MST, by comparison, slavery is wrong because it necessarily involves treating some persons as mere means to the ends of others ("whatever the interests or concerns of those so treated may be in the matter"); and it therefore involves a moral sphere-breaking way of life. So the goods realized by enslaving others (in the form of pleasure, well-being or flourishing of the enslavers) are ill-gotten goods; and, by the IGG restriction, they do not count at all in determining whether slavery does or does not promote the best overall consequences. Slavery would therefore not *become* right even if the aggregate well-being or flourishing of the enslavers (considered from the point of view of the first three dimensions of value) should in some cases, however rare, outweigh the suffering of those enslaved. For the goods realized by enslaving others are not objectively worthy of being realized and therefore do not count as goods in the relevant sense (i.e., fourth-dimensional goods).

Even when act-utilitarians correctly flag actions as wrong, they can often seem to be getting the right results for the wrong reasons because ill-gotten gains are not excluded from the calculations. Consider, for example, torture. Act-utilitarians typically argue that the act of torturing a person for pleasure would normally be wrong because the suffering of the tortured person would far outweigh any pleasure or well-being the torturer might realize by the act.[8] And that may be so in many cases. But what if many torturers were involved, each of a particularly sadistic nature, who derived enormous pleasure and satisfaction from the act?

---

[7] Hare 1979. Shaw (1999: 122–24) also makes this case.
[8] E.g., Smart in Smart and Williams 1973.

What if the act of torture was beamed on the internet to thousands of sadists throughout the world who also derived enormous satisfaction from it? Could there come a point where the collective pleasure of these thousands of sadists outweighed the suffering of the victim?

Maybe such a point could in principle be reached, maybe not. Yet it seems irrelevant to the rightness or wrongness of the act of torture *whether or not* such a point is ever or could ever be reached. How many people gain pleasure or satisfaction from taking part in an act of torture or observing the act, or how much pleasure they derive from the act, seems irrelevant to its rightness or wrongness; and the IGG restriction tells us why. Since the tortured person is being used by those persons who take pleasure in the torturing as a mere means to their ends, the amounts of pleasure they derive from the act of torturing are ill-gotten gains and do not contribute to its rightness.

### 4. CONSTRAINED CONSEQUENTIALISMS

One way consequentialists may avoid familiar objections of the preceding kinds is to import into their account of the "best consequences" of actions considerations of *fairness, justice* or *desert*. Consequences that are undeserved or result from actions that are unfair or unjust would not be counted among *relevant* consequences when deciding which actions produce the best overall consequences. Some consequentialists have suggested such a move as a way of answering objections of the above kinds.[9] Though such a move would bring their views closer to the MST, the resulting views would also no longer be *utilitarian* in the sense usually defined. For right actions would not be determined solely in terms of promoting the greatest amount of welfare or well-being. Critics have further questioned whether such views should even be considered consequentialist.

For example, critics such as Shelly Kagan, Bernard Gert, Brad Hooker, and others, argue that views constraining the relevant consequences to those satisfying conditions of fairness, justice or desert, are ad hoc and question-begging from a consequentialist perspective.[10] Requiring that the consequences of morally acceptable actions be fair, according to Kagan, is question-begging from such a perspective because usually "to say of something that it is unfair is to say nothing more than that it is [morally] illegitimate or unjustified."[11] Gert adds in a similar vein that "fair"

---

[9] E.g., Feldman (1997, 2004) suggests such a move.
[10] Kagan 1998: 54; Gert 1998: 195; Hooker 2000: 45–52.   [11] Kagan ibid.

is now often colloquially used as a synonym for "just" or "deserved" and both as synonyms for "morally acceptable."[12] Thus, Kagan and Gert both argue that views appealing to fairness, justice and desert are importing considerations of moral "rightness" into the definition of the "best consequences" rather than defining the best consequences independently of the right, as consequentialists should. Such views are thereby able to deal with familiar objections to act-utilitarianism and act-consequentialism, but only in an ad hoc and question-begging fashion.

This objection raises an interesting question regarding the MST: By defining the "good" in terms of fourth-dimensional value and thereby restricting what are to count as "good" consequences to those that are not produced by moral sphere-breaking plans of action, is the MST not also restricting good consequences to those that are in a certain sense "fair," "just" and "deserved"? Indeed it is, but not in a question-begging way. For the MST does not pretend to be a consequentialist theory in the sense that the ultimate good to be promoted is to be defined independently of the right. In general, in determining the rightness of actions, the MST does not consider consequences, qua states of affairs, in terms of their value for individuals independently of how they are produced or brought about.

### 5. MAXIMIZATION AND VALUE EXPERIMENTS

There is another, equally important, reason why the MST is not a consequentialist theory in the sense in which consequentialist theories are usually understood: It is not a "maximizing" theory. The rightness of moral actions or rules in the MST is not determined solely by whether or not they promote the most good, *even in a fourth-dimensional sense.* The goal of moral actions and rules is rather to enable it to be the case that whatever good is realized in the first three dimensions of value will *also* be objectively worthy of being realized in the fourth. Promoting such a goal will not guarantee that the greatest amount of objectively worthy good or fourth-dimensional value will result.

The reason there is no such guarantee is that fourth-dimensional value is produced by many different beings engaging in *value experiments* of many different kinds in different forms of life in the first three dimensions of value. One cannot anticipate how all these value experiments will turn out, much less always try to determine how one should act here and now in terms of how all the affected value experiments will turn out. Goods in

---

[12] Gert 1998: 195.

the first three dimensions of value take many forms, as noted. There are indefinite numbers of ways in which beings can pursue such goods through individual projects, personal relations, valued roles in communities, exhibiting virtues, seeking excellences, and so on. Of these innumerable ways of seeking the good, one cannot necessarily anticipate them all, or even appreciate them all, from any one of the finite points of view we inhabit.

It is of the nature of experiments in general that one usually does not know how they will turn out until they are completed. And it is a central thesis of the MST (which includes both a "moral sphere theory" of the right and a "dimensional theory" of the good) that value-seeking and value-creation for beings such as we humans are experimental to the core. Human value is sought and created through value experimentation or "experiments in living." I call this view *value empiricism*.[13] Morality – acting morally – cannot guarantee that the outcomes of these experiments in living (of other persons *or even of ourselves*) will turn out to have the best consequences in the first three dimensions of value (in terms of happiness, well-being or flourishing). If one could tell this in advance, or in some a priori fashion, ways of life would not be "experiments" in living.

What *moral* action aims at in the MST is rather allowing such experiments in living to proceed and to enable it to be the case that whatever good is produced by them will be worthy of being recognized as good from all points of view. Whether the greatest aggregate or average good will result from allowing these experiments to proceed is itself an empirical matter. In determining the rightness of actions therefore, the emphasis in the MST is on the requirement of treating others as ends, or with respect in the sense of openness, rather than as mere means. Promoting the most good is an *ideal* worth striving for, so long as the good in question is fourth dimensional. But the *rightness* of actions is not defined in terms of the ideal of promoting the most good, *even* in the fourth-dimensional sense; nor can it guarantee that the most such good will be produced. For that can only be determined by experiments in living. What the rightness of actions can guarantee is only that the good which is produced by such experiments will be objectively worthy (i.e. fourth-dimensional) good.

6. MILL AND VALUE EMPIRICISM

It is worth noting that the idea of "experiments in living," or value experiments, that plays so important a role in this view was taken over from

[13] I have defended such a view in earlier works, notably Kane 1996: 208–11 and 1985: chapter 5.

John Stuart Mill – an interesting fact, in view of Mill's utilitarianism. In truth, my first intimation of the importance of experiments in living for value theory and ethics came from reading another philosopher – a near contemporary of Mill's who was as different from Mill in temperament and style as any philosopher could be, namely, Soren Kierkegaard. Kierkegaard's account of how various ways of life – the aesthetic, the ethical and others – may break down in despair, guilt or dread started me thinking about the idea of value experimentation.[14] It was interesting to find a similar notion of "experiments in living" also prominent in Mill's writing, where it plays a significant role in his classic work *On Liberty*.

Yet another, very different, philosophical tradition in which the notions of value experiment and value empiricism play a role is that of the American pragmatists, C. S. Peirce, William James and John Dewey. In an earlier work, I made the point that the emphasis of these philosophers "on the ineliminable experimental nature of knowledge (of fact in science) and of value (through choice and experiments in living) is to my mind the most important contribution of classical American pragmatism to modern philosophy."[15]

But it was through Mill that I first saw the connection between "experiments in living," "value empiricism" and the freedom of the will, a connection developed in an earlier work (just cited) on the freedom of the will (*The Significance of Free Will*, 1996). In that work I made the following comment about Mill's *On Liberty* that is pertinent to our current discussion of utilitarianism and consequentialism:

> Value empiricism is the view that we must address questions about values and ultimate ends through freely chosen experiments in living and cannot settle these questions by a priori reasoning from certain or necessary premises that no rational person could deny. Such a value empiricist view is consistent with Mill's empiricism generally. It is, indeed, a plausible extension of empiricism to the domain of values, and I suggest that *On Liberty* is more a reflection of Mill's value empiricism than of his utilitarianism. (1996: 210)

This last suggestion is, of course, controversial. But in support of it, I noted that free societies *may* produce the greatest good of the greatest number. But then again they may not. One cannot guarantee that free societies will produce the greatest good of the greatest number simply because they are free societies. Freedom means the capacity to choose good *or* evil; and what people will do with their freely chosen experiments in living is something we can only learn from experience. Free societies

---

[14] Kierkegaard 1959 passim. [15] 1996: 209.

are themselves "experiments in living" through which humans seek the good in diverse ways and sometimes find the bad.

Similarly, by initially respecting other persons and ways of life in the sense of openness, the retreatants cannot guarantee that the greatest good of the greatest number will result. The "openness" they practice toward other peoples and ways of life is not a guarantor of producing the greatest good. It is a way of finding out *which* ways of life are objectively worthy of being allowed to be pursued and which are not. Indeed, one finds *that* out as well through experiments in living, by way of practical engagements with others. By their plans of action and ways of life, some persons make it impossible for others to treat them with openness and everyone else too. Rightness of actions in the MST is thus determined by initially practicing openness impartially and universally until one can no longer do so, rather than by determining which actions would produce the greatest good.

In arguing this way, I am not saying that the guiding idea of utilitarianism – which Fred Feldman aptly describes as "promoting as much good in the world as you can"[16] – is not in any sense an important and significant moral goal. I am merely noting that it is devilishly difficult to translate this guiding idea of utilitarianism *directly* into a criterion for the *moral rightness* or *wrongness* of particular actions – as the history of utilitarian thought amply demonstrates.[17] I am suggesting that we must look for moral rightness in a different direction – as ensuring that whatever good is realized will be objectively worthy of being realized. Proceeding in this way will also leave room for supererogatory action, since promoting the most objectively worthy (i.e., fourth-dimensional) good may remain a supererogatory ideal, as suggested a few paragraphs earlier, though it cannot be guaranteed merely by *right* action.

## 7. SUPEREROGATORY ACTION

This latter point about supererogatory action is worth further discussion. Additional light may be thrown on it by returning to the example of Chapter 4 of five men in a disabled aircraft who have only four parachutes. The moral sphere has badly broken down in such a situation, though no one of the men is guilty (a "level 2" breakdown). I argued that if one of the men heroically volunteered to sacrifice himself, allowing the

---

[16] Feldman 1997: Introduction.
[17] Sumner (1998: 176) makes this point eloquently in a review of Feldman 1997. He says Feldman's "guiding idea behind utilitarianism ... has long seemed obvious to me, but no particular formulation of this idea has had the same compelling power."

other four to have the parachutes, that would be an ideal solution because the moral sphere would be instantly restored: The four men would have their parachutes and the fifth would have chosen to be a hero of his own free will. All of them could thus be treated unqualifiedly as ends in the sense of being allowed to pursue their freely chosen purposes. In this way, it was suggested, heroism may serve the moral ideal by restoring the moral sphere when it has badly broken down.

But it was *not* assumed in this argument that the man who volunteered had a moral *duty* to sacrifice himself in this way. Why not? Because he had as much right to be treated as an end rather than as a mere means as the other four (impartiality and universality); and this meant that if he was to choose the heroic path, he had to do it of his own free will rather than being forced. His act was supererogatory; and yet it did serve the moral ideal of restoring and preserving the moral sphere.

Pursuing the example further, I argued that if none of the five chose to sacrifice, the next best option was to find some impartial way to settle who would get the parachutes, such as drawing lots. This was a favored ethical option because it was as close as they could come to maintaining the ideal of a moral sphere in which the ends of each were respected in adverse (non-ideal) circumstances when they had to depart from that ideal to some degree. Finding such an impartial solution therefore, if no one chose to sacrifice, *was* a moral duty, since maintaining a moral sphere to the degree possible is what treating persons as ends requires in non-ideal circumstances. Thus, while each did not have a moral duty to sacrifice, each did have a moral duty to find a fair way of deciding who would fail to realize his desired ends. And while choosing to sacrifice was not a moral duty, doing so would have been a laudable supererogatory act since it would have served the moral ideal by restoring the moral sphere.

To sum up, I have been arguing that the MST is not a consequentialist theory in the sense usually understood in modern ethical discussion, for several reasons. First, the good to be promoted – objectively worthy, or fourth-dimensional, good – is not defined independently of the right. Second, the MST is not a "maximizing" theory. The immediate goal of following moral rules is not to promote the most good in either third- or fourth-dimensional senses. The goal of following moral rules is rather to enable it to be the case that whatever good is realized in the first three dimensions of value will also be objectively worthy good in the fourth. Finally, by defining the aim of moral rules in this way, the MST can allow that promoting the most (objectively worthy) good is a laudable moral ideal, though not always a moral duty, and can thus make room for supererogatory action.

These features of the MST are deontological features, placing it closer in spirit to Kantian theory than to Mill's utilitarianism (or to other forms of utilitarianism or consequentialism). So it is noteworthy, as I have emphasized, that the MST *sides with Mill* and parts company with Kant on the topic of *value empiricism* – the view that we must address questions about values and ultimate ends through freely chosen experiments in living and cannot settle these questions by a priori reasoning from certain or necessary premises that no rational person could deny.

My complaint with Kant is not with his Formula of Humanity, which I think is a better candidate for a supreme moral principle (defeasibly understood) than Mill's principle of utility. My complaint with Kant is rather with the idea that the Formula of Humanity, or any other version of the CI, can be derived on rationalist grounds. Mill's value empiricism is a better guide on this point, for reasons that are nicely expressed in the following quote from Isaiah Berlin (quoted also in my book on free will, cited earlier), with which I conclude this section:

At the centre of Mill's thought and feeling [in *On Liberty*] lies, not his utilitarianism, nor the concern about enlightenment, nor about dividing the private from the public domain – for [Mill] himself at times concedes that the State may invade the private domain in order to promote education, hygiene or social security or justice – but his passionate belief that men are made human by their capacity for choice – choice of evil or good equally. Fallibility, or the right to err as a corollary of the capacity for self-improvement; distrust of symmetry and finality as enemies of freedom – these are the principles which Mill never abandons ... because he believes ... there are no final truths not corrigible by experience, at any rate in what is now called the ideological sphere – that of value judgments and of general outlook and attitude to life.[18]

## 8. RULE-CONSEQUENTIALISM

Utilitarians and consequentialists have other options not yet considered for dealing with standard objections to act-utilitarianism and act-consequentialism of the kinds considered thus far.[19] They may opt, for

---

[18] Berlin 1965: 190, 192. Quoted in Kane 1996: 211.

[19] I focus on versions of rule-consequentialism in the sections that follow since it is the most widely discussed alternative to act-utilitarianism and act-consequentialism. A full accounting of contemporary consequentialist views, which I cannot undertake here, would have to also consider a variety of sophisticated contemporary views, including "motive consequentialism" (R. Adams 1976), "global consequentialism" (Parfit 1984, Pettit and Michael Smith 2000), "scalar

example – and many do opt – for some kind of indirect utilitarian or consequentialist view, such as *rule-* (or *motive*) utilitarianism or consequentialism.

I cannot discuss all options of these kinds here. But I want to say
something about *rule-consequentialism* (which has made a comeback in
recent ethics) because it can be instructively compared to the MST. In a
recent anthology discussing new versions of rule-consequentialism, Brad
Hooker, Elinor Mason and Dale Miller note that the alleged advantages
of "rule versions of utilitarianism and consequentialism" arise from the
fact that they "are more complicated than act-versions. The rule versions
evaluate rules in terms of their consequences and then require conformity
with optimal rules. The act versions evaluate acts directly in terms of their
consequences" (2000: 1).

Contemporary rule-consequentialists generally try to determine
what the correct moral rules are by asking which set of rules or code,
if accepted by a substantial majority of the population, would promote
the most good or best consequences for all members of the population,
considered impartially. As with other forms of consequentialism, the
"good" might be defined variously in terms of welfare, well-being or some
kind of flourishing in the first three dimensions of value. This being the
case, it seems that rule-consequentialism, so understood, would run into
similar problems to act-consequentialism in one respect at least. If rule-
consequentialism remained purely consequentialist and avoided introdu-
cing deontic constraints of fairness, justice or desert into its assessment
of the best consequences, rule-consequentialism would not distinguish
ill-gotten consequences from those that were not ill-gotten. Then, like
pure act-consequentialism, rule-consequentialism would fail to take into
account the IGG restriction and hence how various goods were brought
about. But neglecting the IGG restriction causes difficulties for rule-
consequentialism as it does for act-consequentialism.

Consider slavery again. If it is empirically possible that in certain
circumstances the best aggregate welfare or flourishing of a population
would result from enslaving a minority, then a code of rules endorsing
slavery in such circumstances would be the optimal code. No similar outcome is possible in the MST because the consequences in the form of
well-being or flourishing of the majority realized by enslaving a minority
are ill-gotten gains and cannot be counted in the assessment of whether

consequentialism" (Norcross 1997), "multiple-act consequentialism" (Mendola 2006), "multi-
level indirect consequentialism" (Kupperman 2007) and the discussions of Carlson 1995, among
others. Kagan 2000 identifies a large variety of possible consequentialist views that can be distinguished in terms of their differing "evaluative focal points."

a code of rules leads to the best consequences. Rule-consequentialists, it seems, could not proceed in this way without begging certain questions. For they must determine which code of rules is right by determining which code would lead to the best consequences without assuming, as does the MST, that a set of basic moral rules (don't kill, don't steal, etc.) is already in place separating ill-gotten from well-gotten consequences.

Rule-consequentialists might respond by importing criteria of fairness, justice or desert into their account of the best relevant consequences, thus affirming a *constrained rule*-consequentialism. But critics such as Kagan and Gert would surely respond that such a move would be no less question-begging from a rule-consequentialist perspective than it is from an act-consequentialist perspective.[20] The constraints would not be derived from considerations of what promotes the best consequences, where the consequences are defined independently of the right.

Another familiar difficulty with rule-consequentialism is that, in order to settle the question of which rules or code would produce the best consequences, rule-consequentialists must answer a long list of difficult and complicated questions, some of them empirical. Are we to count the best consequences of everyone's *complying* with the rules or merely *accepting* the rules, and thus being disposed to comply with them? Are we to count the consequences of *everyone's* complying or accepting the rules or only of a *majority* of the population's doing so? And if a majority, how great a majority (70%?, 80%?, 90%?). In addition there are the usual questions about what we are to count as the *good* consequences (pleasure, well-being, flourishing) and about how to measure amounts of the relevant good consequences of various codes of rules (not an easy task when the goods are multiform and not easily compared).[21]

One must also calculate the *costs* of getting people to accept and/or comply with a code of rules and the cost of teaching or inculcating the rules to each new generation. And one must decide whether the right rules are those that would *actually* lead to the best consequences or merely those that could reasonably be *expected* to lead to the best consequences. If one chooses expected consequences, which seems to be the only practical alternative, then it may turn out that the *right* rules will not be those that do in fact lead to the best consequences. In general, different answers

---

[20] Cf. Hooker (2000: 45–51) who, though a rule-consequentialist, rejects the view "that rule-consequentialism should evaluate codes of rules in terms of aggregate well-being *and fairness*" in the light of such criticisms.

[21] These issues are discussed in Hooker, Mason and Miller 2000, among other sources cited earlier.

to all these questions may lead to different answers about what the right code of moral rules would be; and this leads to a troubling arbitrariness in rule-consequentialist accounts of rightness, according to their most noteworthy critics, such as David Lyons (1965, 2000).

One thing that is clear is that answering all these questions is quite complicated – and it is needlessly complicated from the point of view of the MST, *if* determining *basic moral rules and duties* is the goal. In the MST, basic moral rules and duties familiar to common-sense morality are derived in a more direct and simple way from the goal of ensuring that whatever good is produced in the first three dimensions of value will not be produced by moral sphere-breaking plans of action and ways of life. Thus, one does not have to answer all the complicated questions cited in the previous paragraphs about compliance, acceptance, the size of majorities, costs of inculcating, and so on, in order to determine what one's basic moral duties are and what basic moral rules one should follow.

Indeed, thinking about moral rules and duties in terms of the moral sphere and its breakdown is itself a procedure that could be fairly easily taught to the young; and so the costs of inculcating it in the next generation would be comparatively low. The MST procedure thus has considerable merit in this regard, even by rule-consequentialist standards. But, more importantly, the moral sphere procedure provides an appealing systematization and rationale for our common-sense moral rules and duties; and it does so without requiring definitive and non-arbitrary answers to complicated questions about the consequences of different numbers of people's complying or not complying with, accepting or not accepting, candidate rules and duties – questions that must be answered by rule-consequentialists in determining which moral rules and duties are the right ones.

### 9. COLLAPSE AND INCOHERENCE OBJECTIONS: LYONS AND OTHERS

Another objection to rule-consequentialism, the main objection to it over the past several decades, takes the form of a dilemma suggesting that rule-consequentialism is an "unstable compromise": Either it *collapses* into act-consequentialism and is therefore not an improvement over act-consequentialism; or rule-consequentialism lapses into an unacceptable kind of *incoherence* or "rule-worship."[22] The first half of this dilemma, the "collapse" objection, begins by maintaining that if following a general

---

[22] Lyons 1965 is a classic statement.

rule would not have the best consequences in particular circumstances, one could formulate a rule with better overall consequences by adding an exception clause to cover the particular case. When exception clauses are added to cover every particular situation in which following some rule would not bring about the best consequences, the lengthy rules that result, with numerous exception clauses, would have the same consequences for action as act-consequentialism has.[23]

The usual response to this collapse objection is to note that if we tried to list all of the exceptions in the rules themselves, the rules would "be so long and complex that they could not possibly be formulated, let alone taught" (Gert 1998: 214). And even if such rules could be formulated, the costs of teaching or inculcating an overly long and complicated list of rules would be too high. Since the costs of teaching and inculcating a moral code must be taken into account, an ideal rule-consequentialist code will therefore "contain rules of limited number and limited complexity"; and such a rule-utilitarian code would "not collapse into act-consequentialism" (Hooker 2000: 97).

Critics of rule-consequentialism respond in turn that rule-consequentialists can avoid the collapse objection in this manner only by lapsing into incoherence. To avoid collapse, rule-consequentialists must require that we follow simple, easily teachable rules, even in those cases where we may be able to see that breaking the rule would do more good than following it. But if the ultimate goal is to maximize the good, then following the rule when one knows it will not maximize the good seems incoherent, say the critics. Indeed, it is a kind of "rule-worship." If the rules are a means to an end (the end being to promote the most good), why stick with the rules even in cases where they do not realize that end? (Cf. Lyons 1965; Williams 1973, among others.)[24]

It is not my purpose here to follow the complex debates surrounding these objections of collapse or incoherence that have led many philosophers to believe rule-consequentialism is an unstable compromise. Rather I want to emphasize how the MST avoids these problems about collapse and incoherence. It does so by denying that the overarching aim of moral rules is to maximize good consequences, where the goodness of consequences is considered independently of how they are produced or brought about. Since exceptions to the rules arise only where the moral sphere

---

[23] See, e.g., Smart in Smart and Williams 1973: 11–12.

[24] Some *act*-consequentialists argue that act-consequentialism can avoid these charges of incoherence and rule-worship in ways that rule-consequentialism cannot. Cf. Hare 1981, Railton 1984, Frey 2000.

breaks down and not just at any time when it is possible to produce more good, however slight the amount of good produced, there is no danger of a collapse into act-utilitarianism. And where the moral sphere has not broken down, there is no incoherence in sticking to the rules when some more good, however slight, may come from breaking them. For the goal, when the moral sphere has not broken down is to treat everyone with respect in the sense of openness, which will not ensure that the greatest amount of good results, but will ensure that whatever good is realized will be objectively worthy of being realized.

I repeat that this line of reasoning does not mean that promoting the greater good in terms of welfare or well-being in the first three dimensions of value is not a worthy goal that should never enter moral decision-making, according to the MST. The point is simply that producing the greater aggregate good in the first three dimensions is not an *overarching* moral goal that *always* trumps treating persons as ends. Indeed, it is the other way around. The idea of promoting the most good comes into play as a default condition in certain circumstances *when the moral sphere has broken down,* so that all persons cannot be unqualifiedly treated as ends, no matter what one does, though none are guilty.

Thus in the airplane example, the men can agree that, while only four of them can be saved, *it is better that four be saved* than less than four. The residual ethical problem for the men was figuring out *which* four would be saved, not whether it would be four who should be saved rather than three or two or one. In such manner, consequentialist and utilitarian considerations can enter ethical deliberation in the MST. But they do not trump respect for persons. They enter when one can no longer respect all persons equally, no matter what one does.[25]

## 10. RULE-CONSEQUENTIALISM AND COMMON-SENSE MORALITY: HOOKER

In response to the collapse and incoherence objections against rule-consequentialism, one influential contemporary rule-consequentialist, Brad Hooker, has suggested taking a whole new approach to defending rule-consequentialism. In view of the debates surrounding the collapse and incoherence objections, Hooker says,

---

[25] It is noteworthy that the conditions allowing one to draw such conclusions in this airplane example also apply to familiar cases of "aggregation," such as the much-discussed Trolley case, where questions arise about whether it is permissible to sacrifice, e.g., one person to save five. In Trolley, a trolley heading down a track will kill five, unless one pulls a switch that will divert it

Most philosophers seem convinced that defending rule-consequentialism is a lost cause once one accepts an overarching commitment to maximize the good. Suppose rule-consequentialism is indeed a lost cause if one accepts an overarching commitment to maximize the good. This need not be the death-knell of rule-consequentialism. For the best argument for rule-consequentialism is *not* that it derives from an overarching commitment to maximize the good. The best argument for rule-consequentialism is that it does a better job than its rivals of

to a track where one person will be killed. Most philosophers who discuss this case, including not only consequentialists, but some staunch deontologists as well, such as Frances Kamm (1989, 1996), believe that it is permissible to divert the trolley, sacrificing one to save five. Similar conclusions are applicable to so-called Rescue cases, where one can save five persons from drowning in one direction or one person in another direction, but not all six. It is noteworthy that, in these much-discussed cases, the following conditions of the airplane example also apply: (1) The moral sphere has broken down, since at least one of the parties must die, no matter what is done (2) all parties involved are innocent victims of tragic circumstances and (3) no one volunteers to sacrifice for the others. Note, for example, that if one person on the diversionary track in Trolley or the one person drowning in one direction in Rescue should freely choose or consent to sacrifice himself or herself, then the moral sphere would be restored by this heroic act, just as in the airplane example, since the other five could then be saved. It might be suggested as a result that conditions (1)–(3) are necessary conditions for the permissibility of sacrificing one to save five in aggregation cases, such as Trolley and Rescue. But, even if that should be true, these conditions would not be *sufficient*. For there are other equally well-known cases where these three conditions apply and most philosophers, even staunch consequentialists, would agree that it is *impermissible* to sacrifice one to save five. Examples are Harvesting, where a surgeon sacrifices an innocent man in order to harvest his different organs in order to save five others who need transplants (see, e.g., Kagan 1998: 71) and Big Man, where there is no track to which the trolley can be diverted, but the bystanders push a large innocent man onto the track who dies in the process of stopping the trolley, saving the five. Once again, if the innocent persons so treated in Harvesting and Big Man had freely chosen to sacrifice themselves, the moral sphere would have been restored, as in Trolley and Rescue, but they did not so choose. Conditions (1)–(3) are therefore not sufficient for the permissibility of sacrificing some to save more, even if they should be necessary. One must bring in further conditions to distinguish permissible from impermissible cases having to do I believe, among other things, with the *intentions* of the agents involved. The following criterion is suggested, for example, by Kamm (2007: 92). She calls it the Doctrine of Triple Effect (DTE) and suggests it as an improvement of the traditional Doctrine of Double Effect, which she criticizes: "A greater good that we cause and whose expected existence is a condition of our action, but which we do not necessarily intend, may justify a lesser evil* that we must not intend but may have as a condition of action" (p. 118). Kamm uses this criterion to distinguish permissible cases of sacrificing some to save more, such as Trolley and Rescue, from impermissible cases, such as Harvesting and Big Man; and she also applies it to even more complicated cases, including the Loop Trolley case. It is not my purpose to defend this specific principle DTE of Kamm's here. (Objections to it have been made by Otsuka (1997) and others; and Kamm has attempted to respond to these objections by formulating a more complicated principle along similar lines (2007: 164ff.).) Rather I want to make the more general point that *some* principle or other concerning the *intentions* of agents, whether the traditional principle of Double Effect or Kamm's Triple Effect, or some still more complicated principle, is required to distinguish cases where it is permissible to sacrifice some to save more; and I would argue that this is significant from the perspective of the MST. For note that the need to appeal to the intentions of agents is consistent with the account of moral sphere breakdown of Chapter 4, where it was argued that one needs to appeal to the intentions or plans of agents in order to distinguish *guilty* from *innocent* parties in moral sphere breakdown situations generally. Appeals to intentions would be needed in the present cases as well, though for a different purpose. I would thus suggest that, from the point matching and tying together our moral convictions, as well as offering help with moral disagreements and uncertainties. (2000: 101)

By abandoning "an overarching commitment to maximize the good" and arguing for rule-consequentialism on the grounds that it does the best job of systematizing and explaining common-sense moral convictions, Hooker manages to avoid collapse and incoherence objections and some other common objections to rule-consequentialism. So one clearly has to argue against his rule-consequentialism in a different way. Some critics maintain that his view is no longer strictly speaking a consequentialist view. Hooker responds that "consequentialist" can be defined in different ways and there is much in his theory of a rule-consequentialist nature, despite the differences in its justification. He adds as well that what counts "is the plausibility of a theory, not its name" (p. 111).

I cannot do full justice to Hooker's sophisticated defense of rule-consequentialism here.[26] But I can say what the strategy of my argument against such a view would be. I would argue that rule-consequentialism, as he understands it, does not, as he argues, do "a better job than" *all* of its possible rivals "of matching and tying together our moral convictions as well as offering help with moral disagreements and uncertainties." Hooker argues that his rule-consequentialism does better at these tasks than familiar rival theories, including act-utilitarianism, Rossian pluralism, contractualism, and so on. But, of course, he does not consider the MST as a possible rival; and my strategy would be to argue that the MST does a better job of systematizing and explaining common-sense moral convictions than his rule-consequentialism.

On Hooker's view, common-sense moral rules to which we have frequently alluded, "don't kill, lie, steal, coerce, etc.," would be systematized and explained by the rule-consequentialist principle: "An act is wrong if and only if it is forbidden by a code of rules whose internalization by an overwhelming majority [he suggests 90 percent] of everyone everywhere in each new generation has maximum expected value in terms of well-being (with some priority for the worst off). The calculation of the

of view of the MST, cases of aggregation, where it would be permissible to sacrifice some to save more, would be cases of (i) *moral sphere breakdown* satisfying conditions (1)–(3) and (ii) *some* further condition having to do with the *intentions* of the agents involved, along the lines of the principle of Double Effect or Kamm's Triple Effect, or some still more complicated principle of a similar type. What the latter principle should be in detail is a complex and difficult question that I'd prefer to leave to others, like Kamm, with more energy than me, to figure out.

[26] For criticisms of Hooker's view from different perspectives than mine, see Stratton-Lake 1997, D. Miller 2000, A. Thomas 2000, Montague 2000 and Mulgan 2000. Hooker responds to these and other criticisms in 2000 and 2000a.

code's expected value includes all costs of getting the code internalized" (p. 32). The qualification "with priority for the worst off" requires giving extra weight to the well-being of the worst off in the overall calculation. It amounts to a constraint needed to avoid variances from common moral convictions that may arise from requiring simply that the code of rules maximize expected value without restriction. Common-sense moral rules are to be derived from such a formula.

Compare this procedure to the way in which common-sense moral rules are introduced in the MST: Killing, lying, stealing, etc. are wrong because they involve plans of action that are moral sphere-breaking – plans that involve "using other persons as mere means to the ends" of the agents. Common moral rules forbid actions that carry out such plans. I submit that this MST explanation not only systematizes these common-sense moral rules, but provides a rationale for them that is simpler and closer to common moral intuitions and convictions than does Hooker's complex rule-consequentialist formula.

The MST explanation does not require specific answers to all the complicated questions cited in previous sections about compliance, acceptance, the size of majorities, costs of inculcating, and so on, in order to determine what one's basic moral duties are and what basic moral rules one should follow. Nor does one have to calculate whether the acceptance or internalization of the rules "by an overwhelming majority of everyone everywhere in each new generation has maximum expected value in terms of well-being (with some priority for the worst off)" – a formidable calculation indeed – to determine what basic moral rules one should follow. Yet, as argued in the previous chapter, the MST supplies a plausible rationale for the common-sense rules and duties commonly cited by intuitionists, in terms of a guiding idea of a certain kind of respect for persons, without the need for such complex calculations.

Note also that, in the MST, common-sense moral rules as well as duties have exceptions (they are defeasible), as Rossian pluralists insist. If the debate is about systematizing and explaining common moral convictions and "offer-ing help with moral disagreements and uncertainties," then it is a further point in favor of the MST that it gives a plausible account in terms of moral sphere breakdown of the *prima facie* status of common-sense moral rules and duties and of where and why commonly recognized exceptions to them arise. It also provides a plausible way of dealing with conflicts of duties, as argued in the previous chapter in the discussion of Rossian intuitionism.

In summary, I want to reiterate that the arguments of this section are meant to be suggestive and not decisive. Much more would have to be said in comparing the MST to Hooker's rule-consequentialism, which is undoubtedly closer to the MST than other consequentialist views because of the primacy it assigns to systematizing and explaining common-sense moral convictions. But these remarks at least suggest a strategy for a longer argument comparing the merits of the two views.

## II. DEMANDINGNESS

To conclude this chapter, I want to consider one further issue that frequently arises in discussions of utilitarian and consequentialist views and ask how this issue would be dealt with by the MST. The issue in question is the so-called "demandingness problem," the problem that in a world (or in conditions) of widespread chronic need, such as widespread poverty, malnutrition and even starvation, morality may become too demanding. It may require that persons abandon the pursuit of their own ways of life in order to devote themselves to helping others with chronic needs. (Cf. Singer 1972, Kagan 1986, Scheffler 1992, 1994, Unger 1996.)

The problem is thought to be especially acute for utilitarian and consequentialist theories requiring that actions always maximize the good. Elizabeth Ashford and Tim Mulgan summarize the problem for such theories, using utilitarianism as an example: "Utilitarianism tells me to put my dollars wherever they will do the most good. In the hands of a reputable aid agency, my dollar could save a child from a crippling illness, and so I am obligated to donate it to the aid agency. I should give my next dollar to an aid agency, and I must keep donating till I reach the point where my own basic needs, or my ability to keep earning dollars, are in jeopardy. Most of my current activities will have to go. Nor will my sacrifice be only financial. According to utilitarianism, I should also spend my time where it will do most good. I should devote all my energies to aid work, as well as all my money ... This leads to the common objection that utilitarianism is unreasonably demanding, as it leaves the agent too little room (time, resources, energy) for her own projects or interests."[27]

Some utilitarians and consequentialists bite the bullet here with varying qualifications contending that morality is indeed extremely demanding in the way suggested by the above argument.[28] But most philosophers, including most utilitarians and consequentialists themselves, argue for a more "moderate" position in this issue: Our obligations to the needy are

[27] Ashford and Mulgan 2007: section 7.
[28] E.g., Singer 1972, Unger 1996. Goodin 1985 also argues for demanding aid obligations.

real and non-trivial, but they cannot be so extensive as to rule out entirely the pursuit of ordinary projects, relations and special obligations that are the substance of our lives. To devote all one's energies and resources to aid work is an admirable supererogatory ideal, as Ashford and Mulgan put it, but most philosophers think it implausible to regard it as a moral obligation imposed on all; and ordinary moral thinking seems to agree.

The goal of morality, according to such a "moderate" position, is to find an appropriate balance between the *partialist* commitments to projects, relationships and special obligations (to children, family, friends, etc.) that are part of a human life and the *impartialist* concerns for all persons demanded by morality. Indeed, philosophers such as Samuel Scheffler (1992) and Thomas Nagel (1991) have argued that finding an appropriate balance between partialist and impartialist perspectives, not allowing one to completely override or trump the other, is a central problem of the moral life[29]; and many consequentialists agree. Peter Railton, for example, a consequentialist, argues that "no plausible moral theory should eliminate the tension between the motivational demands of a moral theory and the agent's personal projects and commitments."[30]

It is not my purpose here to discuss the many modern attempts of utilitarians and consequentialists to respond to the demandingness problem by arguing that utilitarian and consequentialist theories need not be extremely demanding and, suitably modified, can support a moderate position.[31] My purpose is rather to ask how the demandingness problem would be dealt with by the MST and how its treatment of the problem compares to that of other theories, including utilitarian and consequentialist ones.

The first point to note is this: As many philosophers, such as Nagel, Mulgan, Garrett Cullity and others have effectively argued, the demandingness problem, while it may be especially acute for certain utilitarian and consequentialist theories, also arises in some form or another for any moral theory that requires universal moral concern for persons.[32] As Nagel says, "given existing world circumstances, not just act-utilitarianism, but

---

[29] See also M. Friedman 1989, 1991, Cottingham 1983, 1991 who make sophisticated cases for the partialist perspective.

[30] Railton 1984: 138. By deploying a distinction between "objective consequentialism" and "subjective consequentialism," Railton argues that even act-consequentialist views can support a "moderate" position.

[31] Also defending a moderate position from a consequentialist perspective is Mulgan 2001. Mulgan's careful study includes a comprehensive critical survey of recent literature on the problem. Murphy's (2000) moderate position is discussed in the next section. Brandt 1992, Hooker 2000 (chapter 8) defend rule-consequentialist solutions.

[32] Nagel 1986: 188ff., 1991 passim; Mulgan 2001: chapter 1; Cullity 2004: chapter 1.

any morality with a substantial [impartialist] component will make voracious demands."[33] Since the MST does require universal moral concern, the demandingness problem arises for the MST as well. But the demandingness problem arises differently in the MST than in utilitarian and consequentialist theories because the MST is not a maximizing theory.

The goal in the MST is to treat all persons *including oneself* as ends and not as mere means to the degree possible. Such a requirement does impose demands to assist others in extreme need, and can impose very heavy burdens in a world of widespread chronic need. But the requirement to help others in such a world must be balanced against the need to treat oneself as an end; and such balance means the need to treat others as ends should not require that one abandon the pursuit of one's own way of life, including the particular obligations entailed by that way of life by special relations to others, to one's roles and commitments, and so on, as described in Chapter 15.

As a result, the MST supports a "moderate" position on the demandingness problem requiring a balance between partialist and impartialist concerns. Thus, the retreatants, when they took an attitude of openness in the attempt to ascend to the impartial perspective of the fourth dimension, were not thereby required to give up their particular ways of life, including the special obligations entailed by their ways of life and by their particular relationships to others. What they were required to do by taking an attitude of openness was rather to strive to maintain a moral sphere of life in which all partialist perspectives and ways of life, *including their own ways of life*, were respected to the degree possible. Scheffler speaks aptly in this connection of an "ideal of humanity" (in which a balance is struck between partialist and impartialist moral demands) rather than an "ideal of purity" (in which impartialist moral demands completely override partialist ones).

In the language of the MST, what we have in a world of widespread chronic need is an extreme case of moral sphere breakdown. We are definitely in the realm of "non-ideal" moral theory, far from the ideal moral sphere, where treating all persons unrestrictedly as ends would be possible. I believe Nagel and others are correct when they argue that in such a non-ideal world, the only way to attain a proper balance between partialist and impartialist demands is for persons to act *collectively* in some way or another by contributing through various governmental or non-governmental aid organizations to assist those in chronic need. (Others

[33] Nagel 1986: 190.

have made similar arguments, including Scheffler 1992, Pogge 2002, Dasgupta 1993, Mulgan 2001, Cullity 2004.[34])

The MST supports such a conclusion. For only in that way can one fulfill obligations to help others in need in a world where the moral sphere has badly broken down, while protecting to some degree one's own way of life with its partialist commitments. Nagel puts the matter nicely when he says "a well designed set of political and social institutions should function as a moral buffer to protect personal life against the ravenous claims of impersonal good, and vice versa."[35] In the absence of such institutions, it seems to me, as to Nagel, that the impartialist demands of morality (to treat all persons as ends, including oneself) cannot be satisfactorily met and the moral sphere has edged toward complete breakdown (level 4). So there is a moral obligation to strive to put such effective institutions of mutual aid in place internationally, nationally and locally. Doing so should be a central goal of maintaining and preserving the moral sphere to the degree possible, as the MST demands.

## 12. FAIR SHARES, PARTIALIST AND IMPARTIALIST DEMANDS

But there is a further and more difficult question posed by the demandingness problem: Just how much should comparatively affluent individuals give to aid the world's needy *when* such institutions of mutual aid are *not* in place, or are defective or only partially effective, as in the real world today. On this question, I also incline to agree with Nagel and others who argue that no satisfactory answer to the question has been given by any contemporary moral theory that makes impartialist demands and that no *general*, algorithmic solution to this problem may be possible.[36] One original, though controversial, attempt to solve the problem of how much individuals are obliged to give to aid the world's needy is suggested by Liam Murphy in his insightful book *Moral Demands in Nonideal Theory* (2000). Simplifying to some degree, Murphy argues that the comparatively affluent are obligated to donate to the needy of the world as much of their own money or resources as would be their fair share if all of the other comparatively affluent in the world contributed their fair share. Contributions to the needy beyond what one's fair share would be if all contributed would be supererogatory, but not obligatory. This is

---

[34] See discussions of the topic by many others in Chatterlee 2004.
[35] In Scheffler 1988: 154.    [36] Nagel 1991, chapters 1 and 2.

sometimes referred to as a Fair Share View.[37] (Similar Fair Share Views have been defended by others, including Kwame Anthony Appiah in his book *Cosmopolitanism* (2006).)

Fair Share Views have often been criticized, however, on the grounds that they do not properly account for our moral obligations when others in a position to help are *not* contributing their fair share.[38] As one critic, Cullity, puts this objection: "When some of us have done our fair share of what everyone ought to have done, it can still be the case that, because some people are not doing their fair share, there remain many people needing help. We know that other people who should be helping them are not. But that does not affect the powerful reason that there is for us to go further, and help the remaining people."[39]

Such criticisms of Fair Share Views have considerable force. Yet I think Fair Share Views, like Murphy's, have something important to contribute to the demandingness problem. It is noteworthy, for example, that practices of *tithing*, which have been a part of various religious and other traditional communities, are attempts to put Fair Share Views into practice by requiring general compliance so that a line may be drawn between what is obligatory and what is supererogatory with regard to helping the needy. The Islamic pillar of charity, for example, requires a certain percentage of income be given annually by all believers. It is also noteworthy that in the secular order and at a national level, progressive *taxation* plays a similar role to tithing, to the extent that taxation provides a safety net for the needy of a society or nation.

It seems to me that a moral argument for progressive taxation of this sort can be given within the MST and other impartialist moral theories, provided of course that the taxation is fair and is used among other things to aid the needy. If these conditions are satisfied, taxation used for such purposes would contribute to maintaining and preserving a moral sphere in which all persons in a society are treated as ends, as the MST requires. Moreover, like tithing, taxation directed at helping the needy may also be viewed as a way of putting Fair Share notions into practice by requiring general compliance, so that a line *may* be drawn between what is obligatory for all in the society with regard to helping the needy and what is supererogatory.

---

[37] Hurley 2003 is a penetrating discussion of Murphy's view and Fair Share Views generally.

[38] See, e.g., Mulgan 2001, chapter 2; Cullity 2004: 74–9. Appiah (2006), though a defender of Fair Share approaches, also concedes that this is a serious objection to which he sees at present no satisfactory answer.

[39] Cullity 2004: 77.

Taxation for this purpose would thereby provide a moral buffer against what Nagel calls the "ravenous demands" of the moral life in a world or society where there is chronic need. It would allow persons to turn their attention to their partialist commitments, relationships and personal projects – to their work, supporting their families, raising their children, helping aged parents and friends, all of which are plenty demanding tasks in themselves – while feeling at the same time that they have contributed a fair share to help the chronically needy. Further acts of charity would be encouraged, but would be supererogatory. Such moral "buffers" provide a way of balancing the partialist commitments of everyday life with the impartialist demands of morality, as the maintenance of a moral sphere requires.

With regard to the distant needy in foreign lands, the demandingness problem is even more daunting. But it seems to me that the general principle enunciated by Nagel remains the same and is consistent with what the MST would require: In a non-ideal world of widespread chronic need, the only way to attain a balance between partialist and impartialist demands is for individuals to act collectively in some way by contributing through various governmental or non-governmental aid organizations to assist those in chronic need. Such organizations and agencies provide the moral buffers needed to balance partialist and impartialist commitments that Nagel demands.

The problem of aid to the distant needy is complicated, however, by a number of common objections to the efficacy of contributing to international aid agencies. It is commonly alleged for example that much aid in the form of cash donations is known to be appropriated by corrupt middle-persons and does not get to those who need it, that such aid may often be counter-productive, promoting passivity and dependence in those to whom it is given, that it does not get to the root of the socio-economic problems of poor countries, and so on.

Garrett Cullity, in his book *The Moral Demands of Affluence* (2004) persuasively argues that, while there is some justice to at least some of these common objections to contributing to international aid agencies, the objections do not absolve individuals in affluent nations from the obligation of contributing through some such agencies to the distantly needy. Indeed, the familiar objections against aid agencies, to the degree that they have merit, point, in Cullity's view, to the individual and collective moral goals that ought to be sought by individuals and nations in contributing to the distant needy: To seek out and donate to agencies (which do exist in his view) that are not corrupt and through which aid does get to the genuinely needy; to support programs of international aid that, where possible, empower the needy rather than merely promoting passivity and dependence; to seek to create international institutions that attack the root causes of malnutrition and deprivation in poor countries, and so on. There would be a moral obligation in a world of widespread chronic need to strive to put effective institutions of mutual aid of such kinds in place, daunting as the task would be.[40] Doing so would be a central goal of maintaining and preserving the moral sphere to the degree possible, as the MST requires.

There remains, however, the problem of how much comparatively affluent individuals should contribute to aid the world's needy when adequate institutions of mutual aid are not in place, or those in place are only partially effective, as in the real world. I said earlier that I agree with Nagel and others who argue that no satisfactory answer to this question has been given by any moral theory that makes substantial impartialist demands and that no general answer to the question may be possible for such theories. The reason is that, in conditions of widespread non-compliance, where giving a fair share will not be adequate to meet the needs, no definitive line can be drawn between what is obligatory with regard to giving to aid the needy and what is supererogatory. The moral sphere has broken down in such circumstances. There remains an obligation to give to the needy since the theories do make impartialist demands. But just how *much* one is obliged to give is not clearly defined and must be left to particular judgments of individuals based on their circumstances.[41]

This result throws light on a point made earlier – namely, that the demandingness problem not only arises for utilitarian and consequentialist theories, but also in some form or another for any moral theory that requires universal moral concern or makes, in Nagel's terms, "substantial impartialist demands." That includes the MST. But, as I noted, the demandingness problem arises differently for theories that take a "moderate" position on demandingness, such as the MST, than it does for utilitarian and consequentialist theories requiring that actions

---

[40] Pogge (2002) offers influential arguments for aid to the global poor on the grounds that persons in affluent nations have harmed the impoverished of the world by supporting and benefitting from a global order that bars their secure access to basic goods. Such arguments complicate the debate over demandingness in ways that I do not have the space to discuss here. On this issue, also see Kuper 2002.

[41] Some Kantians argue for a similar line with respect to "imperfect" duties such as beneficence and mutual aid. Herman (1993: 69), for example, speaks of the "casuistry of beneficent action," in which "there is no simple rule that will guarantee correct judgment."

always maximize the good. Theories requiring that actions maximize the good seem to require, as Ashford and Mulgan put it, giving all or nearly all of one's resources, time and energy to aiding the needy, leaving little or no time, energy and resources for partialist projects and commitments.

Moderate theories, such as the MST, are not extremely demanding *in that sense*, since they require that a balance be struck between the impartialist and partialist demands. But moderate theories, including the MST, are nonetheless subject to a less extreme version of the demandingness problem: In a world of widespread chronic need, *where giving a fair share will not meet the demand* because many who could contribute are not doing so, no clear line can be drawn in the form of general principles telling us when we have given enough to fulfill our impartialist moral obligations to the needy while at the same time allowing sufficient room for partialist projects and commitments. We may thus feel that no matter how much we have given, we could, and perhaps should, have given more, since there are more people out there who desperately need our aid.

This thought, of course, is the very one that inclines persons toward maximizing theories which demand that we should keep giving more, as long as we can. For moderate theories, however, that is not the solution, since it amounts to allowing impartialist commitments to completely override partialist ones, whereas the goal is to find a balance between the two. Being afflicted with uncertainty about *whether or not we have given enough* is not the same thing as *being certain we have not given enough* until we have given all or most of what we have.

Accordingly, the demandingness problem for moderate theories, such as the MST, is not that, in a real world of widespread need, we must abandon partialist commitments altogether. The problem is that in such a world, when fair shares are not enough, there is no principled way to definitively tell when we have attained the required moral balance between partialist and impartialist commitments, between what is obligatory with regard to giving to the needy and what is supererogatory. This is a tragic situation because we will always be uncertain whether we have given enough.

I believe that *this* form of the demandingness problem is inescapable for any moral theory that requires universal moral concern, including the MST, in a world of widespread chronic need. But I do not think this problem is an indictment of such theories, so much as it is an indictment of a morally broken world in which we cannot treat everyone as an end, including ourselves and those close to us, no matter what we do. In such a world, we can never be confident that our "aspirations" to be moral – understood as treating ourselves as ends and everyone else as ends as well – are fully realized. That is why there is a moral mandate to change such a world by political or other action to bring it closer to the moral sphere.[42]

---

[42] I have benefitted greatly by conversations with John Deigh on many of the topics discussed in this chapter.

# CHAPTER 17

# The good and the right (III): contractualism

## I. CONTRACTUALISM AND THE MST: SCANLON

The further ethical theory I want to discuss in this chapter is *contractualism*, in the influential form given to that theory in recent philosophy by T. M. Scanlon. If Hooker's rule-consequentialism is the closest theory of its kind to the MST, Scanlon's contractualism as formulated in his major work, *What We Owe to Each Other* (1998),[1] is the closest of any contractarian or contractualist moral theory to the MST.[2] I find myself in sympathy with many of Scanlon's basic motivations in moral theory – e.g., his rejection of pure utilitarian and consequentialist approaches; his rejection of Kantian rationalism, Rossian intuitionism, and virtue ethics (despite borrowing insights or themes from all three); his rejection of contractarian moral theories of the Hobbesian kind; and his rejection of other ideal contract approaches to moral theory, notably that of Rawls (despite owing much to Rawls). I also agree with some (though not all) of what Scanlon says about the nature of value. Despite these agreements, however, there are significant and enlightening differences between Scanlon's contractualism and the MST that are worth exploring. (Throughout the chapter, when I speak of contractualism, I will mean Scanlon's version of it.)

Because of the similarities between the two theories, however, I will proceed as follows in this chapter. First, I will discuss the demands that Scanlon believes a successful moral theory and account of moral motivation must meet and will consider how contractualism, in his view, meets these demands. Second, I will discuss how these demands are met by the MST. Third, I will consider objections to Scanlon's contractualism and show how the MST avoids these objections. Whatever the final verdict

---

[1] Page numbers in the text of this chapter hereafter refer to this work.
[2] B. Barry 1995 offers an important alternative contractarian theory that owes much to Scanlon's contractualism, but also contains other (e.g., Rawlsian) elements.

on these arguments, I think the comparison between the two theories throws interesting light on both.

My general theme will be this: The MST provides an alternative way of developing certain basic and attractive ideas of contractualism (such as the ideas of "justifying oneself to others" and what is "reasonably reject-able" by others).[3] This alternative way of developing these ideas through the MST has not previously been considered by contractualists or their critics and is worth exploring since it avoids certain problems with contractualism.

## 2. THE CONTRACTUALIST FORMULA: REASONS AND DESIRES

At the beginning of the pivotal chapters 4 and 5 of *What We Owe to Each Other* (hereafter *WWO*), Scanlon states his task in the following way: In order to give an adequate account of moral motivation, "what we need to do … is to explain more clearly how the idea that an act is wrong flows from the idea that there is an objection of a certain kind to people's being allowed to perform such actions, and we need to do this in a way that makes clear how an act's being wrong in the sense described can provide a reason not to do it" (p. 153). Contractualism, he says, offers such an account of moral motivation. It holds that

(C) An act is wrong if its performance under the circumstances would be dis-allowed by any set of principles for the general regulation of behavior that no one could reasonably reject as a basis for informed, unforced general agreement. (ibid.)

Behind this well-known Scanlonian formula lies the basic idea that moral thinking is concerned with what we can justify to other people. Explaining the formula, Scanlon says: "Thinking about right and wrong is, at the most basic level, thinking about what could be justified to others on grounds that they, if appropriately motivated, could not reasonably reject" (p. 154). Other persons are "appropriately motivated," if they are also "moved to justify their actions on ground that others could not reasonably reject" (2002: 519).

The key to this contractualist formula, C, and much of the contro-versy surrounding it, therefore lies in what is to count as "reasonable

---

[3] Prominent philosophers such as Gibbard (2008) and Parfit (unpublished) have also found these ideas of Scanlonian contractualism attractive and have tried to develop them in ways that differ from Scanlon's and from the way I develop them here.

rejectability" of principles of action – and in particular what makes it "reasonable" for persons to reject certain principles for the general regulation of behavior. On this important issue Scanlon's view has undergone significant changes between his earlier influential essay "Contractualism and Utilitarianism" (1982) and his book, *WWO*. In the earlier essay, as he notes in *WWO*, what motivated one to be moral on the contractualist view was "a *desire* to be able to justify one's actions to others on grounds that they could not reasonably reject" (p. 7). Scanlon was concerned, however, with the objection that persons who lacked this desire (egoists, classist amoralists, elitists, and others) would have no reason to seek agreement with others that *no one* could reasonably reject. Hence persons without the *actual* desire to justify their actions to others would have no reason to be moral.

In *WWO*, Scanlon moved to remedy this problem by distinguishing "having a reason" to do something from having a "desire" or actually "being motivated" to do it. This change required that he distance himself from Humean or internalist ideas about reasons for action, according to which having a reason to act required having a desire or actually being motivated to act. Having distanced himself to his satisfaction from such views in the earlier chapters of *WWO*, Scanlon could argue that even persons who lack any desire or actual motivation to reach agreement with others and hence to act morally, nonetheless can have a *reason* to act morally. Their reason would be to "live with others on grounds they could not reasonably reject insofar as [those others] are also motivated by this ideal" (p. 153). Since some others may not in fact recognize this reason and will therefore not be motivated to be moral, actual agreement to live with others on grounds they could not reasonably reject is not what justifies morality. Rather it is "the ideal of hypothetical agreement which contractualism takes to be the basis of our thinking about right and wrong" (p. 155). The principles defining morality would be those that others who are also suitably motivated to find such agreement could not reasonably reject.

Having laid out these basic ideas, Scanlon then asks:

> Why accept this account of moral motivation? I accept it, first, because it seems to me to be phenomenologically accurate. When I reflect on the reason that the wrongness of an action seems to supply not to do it, the best description of this reason I can come up with has to do with the relation to others that such acts would put me in: the sense that others could reasonably object to what I do (whether or not they would actually do so). (p. 155)

Scanlon continues in subsequent chapters to discuss other reasons for thinking such a contractualist account of moral motivation is superior to alternatives in ethics. Before discussing these further arguments, however, let us pause for a moment to consider how the MST compares with contractualism on the points so far considered.

### 3. REASONABLE REJECTABILITY AND THE MST

I noted earlier that two basic ideas that have made contractualism an attractive option in ethical theory are the ideas of "justifying oneself to others" and "reasonable rejectability" of one's actions by others. I believe these ideas do have an important role to play in moral theory. But it is worth noting that acknowledging their importance *does not necessarily commit one to accepting contractualism.* Much depends on how the ideas of justifiability to others and reasonable rejectability are incorporated into moral theory; and there are different ways of doing it. The MST provides an alternative.

To see this, think of the MST as offering a somewhat different procedure from Scanlon to come up with basic moral rules or principles. Instead of initially asking what *"principles for the general regulation of behavior"* are such that no one could reasonably reject them, one would initially ask in the MST the question: "What *plans of action* or *ways of life* (understanding ways of life as the most comprehensive plans of action) are such that *someone* could reasonably reject them?" Moral sphere-breaking plans of action and ways of life fail this test insofar as they license agents acting on them to "treat some persons as mere means," as defined in Chapter 4.

Persons who would be treated as mere means by such (moral sphere-breaking) plans of action have a *reason* to *reject* such plans of action and ways of life. They have such a reason by virtue of caring about their *own* interests and purposes and hence caring about the pursuit of their own plans of action and ways of life, which would be thwarted by the moral sphere-breaking plans of others, as argued in Chapter 12. The assault victim and Jewish family have reasons to reject the plans of action of the assailant and Gestapo in this sense and so would others treated as mere means by moral sphere-breaking plans. Putting the matter in another way, one can also say that the assailant and Gestapo cannot "justify their plans of action" to the assault victim and the Jewish family respectively, to the extent that the victim and the Jewish family care about their own well-being or flourishing (or "how things would go for them").

This is the first step in the MST procedure. But there is more to it. For, it turns out that moral sphere-breaking plans of action, *as a consequence* of treating some persons as mere means, do something else: They also make it impossible for *all other persons* to unqualifiedly "treat as ends" (or with "respect in the sense of openness") those who pursue the moral sphere-breaking plans of action *and* at the same time to treat everyone else as ends or with similar respect as well. For one cannot be open to the plans of action of the moral sphere breakers (allowing them to be pursued without interference) and at the same time be open to the plans of action of those they are treating as means as well.

Recall further that the reason in the MST for initially being open to all ways of life was to find out which ways of life were, and which were not, unqualifiedly worthy of such respect by everyone (from all points of view). And it turned out that the way one finds that out is also the way one shows one's own plans of action and way of life are objectively worthy of being lived: One does it by striving to "maintain a moral sphere in which all persons are treated with openness by all others" and departing from this ideal as little as possible when one must depart from it. From the point of view of the MST, therefore, persons have further *reason* to reject moral sphere-breaking plans of action and ways of life to the extent that *they are striving to live lives that are objectively worthy of being lived*. Persons who are so striving have such a reason, since rejecting moral sphere-breaking plans is required of those who are striving to maintain a moral sphere in which all persons are treated with openness. And that is *what striving to live an objectively worthy life requires*.

The same reasoning applies to those persons themselves who are used as "mere means" by the moral sphere-breaking plans (the assault victim, Jewish family, etc.). For such plans make it impossible for those used as mere means to pursue their own purposes without interference *and* at the same time to allow those pursuing the moral sphere-breaking plans to pursue their purposes without interference. Crucial to this inference is a point noted earlier, namely, that the requirement to treat all persons as ends, the EP – like the Kantian Formula of Humanity – includes treating *oneself* as an end as well.

Persons used as mere means can therefore appeal to the thwarting of their own well-being or flourishing as a *reason* to *reject* moral sphere-breaking plans of action, as noted earlier. But (and here is the key point) such an appeal to one's own well-being has moral legitimacy from the point of view of the MST only to the extent that one's *own* plans of action and ways of life are themselves *objectively worthy of being pursued* and therefore not moral sphere-breaking – as we assumed was the case for the assault victim and the Jewish family. In other words, the fact that persons are striving to live lives that are objectively worthy of being lived (and therefore not themselves engaging in moral sphere-breaking plans of action) is what *morally* legitimizes appealing to the harm done *to their own well-being* as a reason for rejecting the plans of action of others.

## 4. AN MST ANALOGUE OF THE CONTRACTUALIST FORMULA

With these points in mind then, let us return to Scanlon's contractualism. Much is revealed about the relation of the two theories, I suggest, by noting that one can derive a formula from the MST procedure just described that is analogous to Scanlon's contractualist formula C, but with two significant differences. (1) The analogous formula in the MST would not define what moral rightness and wrongness *consist in* (so it would not play the foundational role that Scanlon's formula C plays in contractualism); and (2) the analogous formula in the MST would presuppose explicit moral content *that is grounded independently* of the formula, i.e., on non-contractualist grounds.

Regarding point (1), *moral rightness* in the MST *consists in* "striving to lead a good life that is objectively worthy of being lived and striving thereby to realize goods by virtue of the living of such a life that are objectively worthy of being realized" (as expressed by the "MST formula" of Chapter 15). Striving to live such a life (hence moral rightness) entails in the first instance not treating others as mere means (not breaking the moral sphere) and then doing what one can to maintain (restore and preserve) the moral sphere when it has broken down. *Moral wrongness* in the MST consists in treating others as mere means by imposing one's will on them in situations in which one is not doing what one can to maintain the moral sphere when it has broken down. What *makes* such behavior wrong are the diverse harms that befall individuals as a result of being so treated as mere means and of moral sphere breakdown: loss of life if one is killed, loss of life-savings if one is cheated, suffering if one is tortured, physical injury if one is assaulted, and so on.

With these notions in mind, one can formulate an MST version of the contractualist formula as follows:

(C*) An act is wrong if its performance under the circumstances would be disallowed by any set of principles for the general regulation of behavior that no one *who is striving to live a good life that is objectively worthy of being lived* could reasonably reject as a basis for informed, unforced general agreement.

This is Scanlon's contractualist formula C with the addition of the italicized phrase. But the italicized phrase imports into the formula *moral content* that is presupposed by the formula and derived independently of it (point 2 above). For, as we have seen, persons striving to live a good life that is objectively worthy of being lived are thereby already committed to a host of defeasible moral rules entailed by the Ends Principle (don't kill, don't lie, don't coerce others, etc.), the following of which is a necessary condition for living such a life. Such persons have no good *reason* to reject rules *the following of which is necessary for the kind of life they are striving to live*.

If C* were meant to be a foundational principle in the MST, defining what moral wrongness of actions consists in, it would therefore be subject to the charge of circularity. But C* is not meant to be a foundational principle in the MST, as the corresponding formula C is in Scanlon's contractualism. In the MST, principles of moral rightness and wrongness are defined independently of social contracts and agreements (actual or hypothetical). Indeed, the moral legitimacy of (actual or hypothetical) social contracts or agreements in the MST depends on prior principles of moral rightness independently defined rather than the other way around. One might therefore view C* as a derivative principle in the MST specifying the conditions for *morally* legitimate social contracts or agreements in social ethics and politics.

## 5. SCANLON'S CONTRACTUALISM AND THE CIRCULARITY PROBLEM

Reflecting on C* is an interesting way of comparing the two theories. For, Scanlon himself concedes that his own contractualist formula C must presuppose some moral content in judgments about what is "reasonably" rejectible, if the formula is to yield the results he desires (p. 194). And this concession that moral content must be presupposed in his formula presents a problem from the point of view of Scanlon's contractualism, because, as he is aware, it invites charges of circularity against his theory. Indeed, such charges have been made by many of his critics, as we shall see. Scanlon himself aptly states the problem in *WWO*:

According to my version of contractualism, deciding whether an action is right or wrong requires a substantive judgment on our part about whether certain objections to possible moral principles would be reasonable ....If my analysis is correct then the idea of what would be reasonable in this sense ... is thus an idea with moral content. This moral content makes it inviting as a component in moral theory, but also invites the charge of circularity. By basing itself on reasonableness, it may be charged, a theory builds in moral elements at the start.

This makes it easy to produce a theory which *sounds* plausible, but such a theory will tell us very little, since everything we are to get out of it at the end we must put in at the beginning as part of the moral content of reasonableness. (p. 194)

It is important to consider why Scanlon thinks moral content must be assumed by his formula and how he tries to answer this charge of circularity. Elaborating on the nature of the moral content that must be assumed, he says that principles violating standards of *fairness*, or treating persons differently in arbitary ways, or principles that do not take into account the *responsibility* of agents in certain ways, or do not take account of various *rights* or *entitlements* of agents, are "reasonably" rejectable, according to his formula.[4] In saying this, he explicitly rejects what he calls a "welfarist contractualism," according to which reasonable rejection of a proposed principle can be based solely on how the principle affects the welfare or well-being of the persons rejecting the principle (pp. 141–43). Principles are not reasonably rejectable in the required sense simply because they would disadvantage one's welfare or that of one's group. Other considerations of a moral kind, for example, of fairness and responsibility, must be factored in.

To illustrate these points, Scanlon offers the following example: Suppose "we are negotiating about water rights in our county and ... there is one landowner who already controls most of the water in the vicinity. This person has no need for our cooperation. He can do as he pleases and what he chooses to do will largely determine the outcome of the negotiations" (p. 192). In such a situation, Scanlon says "it would not be unreasonable for one of us to maintain that each person is entitled to at least a minimum supply of water, and to reject any principle of allocation that does not guarantee this. But it might not be rational to make this claim or reject such principles, since it is very likely to enrage the large landowner and lead to an outcome that is worse for almost everyone" (ibid.).

Scanlon thus distinguishes between the *rationality* and the *reasonableness* of "rejecting" principles. He concedes that it would be *rational* for the large landowner to reject our request for principles guaranteeing minimum water rights since he gains no benefit from cooperating with us. What is *rational* in this sense is related to the advancement of his self-interest. Scanlon associates such rationality with contractarian ethical theories of the Hobbesian kind, in which the rationality of agreeing to cooperate with others is based on mutual advantages gained from such cooperation (pp. 192–93). He rejects such Hobbesian theories because he

---

[4] On fairness, arbitrariness and entitlements, see 191–218. On responsibility, chapter 5.

does not believe they will yield appropriate moral principles (pp. 190–91). Thus, he rejects the idea that "rightness is determined by … principles that no one could *rationally* reject" (p. 193) in the self-interested Hobbesian sense and chooses instead to talk about what persons could *reasonably* reject.

In the water rights case, for instance, Scanlon grants that it would be rational for the large landowner to reject principles guaranteeing minimum water rights. But he adds that it would nonetheless be "natural to say that it would be *unreasonable* of the large landowner to reject our request for principles guaranteeing minimum water rights. What it would be rational for him to do (in the most common understanding of that term) is a different question, and depends on what his aims are" (pp. 192–93).

But in what sense, one might ask, would it be *unreasonable* to reject the neighbors' request for minimum water rights? Scanlon's answer in brief is that it would be *unfair*. Since the large landowner would not be disadvantaged very much by granting minimal water rights to the neighbors, "our judgment that it would not be unreasonable for the neighbors to demand better terms than the large landowner is offering reflects a substantive judgment about the merits of their claims" (p. 194). He goes on to say that this substantive judgment about the merits of their respective claims has "moral content" since the judgment is based on notions of fairness and on the neighbors' entitlement to "mutual recognition and accommodation" from the landowner that would allow them the minimal amount of water necessary to survive (p. 192). This is the point at which Scanlon acknowledges that presupposing such "moral content … invites the charge of circularity" (p. 192).

## 6. HOLISM, FAIRNESS AND PRINCIPLES

Scanlon takes this charge of circularity quite seriously and he offers a number of responses to it throughout *WWO* that I will consider in turn. His first response is the following:

> While it would be objectionably circular to make "reasonable rejection" turn on presumed entitlements of the very sort that the principle in question is supposed to establish, it is misleading to suggest that when we are assessing the "reasonable rejectability" of a principle we must, or even can, set aside assumptions about other rights and entitlements altogether …. What this illustrates is that a sensible contractualism, like most other plausible views, will involve a holism about moral justification: in assessing one principle we must hold many others

fixed. This does not mean that these other principles are beyond question, but just that they are not being questioned at the moment. (p. 214)

Many critics of Scanlon's contractualism have questioned whether this appeal to the "holism" of moral justification really answers the charge of circularity (e.g. Joseph Raz, Brad Hooker, Gerald Dworkin, Robert Adams, Philip Pettit, Simon Blackburn, among others).[5] If contractors considering a proposed moral principle must appeal to other background principles they may hold regarding fairness, responsibility, desert, rights or entitlements (even if those other principles are treated as merely provisional), might not the contractors hold different background and competing principles (different conceptions of fairness or entitlements, for example)? And if so, the proposed moral principle would be reasonably rejectable by some, but not by others.

As Adams, Pettit and Hooker point out, notions of fairness and entitlement may differ from individual to individual, society to society.[6] A contractualist view must be able to separate the *right* notions of fairness and entitlement from wrong ones *in contractualist terms*. But, as Hooker says, "virtually all the references to fairness in Scanlon's book ... suggest that fairness is a consideration that helps shape what people can reasonably reject, not a concept whose content can be determined by what people can reasonably reject."[7] This point is illustrated by the water rights example where the judgment is made that it is "unreasonable" for the large landowner to reject a principle requiring him to grant minimal water rights to his neighbors since they are "entitled to at least a minimum supply of water" and hence it would be unfair. In such a case, a judgment about what is fair in the situation and what entitlements are valid "shapes what people can reasonably reject" rather than being "shaped by what people can reasonably reject." (Similar arguments are made by Raz, G. Dworkin and others.[8])

Robert Adams adds that "the problem of circularity is aggravated by Scanlon's account of *principles*."[9] Adams cites Scanlon's claim that

[5] Raz 2004, Hooker 2003, G. Dworkin 2002, Adams 2001, Pettit 2000, Blackburn 1999. Other critics with similar complaints include Arneson 2002, R. J. Wallace 2002, McGinn 1999a, D. Sosa 2004. Deigh (2002) implicitly raises such questions in discussing Scanlon on promises. Scanlon responds to Raz in Scanlon 2004: 125–28, to Dworkin, Wallace and Deigh in Scanlon 2002. Two excellent collections on Scanlon's view are Matravers 2003, Stratton-Lake 2004. Defenses of Scanlon against critics include Kumar 2000, Ridge 2001. Arneson 2002, Parfit 2004, Raz 2004 and Brand-Ballard 2000 discuss subtle problems in Scanlon's account of restrictions against harming some to save others. Parfit 2004 also makes interesting suggestions about how a contractualist view might be altered to deal with these problems.

[6] Adams 2001: 564–68; Pettit 2000: 159ff.; Hooker 2003: 57–62.     [7] Hooker 2003: 68.

[8] Raz 2004; G. Dworkin 2002. Ridge 2001 attempts to respond to such charges.

[9] Adams 2001: 567.

"principles may rule out some actions by ruling out the reasons on which they are based, but they also leave wide room for interpretation and judgment .... Even the most familiar moral principles are not rules which can be easily applied without appeals to judgment" (p. 199). To illustrate, Scanlon cites common rules against killing, breaking promises or lying, each of which has exceptions (in the case of killing, he cites "self-defense ... certain acts of killing by police officers and by soldiers in wartime") (ibid.). And he insists that deciding which exceptions to such moral principles are reasonable and which are unreasonable "leaves wide room for interpretation" and requires appeals to "judgment" (p. 200).

As Adams points out, however, in making these judgments about acceptable exceptions to moral principles in *WWO*, Scanlon usually relies on common-sense intuitions that presuppose moral content, thus adding "to the appearance of circularity."[10] Consider, says Adams, "Scanlon's judgment that it is reasonable to reject principles allowing harmless free riding because they are 'unfair.'"[11] (Harmless free riding is exempting oneself from participation in a cooperative scheme when one's participation is not needed to attain the desired goal.) Adams comments:

Unfairness is certainly not the same as wrongness, but this difference does not clearly lead us out of the circle here. For Scanlon will surely agree that there are (minor) unfairnesses that it is not worth the trouble of prohibiting morally. So presumably his judgment here must be, in effect, that harmless free riding is *so* unfair as to be *wrong*, and the judgment weighing reasons threatens to collapse into a judgment of wrong action. His best chance of escaping the circle at this point may be to say that his judgment is rather that harmless free riding is so unfair that it is *reasonable* for us to *require* each other to live in accordance with principles that forbid it. Here Scanlon cannot allow much looseness of fit between the reasonable and the right .... The judgment he needs amounts – transparently, I think – to a judgment that it is *right* to impose the requirement.[12]

In this case and in others, Adams argues, the problem of circularity is aggravated and not solved by Scanlon's contention that the application of moral principles requires "judgment and interpretation."

Scanlon's assertion that "even the most common moral principles cannot be easily applied without appeals to judgment" has also invited criticisms from Rossian intuitionists and moral particularists. McNaughton and Rawling, for example, point out that various principles Scanlon formulates against killing, promise-breaking and lying in Chapters 5 and 7 of *WWO* all include a clause that such acts are forbidden "in the absence

[10] Ibid.   [11] Ibid.
[12] Ibid.: 566–67.

of special justification" (such as self-defense in the case of killing).[13] McNaughton and Rawling then argue that when Scanlon gets around to specifying these "special justifications" throughout these chapters, he inevitably appeals to common moral intuitions about particular cases in the manner of Rossian intuitionists. These moral intuitions, McNaughton and Rawling contend, are doing the real moral work in Scanlon's contractualist theory because the intuitions are determining which principles are reasonably rejectable and which are not. "The digression through reasonable rejectability," they conclude, seems "unnecessary"[14]; and the advantages of contractualism over intuitionist theories of the Rossian kind, they argue, are more apparent than real.

Scanlon might reply that contractualism makes progress over intuitionism on the problem of "systematization" of our common moral intuitions since moral agents, on the contractualist view, have "a unifying aim of seeking principles of a certain kind ... cashed out in terms of reasonable rejectability" (p. 144). But McNaughton and Rawling counter that, *if* common moral intuitions must be appealed to in order to spell out *which* principles are reasonably rejectable, the contractualist claim to systematization in terms of reasonable rejectability is more apparent than real.[15]

## 7. THE APPEAL TO MUTUAL RECOGNITION

These familiar objections to Scanlon's contractualism have considerable force; and I think they would be compelling, if Scanlon's response to the circularity problem involved no more than appeals to a "holism" of moral justification and the need for "interpretation and judgment" in the application of moral principles. But Scanlon has a further response to the circularity problem that plays a crucial role throughout *WWO* and must be considered. It first appears in the following passage.

> The contractualist ideal of acting in accord with principles that others (similarly motivated) could not reasonably reject is meant to characterize the relation the value and appeal of which underlies our reasons to do what morality requires. This relation ... might be called a relation of mutual recognition. Standing in this relation to others is appealing in itself – worth seeking for its own sake. (p. 162)

Scanlon argues in this passage and others that this relation of *mutual recognition* is the "positive value" (p. 162) ("appealing in itself" and "worth

---

[13] 2006: 439.    [14] Ibid.: 441.
[15] Ibid.: 440.

seeking for its own sake") that underlies his contractualist formula. As a consequence, appeals to the value of mutual recognition play a significant role throughout *WWO* when he is applying the formula to specific cases.

But mutual recognition can be interpreted in various ways, as commentators on Scanlon have noted[16]; and much depends on how it is interpreted. Scanlon himself describes mutual recognition in ways that lend themselves to two possible interpretations. On the one hand, mutual recognition may be understood simply as a way of *expressing* the contractualist formula itself: To accord mutual recognition to others on this interpretation would simply mean being willing to act on "principles that those others (if similarly motivated) could not reasonably reject." The expression "mutual recognition" would then merely be a shorthand way of designating what the contractualist formula itself requires. If interpreted in this way, however, the appeal to mutual recognition would make no advance on the circularity problem. Determining what mutual recognition of others required would involve determining what principles were "reasonably" rejectable by them and by us. And in determining what principles were reasonably rejectable, moral content would have to be assumed in the form of background moral beliefs ("holism" of moral justification) and interpretation or judgments about particular cases that would presuppose common moral intuitions.[17]

More interesting is the second possible interpretation of mutual recognition, which is often suggested by Scanlon's references to it. On this interpretation, mutual recognition is not merely a way of labeling or designating what the contractualist formula requires, but a *substantive ideal* or *value* upon which the contractualist formula *depends* – an ideal or value that, as he says, is "appealing in itself" and "worth seeking for its own sake." Elsewhere, Scanlon says that this ideal of mutual recognition expresses the *value of persons* and therefore requires a measure of *respect* for their points of view (pp. 169, 271–72). It represents what one of his commentators, R. Jay Wallace, calls an "idealized reciprocity of respect" between persons.[18] Moreover, Scanlon assumes such recognition must extend to all persons, not merely to those of a favored circle or group. In discussing amoralists who lack the attitude of mutual recognition, for example, he says: "This attitude includes not only us, but everyone else as well, since the amoralist does not think that anyone is owed the consideration that morality describes just in virtue of being a person" (p. 159).

[16] E.g., Wallace 2002: 451ff.   [17] Cf. Wallace 2002: 451–59; Hooker 2004: 57–62.
[18] Wallace 2002: 452.

Scanlon further assumes that mutual recognition can trump other personal, self-interested values and can therefore help to explain the "priority" of morality over self-interested concerns (p. 166).

Interpreted as a substantive ideal with all these features, the notion of mutual recognition can obviously supply moral content to the contractualist formula; and Scanlon often appeals to the value of mutual recognition when deciding whether principles are or are not reasonably rejectable.[19] But such appeals to mutual recognition have also (unsurprisingly) invited the charge from critics that Scanlon is begging the question by assuming that mutual recognition of others based on their value as persons is a master value that trumps all others and is a good worth seeking for its own sake.[20] Such an appeal to mutual recognition seems to solve the problem of moral content in the contractualist formula by fiat and, as a consequence, does not solve the problem of circularity. Indeed, it aggravates that problem. For, the value of mutual recognition is not derived from the contractualist formula. It is presupposed by the formula in determining what is and is not reasonably rejectable.[21] Kantians, for example, could well object that, by appealing to mutual recognition in this way, Scanlon is merely helping himself, without benefit of a derivation, to a Kantian-like principle that all persons are deserving of recognition or respect because they have value as persons; and this Kantian-like principle, they might argue, is doing the real *moral* work in the theory.

To be fair, however, Scanlon does not merely assert that the relation of mutual recognition is "appealing in itself" and "worth seeking for its own sake." He tries to justify these claims by showing how a mutual recognition based on the inherent value of other persons may enhance many human relations and projects, such as friendships and scientific or other collective pursuits (pp. 162–68). Scanlon's discussions of these matters are subtle and interesting; and they do show something of importance. One can, I think, reasonably argue, as he does, that according mutual recognition to *some* other persons in one's life (friends, family, clan, tribe, colleagues, etc.) can "make life go better" for the person who accords such respect. One may even argue that being in a relation of mutual recognition with some other persons, such as friends and family, is a value worth seeking for its own sake and is a necessary ingredient of a happy and flourishing life.

But Scanlon needs to argue for more than that. For, the mutual recognition needed to provide the moral content of his contractualist

---

[19] Scanlon 2002: 511.    [20] See Wallace 2002: 453–59; G. Dworkin 2002: 478ff.
[21] Wallace ibid.

formula has to be accorded to *all* persons, strangers as well as friends and family, those outside one's favored circle as well as those inside. And one cannot argue that life will necessarily "go better" from a person's own point of view if mutual recognition were accorded to all persons in that way rather than to a select few. To assume so would be to beg the "why be moral?" question against classist amoralists (those who are willing to act morally to others in their favored circle, but not to all persons outside their favored circle), as argued in Chapter 8. And to argue that according such recognition to all other persons would "make life go better" *morally* for the person who accords it would beg the question in an obvious way.

The problem here for Scanlon is nicely described by one of his more sympathetic critics cited earlier, R. Jay Wallace. Wallace says that "Scanlon should probably be understood as launching an appeal to his readers to reflect carefully for themselves on the concrete value of being able to enter into relationships with people on terms of mutual recognition. The idea, I suppose, is that they will come through such reflection to grasp the value of complying with moral principles."[22] But Wallace questions whether such reflection on the value of mutual recognition in relations such as friendship will "really suffice for the person who" wonders why moral commitments should have priority over, or override, personal relations and projects. "Such a person," he says, "may concede the value of standing in the relation of mutual recognition with their friends, but wonder whether the logic of friendship equally requires them to value this kind of relationship with all other persons."[23] Wallace concludes that we have reason to be skeptical that reflection on the value of mutual recognition in our lives *alone* will solve the problem of priority of morality over personal relations and projects. (Similar criticisms are made by G. Dworkin, Susan Mendus, and others.[24])

## 8. GRIDLOCK AND IRRECONCILABLE DIFFERENCES

Arguments of the past few sections make a compelling case, it seems to me, that Scanlon's contractualist formula must presuppose significant moral content that cannot be derived on contractualist grounds alone and must be imported into his contractualist formula from other sources. These other sources of moral content involving notions of

---

[22] Wallace ibid.: 452–53.    [23] Ibid.: 453–54.
[24] Dworkin 2002: 480; Mendus 2003: 45.

fairness, entitlement and mutual recognition "shape what is reasonably rejectable" in the contractualist formula rather than "being shaped by what is reasonably rejectable." The arguments of previous sections also make a compelling case, I believe, that Scanlon's attempted responses to this circularity problem (in the form of appeals to holism, to the need for judgment in the application of moral principles and to the value of mutual recognition) "aggravate the problem of circularity rather than solving it," as Adams puts it. These appeals are various ways of importing moral content that must be presupposed by the contractualist formula, but are not derived from it.

Scanlon himself concedes that the contractualist formula must presuppose moral content in these forms to avoid "gridlock" – a situation in which any proposed principles for the general regulation of behavior might be rejected by someone or other (p. 170). He further assumes that the interpretations of the moral content must be *shared* to a large degree by those seeking agreement (p. 204). Wide divergences in the interpretation of what is required by fairness, entitlement and mutual recognition would lead to gridlock as well.

It might appear at this point that Scanlon has other resources with the potential for supplying at least some moral content to his formula. For example, the contractualist formula seeks "principles for the general regulation of behavior that no one could reasonably reject as a basis for *informed, unforced* agreement" (p. 152). Persons seeking agreement of such a kind cannot be *coerced* or *forced* into agreeing on terms favorable to others. Nor can they be *duped* into agreeing on terms favorable to others. In addition to these requirements, persons are not required by the formula to reach agreement with any other persons whatsoever on grounds the others could not reasonably reject, but only with others who are "*similarly motivated*" to also reach agreement with them in return on grounds *they* could not reasonably reject (pp. 152–54).

These requirements eliminate actual contracts arrived at by force or fraud and make the relevant contract at best hypothetical. The requirements also appear to eliminate egoists and amoralists who could not care less what we or others may or may not reasonably reject and are therefore not "similarly motivated" to seek agreement with us on grounds we could not reasonably reject. So the requirements of "informed, unforced agreement" with others "similarly motivated" seem to supply at least some moral content to the contractualist formula. The problem, however, is that *these requirements alone do not eliminate the potential for gridlock*, as Scanlon himself is well aware.

For, persons who are not amoralists and do have sincere moral convictions may nonetheless not be able to agree on principles for the general regulation of behavior even when they are motivated to agree, if their moral convictions are sufficiently different.[25] For example, persons and groups may disagree about the place of women in society, whether women should have exactly the same rights as men or should be subordinate in varying ways, or whether rules about lying or deception apply with the same force to those in one's group or to co-religionists as to strangers, or whether same-sex relations should be allowed or punished, and so on.

The problem is compounded if, as usually happens in the real world, the differing moral convictions are based on world-views or on religious or other beliefs that are felt to be essential to the persons' identities or to what gives meaning to their lives. Persons with such convictions may be motivated to reach agreement with others on grounds the others could not reasonably reject. Yet they may find they *cannot* reach agreement in good conscience without giving up *ideals* that are *uncompromisable* ingredients of their practical identities or world-views or religions that give meaning to their lives. (It should be noted that this is very much like the problem of pluralism faced by the retreatants with which the arguments of this book began.)

It seems to me that Scanlon is acutely aware of this kind of problem; and it factors into his worries about "gridlock." He realizes that if additional moral content is not presupposed in the understanding of what persons can "reasonably" reject, then agreement on principles for the regulation of behavior will founder over irreconcilable differences based on uncompromisable ideals and world-views. (This is what happened at the retreat and why general agreement failed there, provoking many groups to leave.) To avoid gridlock, Scanlon realizes that it is not enough to require that persons are not coerced or duped into agreeing. Nor is it enough to require that they are all similarly motivated to reach agreement on grounds the others could not reasonably reject. For persons may want to reach agreement, but find they could reasonably do so only at the cost of accepting principles that go against their most deeply held ideals and world-views.[26]

---

[25] A persuasive case is made for this in R. Miller 1992. See also Larmore's subtle works (1987, 1996) on related issues.

[26] Scanlon's allows for a "benign relativism" or pluralism (chapter 8). But it is "benign" because he assumes the differing groups share common moral ideals concerning fairness, mutual recognition and the value of all persons; and whether these assumptions are justified on contractualist grounds is the matter in dispute.

It is to avoid this kind of gridlock problem, I believe, that Scanlon feels the need to import additional *shared* moral content into his contractualist formula in the form of appeals to fairness, entitlements, mutual recognition and the value of persons. He wants to be able to say, for example, that it is not "reasonable" to reject principles for the general regulation of behavior that would accord equal rights to women or not allow one to lie to strangers, *even if* such principles would go against one's most deeply held ideals or beliefs or traditions. It would not be "reasonable" to reject such principles because to do so would be *unfair* to the woman or to the strangers and would be to deny *mutual recognition* equally to *all* persons.

In this way, appeals to fairness and mutual recognition allow Scanlon to avoid gridlock, but at a significant cost: They open him up to the charges of circularity. For, the notions of fairness and mutual recognition to which he appeals supply substantial moral content to the contractualist formula that cannot be derived *on contractualist grounds* alone and must be imported from other sources.

### 9. THE MST REVISITED

Is there a systematic way to get the moral content required by the contractualist formula without circularity and without merely appealing to "considered moral judgments" or common moral intuitions about fairness, entitlements and mutual recognition? I have argued that the MST suggests such a way. Something more must be considered than merely seeking to reach agreement with others on grounds that those others, if similarly motivated, could not reasonably reject. Proceeding in that way will founder over irreconcilable differences about what is "reasonably" rejectable based on differing ideals and world-views. Nor, can one merely appeal to one's own "considered moral judgments" or common-sense intuitions about what is fair or what people are entitled to, which may also differ depending on differences of belief and world-view.

What one must show is that the considered moral judgments that may seem correct to oneself upon reflection are not merely right as one sees it, but should be recognized as right by everyone from every point of view, whether others in fact agree with one's considered judgments or not. But this, as it turns out, is just the challenge the retreatants faced in Chapter 3; and the procedure they undertook was aimed at meeting this challenge. That procedure took the form of a search or quest for wisdom in the ancient philosophical sense. Such a search may begin, as it did for the retreatants, by believing one's own considered moral judgments or intuitions are correct. But in order to put those judgments and intuitions to the test, one needs to find out if the form of life of which the judgments and intuitions are a part is objectively worthy of being lived – that is, worthy of being lived, not just from one's own point of view, but from every point of view. Proceeding in this way leads directly to many common moral principles, as we have seen. Since living in accordance with these moral principles is a precondition for showing that one's form of life, or any form of life, is "objectively worthy of being lived," those who are striving to live such an objectively worthy life have *reasons* to accept such moral principles.

Following this MST procedure thus supplies moral content to the contractualist formula by placing further constraints on the motivations of the hypothetical contractors that the contractualist formula alone does not provide. It is not enough that the contractors be informed, uncoerced and want to reach agreement on grounds that others similarly motivated could not reasonably reject. Such conditions may be necessary for morally legitimate contracts. But they are not sufficient, if gridlock is to be avoided, as I think Scanlon was aware in *WWO*. The further motivation needed, according to the MST, is the motivation of the retreatants to find out which of the competing ways of life are objectively worthy of being respected (in the sense of openness) by all other persons and thereby to show that one's own way of life is so worthy. It would be the *reasonable rejections* of persons who are striving to live such objectively worthy lives that would be taken seriously when deciding what principles for the general regulation of behavior are morally acceptable.

One thus arrives at the MST analogue of the contractualist formula stated earlier, namely, (C*) "An act is wrong if its performance under the circumstances would be disallowed by any set of principles for the general regulation of behavior that no one *who is striving to live a good life that is objectively worthy of being lived* could reasonably reject as a basis for informed, unforced general agreement." This formula, however, would not play the foundational role in the MST that Scanlon's formula plays in contractualism. Its moral content would be grounded independently in non-contractualist terms by way of the MST procedure.[27]

---

[27] In an important new manuscript, Parfit (unpublished) develops a version of contractualism that, he argues, converges with versions of consequentialism and Kantianism. There are interesting resemblances and differences to the MST in its approach that I hope to discuss in future writings.

## IO. MUTUAL RECOGNITION

Similar remarks can be made about Scanlon's appeals to *mutual recognition* to provide moral content to his contractualist formula. Scanlon's arguments for the value of mutual recognition, citing friendship and other special relationships and projects, fall short of what his contractualist formula requires, as noted by commentators such as Wallace, since the mutual recognition required must be accorded to *all* persons, not merely to friends, family or a select few. If the relation of mutual recognition in this strong sense is to supply moral content to Scanlon's contractualist formula, that moral content must be supplied in some way other than through the contractualist formula itself.

The MST again provides an alternative. A relation of mutual recognition in the form of reciprocal respect for other persons plays a role in the MST, as it does in Scanlon's theory. But there is a crucial difference. In the MST, the goal worth seeking for its own sake is not mutual recognition or respect for all persons *simpliciter*, but rather the *worthiness* for such mutual recognition or respect from all persons. Actual mutual recognition by others is a good, but it cannot be guaranteed simply by acting morally (since getting the recognition one deserves also requires an "audience fit to render it," as noted in Chapter 12). The goal of moral action is rather the worthiness for mutual recognition by all, which *is* something that can be attained by being moral, whether the recognition is actually accorded or not.

But it is also significant and worthy of note that *actual* mutual recognition of others has an important role to play in the MST as well. For one becomes *worthy* of recognition from all others by *initially* being willing to accord *actual* recognition to others in the form of respect in the sense of openness for their plans of action and ways of life. That is, one takes an initial attitude of "openness" toward others in order to find out which persons and ways of life are ultimately worthy of being treated with openness *and* to show that one's own way of life is worthy of being so treated. So actual recognition or respect for others of a certain kind is a necessary part of "living a life that is objectively worthy of being lived" – i.e., a moral life – though according such recognition or respect is not a good in all circumstances. It is not a good, for example, if given to those who pursue moral sphere-breaking ways of life and hence are not deserving or worthy of it.

## II. CONCLUSION

At the beginning of the chapter, I noted that two basic ideas of contractualism that have made it an attractive option in ethical theory are the ideas of "justifying oneself to others" and "reasonable rejectability" of one's actions by others. I think these two ideas do have a role to play in moral theory. But I have argued that acknowledging their importance does not necessarily commit one to accepting contractualism. Contractualism must presuppose moral content in what is "reasonably" rejectable by persons and hence in determining what is (morally) "justifiable to others" – moral content that the contractualist formula itself does not supply and must be independently derived in non-contractualist terms. I have argued that the MST provides an appealing way of arriving at this required moral content.

# CHAPTER 18

# Politics, public morality and law: justice, care and virtue

## I. POLITICS AND NEUTRALITY

In this concluding chapter, I consider some practical implications of the moral theory of earlier chapters for political philosophy, law, social ethics and moral education. I begin with current debates about state neutrality in political theory and move on to issues about public morality, the legal enforcement of morals, debates about an ethics of justice versus care, the role of virtues in moral education and the relation of ethics to politics.

Influential political and legal philosophers, such as John Rawls, Ronald Dworkin, Bruce Ackerman, Charles Larmore, D. A. Lloyd-Thomas and others,[1] have argued in different ways and with differing qualifications that states or governments in free and pluralist societies should remain neutral with respect to (in Rawls' terms) differing "comprehensive conceptions of the good," not favoring or establishing one such conception over others. The general argument for neutrality so understood is that, in a pluralist state, where citizens have differing conceptions of the good and competing ways of life, if the state favors one conception of the good (a religion or ideology or particular morality) over others, it cannot legitimately claim the full assent of all citizens whose religious or moral views differ from the favored one.[2]

This argument has appeal. But the ideal of state neutrality is controversial and has many critics. Critics argue that complete state neutrality would appear to be an impossibility.[3] Every law, policy or political

---

[1] In an excellent recent critical study of neutrality, Sher (1997) lists the following as defenders of neutrality in one form or another: Rawls 1971, 1993; Nozick 1974; Dworkin 1978, 1985; Ackerman 1982; Larmore 1987; Lloyd-Thomas 1988; Kymlicka 1989; Arneson 1990. If one includes all of these thinkers, however, it is important to note that they differ (sometimes markedly) in the details of their views and many qualify neutrality in significant ways.

[2] Dworkin 1978, Rawls 1971.

[3] Examples include Haksar 1977, Sandel 1983, Raz 1986, Gutmann 1987, Macedo 1990, Galston 2002, Barry 1995, McCabe 1995, Sher 1997, White 1997, Wall 1998. A useful collection on the issues is Goodin and Reeve 1989.

institution will inevitably favor some conceptions of the good over others. By adopting tax policies, environmental regulations, zoning laws, by taking stands either for or against gambling, homosexuality, obscenity, legalization of drugs and many other matters, governments inevitably favor some ways of life and conceptions of the good over others.

Those sympathetic to neutrality frequently concede this point.[4] Government neutrality must be limited only to certain issues or reasons, they say. But then it is difficult to draw a line where neutrality is justified and where it is not without making substantive assumptions about the good favoring some views over others. Ways of life that tolerate and even relish a great deal of freedom of choice and diversity of life-styles will more easily flourish in a state that remains neutral on most moral issues. By contrast, adherents of traditional religious ways of life, and those who hold more conservative moral views, find such a free-wheeling neutral state less hospitable to their beliefs and ways of life.[5] They would prefer greater enforcement of morals and do not want their children exposed to ways of life they regard as corrupt and immoral. As such examples show, any degree of state neutrality will not really be neutral, for it will inevitably favor some substantive notions of the good and some ways of life over others.

Joseph Raz is one of many contemporary political and legal thinkers who concede this point.[6] Raz argues that free societies cannot be neutral with respect to all substantive questions about the good, but indeed must favor a certain kind of good above all others, the good of autonomy – the capacity of individuals to make their own non-coerced choices about how they will live.[7] Whether or not one agrees with Raz on this point, defending autonomy above all other values is not a neutral stance, as he himself concedes. Doing so involves substantive assumptions about the best way for humans to live – assumptions not shared by all groups or persons. Other critics of neutrality (Haksar 1977, MacIntyre 1981, Sandel 1983, Hurka 1993, Sher 1997, White 1997, Wall 1998, and others) agree with Raz that substantive assumptions about the good cannot be ignored in political theory, while differing with him (and with each other) about what the relevant substantive assumptions should be.

---

[4] E.g., Kymlicka 1989: chapter 1.  [5] White 1997 forcefully makes this point.
[6] See Raz 1986: 117ff. (for his critique of neutrality) and 369ff. (for his defense of autonomy). Another philosopher who concedes this point is Jeffrey Reiman (1997), who brings numerous interesting arguments in support of the claim that liberalism is based on the fundamental value to all humans of a "self-governed life."
[7] Ibid.: Part IV.

## 2. NEUTRALITY AND OPENNESS

While complete political neutrality may indeed be an impossibility, I think defenders of state neutrality are aiming at something important for political theory. What they are aiming at, however, can better be captured, I now want to suggest, by focusing on an attitude that bears a superficial *resemblance* to neutrality, but turns out to be something quite different – namely, an attitude of *openness* in the search for the good.

The initial attitude of openness taken by the retreatants did not require that they remain neutral with respect to *all* points of view about values and to all ways of life implied by those points of view. To the contrary, the initial respect for the points of view and ways of life that openness required was a way of separating those points of view and ways of life that were unqualifiedly worthy of such openness respect from those that were not. We might therefore imagine a political order founded on a variation of the retreat of Chapter 3 in which those gathered are members of a single society or nation rather than peoples from all over the Earth. As in the original retreat, those present represent different religions, ideologies, points of view and ways of life; and their goal is the same as in the original gathering – to search for common ethical principles despite their differing points of views. But, in this case, the principles arrived at would be the basis of a "public morality" for their society.

Understood in this way, the political order arrived at in such a manner would not be based on neutrality, but on certain universal ethical assumptions. These would include rights to life, liberty and the pursuit of happiness that lie at the foundation of modern free societies. To respect these rights is an implication of the requirement to "treat all persons as ends in every situation and no one as a mere means" (the Ends Principle) at which the retreatants would have arrived by trying to sustain an attitude of openness to all to the degree possible. Thus interpreted, the principle enunciated by Thomas Jefferson that all humans have "inalienable rights to life, liberty and the pursuit of happiness" – the principle that Abraham Lincoln called "the father of all moral principle"[8] – would be a guiding principle of such a political order founded on openness. To say these rights are "inalienable," however, would not mean that they are "unlimited," for they would be limited at the point of moral sphere breakdown.

---

[8] Lincoln 1953, vol. 2: 499–500. I am indebted to historian George Forgie for this reference.

## 3. THE GROUNDING OF RIGHTS AND
## THE SEARCH FOR THE GOOD

In the light of the previous chapter on contractualism, it is worth reminding ourselves that the retreatants did not arrive at these results by making a social contract; nor did they base them on a social contract. The retreatants did not do so because they wanted their ethical principles to be applicable to all persons, including those who had left the retreat and would not agree or consent to abide by the principles. If all those who left the retreat had actually stayed, the result would have been "gridlock" of the kind discussed in the previous chapter – an absence of agreement because of differing uncompromisable ideals and world-views. Nor were the retreatants merely agreeing for mutual advantage to treat others as ends and not mere means, if those others would treat them in return as ends and not mere means. Their perspective was wider than that. They chose to treat each other (and all persons) initially with openness, in order to find out which persons and ways of life were objectively worthy of being so treated and which were not.

The retreatants were thus engaged in a search for the objective good under conditions of pluralism, guided by an aspiration to be wise; and the shared ethical and political principles they arrived at were the conditions for this search. If they were to form a state or polity in this manner, they would thereby be *retrieving the ancient idea that political life involves a shared search for the good,* as part of an overall search for wisdom, while acknowledging that this search is to take place *under modern conditions of pluralism.*

The public morality of a society thereby arrived at would have considerable content. When translated into law, it would provide a moral basis for both criminal and civil law. On the criminal side, it would cover laws against murder, theft, assault, fraud, bribery, and so on through the criminal code. All such crimes involve breakdowns of the moral sphere described in Chapter 4, specifically moral sphere breakdowns of "level 3" where some persons are using others as mere means to their own ends. Public morality, so defined, would also deal with the criminal justice system, fair trials, punishment and treatment of the guilty and the accused. The level 3 principle of "Using minimum force to restore and preserve the moral sphere" mandates concern for the rights of prisoners and those convicted of crimes, consistent with the fact that by their actions they have forfeited the full measure of respect for such rights due them in level 1 (the ideal moral sphere). The other level 3 principle of "Restraining the guilty, not the innocent," mandates protections against wrongly convicting innocent persons, adequate representation for those accused, right to trial by a jury, and similar protections.

In civil law, public morality defined by the Ends Principle and moral sphere breakdown would be the basis for fair contracts and the just resolution of civil disputes and conflicts of interest under imperfect conditions. Insofar as civil law involves findings of liability or fault for harms done, it also involves level 3 concerns about guilt or innocence. But civil law also concerns level 2 breakdowns of the moral sphere where competing parties have claims that cannot be simultaneously satisfied. The ideal solution for such "conflicts of interests" suggested in Chapter 4 was to seek a resolution that both parties could freely accept, thus respecting both as ends. Since such an ideal solution is often not possible, it was further argued that one must resort to "second-best strategies" for resolving level 2 conflicts – third-party arbitrators, judges, juries, majority vote, choosing by lot and other procedural methods, private, legal and political.

The underlying goal of such second-best strategies is the same as in all moral sphere breakdown: To depart as little as possible from the ideal of treating all parties with openness, when one must depart from that ideal to some degree. Finally, in yet another sphere of public life – the political arena – public morality as defined by the Ends Principle and the moral sphere would be the basis for ethics legislation governing the behavior of legislators, lobbyists, and others involved in the political process as well as the fairness of elections. Indeed, as argued in Chapter 4, democracy itself emerges as a strategy for dealing with conflicting interests that is justified by the same ethical goal of departing as little as possible from the ideal of treating all persons with openness when one must depart from that ideal to some degree.

### 4. LEGAL MORALISM: DEVLIN, DWORKIN, AND OTHERS

A public morality arrived at by a shared search for good of the kind undertaken by the retreatants would in this manner provide a foundation for the legal and political systems of societies founded upon it. But such a public morality would have further ethical implications for the life of such societies beyond these basic ones for law and politics. To see why, it is instructive to critically examine the view of those who argue for greater enforcement of morals in law and society.

A familiar and widely debated argument favoring greater legal enforcement of morals is that of Patrick Devlin (1965), British judge and legal theorist, who first presented his case while arguing against efforts to liberalize England's laws against homosexuality. Arguing against the liberalization of these laws, Devlin first noted that societies are based on a community of ideas, part of which must be a moral foundation, and that society has a right to protect this moral foundation for its own survival. "Society," he says, "is held together by the invisible bonds of common thought. If the bonds are too far relaxed, the members would drift apart."[9]

Devlin's second point concerned the standards by which societal morals would be judged. They should be the "community standards" as determined by the "reasonable person," or "man in the street" or the "person in the jury box."[10] In matters of pornography, for example, questions about what is obscene or outside community standards may be put to grand juries that are supposed to be representative samplings of the community. Devlin insists that the community reaction directly or through such representatives must be a strong one of disgust or indignation to justify legal sanctions. But when there is such a reaction, he argued, liberty can be restricted on moral grounds. A liberty-limiting principle that would justify restrictions of immoral behavior in such cases is called by Joel Feinberg the principle of Legal Moralism.[11]

Devlin's defense of Legal Moralism has been criticized on a number of grounds. Critics such as H. L. A. Hart and Ronald Dworkin argue that Devlin's appeal to the criterion of community standards is vague and potentially dangerous.[12] Community moral standards may be based on ignorance or prejudice. Should they be given the status of law simply because they are widespread? And how widespread must community attitudes be? Will a majority suffice, and if so, is there a potential for the tyranny of the majority? The critics further point out that consensus or near-unanimity is not likely to be found in modern societies on issues that concerned Devlin such as homosexuality, abortion or obscenity in art or literature.

These criticisms are nicely summed up by Dworkin when he says that the problem is not with Devlin's "idea that the community's morality counts, but his idea of what counts as the community's morality."[13] Restrictions on liberty to prevent immoral behavior based on community standards as conceived by Devlin fail to adequately resolve a central

---

[9] Ibid.: 3.     [10] Ibid.
[11] Feinberg 1982–88: vol. 4.
[12] Hart 1965; Dworkin 1978, chapter 10: 240–59. See also Feinberg 1982–88, vol. 4: chapter 1.
[13] 1978: 245.

question of pluralist societies: Whose idea of immoral behavior will be enforced when particular moralities differ?

## 5. THE PUBLIC MORALITY PRINCIPLE

Such objections to Devlin's arguments for Legal Moralism have merit and justify skepticism about the Legal Moralism principle. Yet there is something to be said for Devlin's view that "society is held together by the invisible bonds of common thought," which must include some moral foundation or shared ethical beliefs. Social philosophers from Plato to de Tocqueville to modern communitarians have supported such a claim.[14] And many of Devlin's critics acknowledge it to some degree when they say, as Dworkin does, that the problem with Devlin's position is not his idea that "the community's morality counts" but his idea of what counts as the community's morality.

I now want to suggest that the objections made to Devlin's Legal Moralism do not require that we abandon the idea of shared moral commitments to which de Tocqueville and modern communitarians wish to draw our attention. That idea of shared moral commitments can be embodied, I would argue, in an alternative to the Legal Moralism principle that is entailed by the search for the good in the manner of the retreatants.

The public morality arrived at by such a search goes beyond its embodiment in criminal and civil law and politics of the kinds considered thus far, even if it would not go as far as Devlin would take it. The reason is that commitment to the ideal of treating all persons as ends, as the Ends Principle (EP) requires, also implies a commitment to "doing what one can do to maintain [and hence to sustain and preserve] a moral sphere in which all persons can be treated with openness by all others." Such a commitment implies a further principle of social ethics that might aptly be called the *Public Morality Principle*: *Society has a legitimate interest in protecting and encouraging attitudes, practices, institutions and social conditions that tend to sustain the moral sphere, and in discouraging attitudes, practices, institutions and conditions that would lead to its breakdown.*

Such a principle, which follows directly from the requirement of the EP to maintain the moral sphere to the degree possible, has numerous implications for social policy that go beyond those discussed in Section 3.

---

[14] Plato 1987; De Tocqueville 1974.

Treating persons with respect in the sense of openness (which is equivalent to treating them as ends) does entail according them rights and liberties against the interference of the state, of the kinds discussed in Section 3. These rights and liberties are a central concern in free societies, as Mill and other classical liberal theorists have emphasized. But other political theorists, including communitarians and feminists, have often criticized liberal political theories for putting too much emphasis on individual freedoms, while paying too little attention to social institutions such as the family, the extended family, neighborhoods, schools, churches, associations, and the like, that make it possible for individual liberties to flourish.[15] If such supporting social institutions that are involved in morally educating the young and maintaining societal bonds are dysfunctional, or ineffective, one can scarcely maintain a moral sphere in which individual freedoms can be exercised and everyone is treated as an end and not used as a mere means.[16]

The Public Morality Principle is meant to address these civic concerns by protecting and promoting attitudes, practices, institutions and social conditions that sustain the moral sphere. Such a principle would guide all social policy and private initiatives having to do with the health of families, moral education in the schools, social programs and community efforts – such as Head Start, Big Brothers and Big Sisters, boys and girls clubs, and others, that provide support in educating and morally directing the young. It would guide programs dealing with teen pregnancy, drug abuse, drunk driving, disaster relief, job retraining, child abuse, gang violence, and society's other pressing social problems that lead to breakdown of the moral sphere. It would encourage support groups for mental illness and alcoholism, rape crisis centers, suicide hotlines, shelters for battered spouses, hospices and counseling for runaways, half-way houses for parolees or for the mentally impaired, educational aids for the blind and deaf and others with disabilities, to allow them to become productive and respected members of society. Such efforts and many others of similar kinds would not merely be viewed as social programs, but as matters of public morality.

[15] For example, Bellah *et al.* 1985, Sandel 1983, Taylor 1989, Etzioni 1995 and communitarian contributors to Rasmussen 1990. Kymlicka 2002, chapter 9, develops this theme in persuasive fashion. For feminist theorists see note 20.

[16] Louden 2000 perceptively argues that such issues are addressed by Kant in what he calls the "impure" part of Kant's ethics which is "not about deriving duties from the categorical imperative, but about making morality efficacious in human life." In the MST, this "impure" part of ethics follows from the EP itself insofar as it requires "doing what one can to maintain the moral sphere" in adverse circumstances.

The Public Morality Principle does not require that government provide all these services. What it requires is only that a "good society" should provide them *in some way or another*, public or private. The presumptions of liberty and individual responsibility (which follow from the respect for persons enjoined by the Ends Principle) suggest that services supporting the moral sphere be provided to the degree possible by private institutions and initiatives, beginning with the family, the most important institution of society for supporting the moral sphere, and by local governments to the degree possible to maximize citizen input. But government support at higher levels is usually helpful and often indispensable. Private institutions themselves, such as the family, often need public support to do their job well. Where the line is to be drawn between state and private initiatives should therefore be a matter of continuing political debate in free and democratic societies. But the overriding goal implied by the MST is that social initiatives, falling under the Public Morality Principle, be attended to in some way or another if the moral order of such societies is to be sustained.

## 6. MORAL EDUCATION

Perhaps the most important application of the Public Morality Principle to social ethics and to the maintenance of a moral sphere concerns the moral education of the young. This topic, important in itself for social and political philosophy, has the further merit of returning us full circle to issues about pluralism and relativism with which this book began.

One of the social consequences of relativistic thinking in modern societies, decried by Allan Bloom and other social critics mentioned in Chapter 2, is a method of moral education advocated by many education theorists called "values clarification."[17] This method is based on the premise that in modern pluralist and democratic societies, no one can claim to have *the* right set of values to pass on to other people's children. Teachers in publically supported schools must therefore focus on the means by which people come to have and accept values. Through group discussion, in which the teacher remains non-judgmental, young people are supposed to express and discuss their differing values in order to come to a better understanding of their own values, to self-acceptance, and to respect for the differing values of others.

[17] For an overview of the values clarification method and its role in values education, see Maury Smith 1977. Bloom's critique is in 1987: 61.

Critics of this method of teaching values, such as Bloom, argue that it is a road to relativism and indifference.[18] What, they ask, will students take away from a method in which they are allowed to express their differing values and beliefs and in which no one, including the teacher, is allowed to be judgmental about the beliefs expressed? Such a method is likely to lead to the belief that no view of right or wrong is objectively better than any other, and each is to be respected so long as it feels good to the one who "accepts" it.

It is instructive to look at this controversy through the lens of the ethical arguments of earlier chapters and the Public Morality Principle based upon those arguments. Viewed through this lens, the values clarification method is a reaction to conditions of pluralism and uncertainty in modern societies. Its advocates share the natural reaction of ordinary persons reared in free and democratic societies mentioned in Chapter 2, who believe that openness, or initial respect for differing points of view and ways of life, is the only proper response to pluralism and uncertainty.

What advocates of values clarification fail to note, however, is that consistently maintaining such an attitude of openness *to all* persons and points of view (as they advocate), *if* one does it for the educational purpose of finding out which points of view and ways of life are ultimately worthy of being treated with openness by all persons, would not lead to relativist conclusions. Rather one would thereby be led to ethical principles that *are* judgmental and tell us that some ways of acting are right and others wrong and some ways of life more worthy of being treated with openness than others.

In sum, if one starts with openness, as the values clarification method does, but does so as part of a search for wisdom about what should be regarded as objectively good from all points of view, one would not end by asserting that every view is as good as every other. Some views would be more worthy of respect in the sense of openness by all persons and some less worthy. This theme would be applicable to moral education at all levels, including the home. As children in modern societies are confronted through media and in daily life with different points of view from all over the global city, teachers and parents may say the following:

Be open if you wish to other points of view. This may be a correct attitude *to start with* if you want to learn what is objectively good. But remember that this attitude of openness does not mean anything goes, ethically speaking. To the contrary, trying to sustain an attitude of openness respect toward *all* persons

---

[18] Bloom ibid.

leads to the conclusion that some ways of acting and living are less unqualifiedly worthy of such respect than others.

And note that some of the ways of acting and living that are less worthy are signified by those familiar commandments you have heard from your parents and in your churches: Don't kill or lie. Don't steal or cheat. Don't be unkind or inconsiderate or cause harm unnecessarily or be unfair. Don't treat others as mere means to your own ends unless you are forced into it by their actions. And when you must, when the moral sphere breaks down, do what you can to restore and preserve conditions in this world where such respect for others can flourish once again: Use minimum force and be as fair or just as imperfect conditions may allow. To love rightly is to recognize that you cannot love everything equally – except perhaps in a perfect world – and the world is usually imperfect. But even when you cannot love equally in an imperfect world, you can love well by striving to restore and preserve conditions in which mutual respect and concern can flourish once again.

## 7. VIRTUES AND MORAL EDUCATION

These remarks have further implications for controversies about the teaching of the *virtues*, or more generally "character education," in publically supported school curricula.

The teaching of virtues presents a problem similar to the teaching of values – the problem of pluralism. Which virtues should be singled out, if virtues are to be a part of state-supported education in pluralist societies? Will it not be the case that any chosen table of virtues will privilege some particular morality or religion or some particular conception of the good that will be favored over others? And is this not another case of government or the state – in the person of public school teachers, school boards or local governments – being judgmental and imposing one favored view of the good on other people's children?

These questions may be addressed, I suggest, in a way that is similar to the way in which concerns about values clarification were addressed. Consider, as an example, those virtues that have frequently been suggested by various public interest groups in the United States which have been promoting the teaching of virtues in the schools. Such groups have struggled to come up with a list of virtues that could gain general consensus and avoid dissent; and the lists of virtues they suggest differ in details. But it is interesting that a core set of virtues appears again and again on their lists, including, most commonly, the following six: *honesty, respect, responsibility, fairness, trustworthiness* and *caring.*[19] The proposals usually

---

[19] Such core virtues also play a prominent role in the work of philosophers who discuss the psychology of moral character, e.g., Thomas 1989.

call for encouraging these virtues by simple examples and activities from the earliest grades onward.

I suggest that we take a closer look at this list: honesty, respect, responsibility, fairness, trustworthiness and caring. Are these not just the traits of character one would wish to instill in young people in order to maintain and promote institutions and behavior that would sustain and preserve the moral sphere, as the Public Morality Principle requires? To be dishonest and deceptive in dealing with others is to break the moral sphere. To *respect* others, in the sense of treating them to the degree possible as ends and not mere means to one's own ends, is the essence of what it means to maintain a moral sphere. To be *responsible* about keeping one's commitments and promises to others, including the commitments of marriage, parenthood, work and friendship, is also part of what it means to treat those others as ends and not merely as means to one's own ends; and such commitments (of parenthood, etc.) are essential to the maintenance of a moral sphere. To be as *fair* as possible in resolving conflicts of interest in a manner that respects the interests of everyone involved, and to be *trustworthy* in one's dealings with others in work, business and private life – all are traits that would promote and sustain the moral sphere as required by the Public Morality Principle.

## 8. JUSTICE AND CARE: FEMINIST THEMES

The final virtue on the list, that of *care* for others (including those who are deprived or vulnerable, the young, the elderly, the sick and infirm), has a special place in the argument of earlier chapters. It is related to the objective worthiness for care or concern for the inscapes of others upon which the Ends Principle and the idea of a moral sphere is based. A "good society" intent on maintaining a moral sphere as the Public Morality Principle requires would also make prominent the promotion of such a virtue in its young people.

It is interesting that the virtue of caring also plays a central role in some modern virtue ethical theories, such as that of Michael Slote (2007), as well as in many contemporary feminist ethical theories, which emphasize the virtues.[20] Feminist theorist Virginia Held, along with many other feminist theorists, argues, for example, that society includes persons in

---

[20] Contemporary literature on feminist ethics supporting this claim is voluminous. A mere sampling would include Noddings 2002; Calhoun 1988; Jaggar 1995; Okin 1989; Ruddick 1989; Card 1991, 1999; Held 1995, 2006; Clement 1996; Harrington 1999. Mendus 2002 emphasizes the role of caring to moral education in general.

various degrees of dependency, children, the elderly, the sick and infirm, and so on; and caring is the glue that holds such a society together.[21] The arguments of the MST for the centrality of caring differ from those of a virtue ethicist, such as Slote, or feminist theorists, such as Held. But there is agreement on the point that a good society intent on maintaining a moral sphere of life would promote such a virtue in its young people and indeed in all its people.

A related point of importance concerning contemporary feminist ethical theory is the following: Connecting the virtue of care to the objective worthiness for concern, as in the MST, allows one to give a unified account of what feminist moral theorists call an *"ethics of justice"* and an *"ethics of care."*[22] As argued in Chapter 12, justice in the sense of respecting the ways of life of persons, or allowing them to pursue their freely chosen ends, is the specific *form* that care or concern for the inscapes of others would take, *when* those others are rational beings in their maturity, capable of choosing their own ends. Such mutual respect for mature and reflective beings comprises an "ethics of justice."

But when it comes to persons in various stages of dependency, such as children, the sick, the infirm, the elderly, and so on, the form that care or concern for the inscapes of others must take is one of caring that their basic needs and interests are satisfied and doing what one can to enable these outcomes. Such care for the needs of those in various stages of dependency is characteristic of an "ethics of care." Thus, the demands of both justice and care emerge from a common root in the concern for the inscapes of others which takes different forms depending on the status of those to whom such concern is directed.

In summary, the Public Morality Principle directs our attention to the fact that maintaining a moral sphere in which all persons can pursue ends of their own choosing entails more than preserving individual rights and freedoms against the encroachment of the state. For the rights and freedoms in question are not self-sustaining and do not exist in a vacuum. They require the existence of a moral sphere; and that moral sphere is a vulnerable thing, depending for its preservation on the virtues and

---

[21] Held 2006: 542ff.

[22] This distinction is central in a good deal of the feminist literature cited in note 20. Many of those cited there and other feminists argue that the ethics of justice and ethics of care are not competing theories, but complementary. A case for this is strongly made as well by Sterba 1998 and Kymlicka 2002. Sterba generally argues for common ground among apparently different ethical perspectives. Brock (1999) takes the argument for complementarity one step further by arguing that a coherent conception of just deserts, hence of justice broadly conceived, entails that we must also care about people's starting positions and hence about their basic needs.

character of those who participate in it. As James Madison said: "If there be no virtue among us, no form of government can render us secure. To suppose that any form of government will secure liberty and happiness without any virtue in the people is a chimerical idea."[23]

The Public Morality Principle supports this idea, first, by requiring support for what might be called the "ethical infrastructure" of society – those institutions, such as home, family, schools, churches, neighborhoods, charitable organizations, and the like, that help to sustain the moral sphere; and second, by requiring the cultivation of attitudes and virtues that de Tocqueville called "habits of the heart" that make it possible to maintain a moral order.

### 9. CONCLUSION: POLITICAL THEORY AND THE QUEST FOR WISDOM

Among classical political philosophers, such as Plato and Aristotle, politics was continuous with the ethical search for the good and the good life. Many modern political thinkers have been suspicious of this traditional view because it seemed to imply that one must first determine by the use of one's reason what the good life was and then arrange a political order to which everyone must conform in the light of this knowledge. And the "conditions of modernity," mentioned in Chapter 1 – pluralism, uncertainty and the "sunderings" of fact and value, theoretical and practical inquiry, and so on – have made many modern thinkers less confident than the great ancient thinkers that it was possible to find definitive answers to, or agreement of reasonable people on, such deep questions.[24]

The suggestion of this chapter is that the connection between politics and the search for the good need not be abandoned in the face of pluralism, uncertainty and other conditions of modernity, though it must be reconceived. We do not have to assume that the good or the good life can be known in a definitive way and such knowledge then applied to found a political order to which all should conform. For it is not the attainment of knowledge of the final good that provides the basis for political order. Rather it is the *search* or *quest* for knowledge of a good as yet unknown and always to some degree beyond our grasp that provides the basis for a political order. Ethical principles arise as the conditions for this search or quest.

[23] Federalist Paper #10.
[24] Larmore spells out this theme at length in two astute studies (1987, 1996).

These remarks return us to the central theme of this book, stated in Chapter 1 and more fully in Chapter 2, which is worth restating here in conclusion:

Inquiry into the truth about ethical matters and the nature of the good life must involve practical engagement in the world, including engagement with others. But such practical engagement, if it is to yield ethical insight, must be part of an overall search for wisdom, in the sense of a search for what is objectively true and good from every point of view, not merely what is good for oneself or from one's own point of view. The attitude of openness is an expression of this latter requirement. By opening one's minds initially to all points of view in an effort to find out what is true from all points of view, not just from one's own, and striving to maintain this ideal of openness to all in the face of obstacles in one's practical engagements with others, one finds that some ways of life are more worthy of being treated with openness by others and some less worthy. Practical inquiry about the good may thus be viewed as experimental, like theoretical inquiry into nature, but practical inquiry is experimental in its own distinctive way.

# References

Ackerman, Bruce. 1982. *Social Justice and the Liberal State*. New Haven: Yale University Press.

Actenberg, Deborah. 2002. *Cognition of Value in Aristotle's Ethics*. Albany: State University of New York Press.

Adams, Don. 1993. "Love and Impartiality." *American Philosophical Quarterly* 30: 223–34.

Adams, Robert Merrihew. 1976. "Motive Utilitarianism." *Journal of Philosophy* 23: 167–87.

1999. *Finite and Infinite Goods: A Framework for Ethics*. Oxford: Oxford University Press.

2001. "Scanlon's Contractualism." *Philosophical Review* 110: 563–86.

2006. *A Theory of Virtue*. Oxford: Oxford University Press.

Alexander, J. McKensie. 2007. *The Structural End of Morality*. Cambridge: Cambridge University Press.

Ameriks, Karl. 2000. *Kant and the Fate of Autonomy*. Cambridge: Cambridge University Press.

Anderson, Elizabeth. 1991. "John Stuart Mill and Experiments in Living." *Ethics* 102: 4–26.

1993. *Value in Ethics and Economics*. Cambridge MA: Harvard University Press.

Anderson, Owen. 2005. Review of Audi 2004. *Review of Metaphysics*: 873–74.

Annas, Julia. 1993. *The Morality of Happiness*. Oxford: Oxford University Press.

Appiah, Kwame Anthony. 2006. *Cosmopolitanism: Ethics in a World of Strangers*. New York: W. W. Norton.

Aquinas, Thomas. 1950. *Summa Theologiae*. 3 vols. Rome: Marietti.

Aristotle. 1941. *The Basic Works of Aristotle*. Ed. by R. McKeon. New York: Random House.

1983. *The Ethics of Aristotle: Nichomachean Ethics*. Trans. by J. A. K. Thomson. Harmondsworth: Penguin Books.

Arneson, Richard. 1990. "Liberalism, Distributive Subjectivism and Equal Opportunity for Welfare." *Philosophy and Public Affairs* 19: 158–94.

2002. "The End of Welfare as We Know it: Scanlon versus Welfarist Consequentialism." *Social Theory and Practice* 28: 315–36.

Ashford, Elizabeth and Tim Mulgan. 2007. "Contractualism," in the *Stanford Encyclopedia of Philosophy*. http://plato.stanford.Edu/entries/contractualism/

Audi, Robert. 2001. "A Kantian Intuitionism." *Mind* 110: 601–35.

2004. *The Good In the Right*. Princeton: Princeton University Press.

Augustine. 1948. *Basic Writings of Saint Augustine*. Ed. by A. Pegis. New York: Random House.

Axelrod, Robert. 1984. *The Evolution of Cooperation*. New York: Basic Books.

Baghramian, Maria. 2004. *Relativism*. London: Routledge.

Baier, Annette. 1986. "Trust and Anti-trust." *Ethics* 96: 231–60.

Baier, Kurt. 1958. *The Moral Point of View*. Ithaca NY: Cornell University Press.

1995. *The Rational and the Moral Order*. Chicago and LaSalle IL: Open Court.

Bailey, James Wood. 1997. *Utilitarianism, Institutions and Justice*. New York: Oxford University Press.

Baldwin, Thomas. 1990. *G. E. Moore*. London: Routledge.

Banham, Gary. 2003. *Kant's Practical Philosophy: From Critique to Doctrine*. Basingstoke: Palgrave.

Baron, Marcia W. 1991. "Impartiality and Friendship." *Ethics* 101: 836–57.

1995. *Kantian Ethics Almost Without Apology*. Ithaca NY: Cornell University Press.

Barrow, Robin. 1991. *Utilitarianism: A Contemporary Statement*. Aldershot: Edward Elgar.

Barry, Brian. 1995. *Justice as Impartiality*. Oxford: Clarendon Press.

Barry, Norman. 1990. *Welfare*. Minneapolis: University of Minnesota Press.

Bayles, Michael D. (ed.) 1968. *Contemporary Utilitarianism*. Garden City NY: Anchor Books.

Becker, Lawrence. 1998. *A New Stoicism*. Princeton: Princeton University Press.

Bedke, Matthew S. 2008. "Ethical Intuitions: What They Are, What They Are Not, and How They Justify." *American Philosophical Quarterly* 45: 253–69.

Bellah, R., R. Madsen, W. Sullivan, A. Swidler and S. Tipton. 1985. *Habits of the Heart*. New York: Harper & Row.

Benedikt, Amelie. (Unpublished) *Wisdom: History and Analysis*. Ph.D. Dissertation. The University of Texas at Austin.

Benedikt, Michael. (Unpublished) *Value, Economics, Psychology, Life*.

Berger, Fred R. 1984. *Happiness, Justice and Freedom: The Moral and Political Philosophy of J. S. Mill*. Berkeley: University of California Press.

Berlin, Isaiah. 1965. *Four Essays On Liberty*. London: Oxford University Press.

Bernstein, Mark. 1998. *On Moral Considerability*. New York: Oxford University Press.

Blackburn, Simon. 1993. *Essays in Quasi-realism*. Oxford: Oxford University Press.

1998. *Ruling Passions*. Oxford: Oxford University Press.

1999. "Am I Right?" *New York Times* February 21, 1999.

2005. *Truth: A Guide*. Oxford: Oxford University Press.

Bloom, Allan. 1987. *The Closing of the American Mind*. New York: Simon & Schuster.

Bloomfield, Paul. 2001. *Moral Reality*. New York: Oxford University Press.

2003. "Is There a Moral Highground?" *Southern Journal of Philosophy* 41: 511–26.

Blum, Lawrence. 1980. *Friendship, Altruism and Morality*. London: Routledge & Kegan Paul.

1994. *Moral Perception and Particularity*. London: Routledge & Kegan Paul.

Bond, E. J. 1983. *Reason and Value*. Cambridge: Cambridge University Press.

Bonevac, Daniel. 2004. "Reflection Without Equilibrium." *Journal of Philosophy* 51: 363–88.

Bowlin, John. 1999. *Contingency and Fortune in Aquinas's Ethics*. Cambridge: Cambridge University Press.

Boyd, Richard. 1988. "How to Be a Moral Realist." In Sayre-McCord (ed.): 181–228.

Brand-Ballard, Jeffrey. 2000. "Contractualism and Deontic Restrictions." *Ethics* 114: 269–300.

Brandt, Richard. 1992. *Morality, Utilitarianism and Rights*. New York: Cambridge University Press.

Bratman, Michael. 1987. *Intentions, Plans and Practical Reason*. Cambridge MA: Harvard University Press.

Braybrooke, David. 2001. *Natural Law Modernized*. Toronto: University of Toronto Press.

Brewer, Talbot. 2009. *The Retrieval of Ethics*. Oxford: Oxford University Press.

Brink, David O. 1989. *Moral Realism and the Foundations of Ethics*. Cambridge: Cambridge University Press.

2006. "Some Forms and Limits of Consequentialism." In Copp (ed.): 380–423.

Broadie, Sarah Waterlow. 1991. *Ethics With Aristotle*. Oxford: Oxford University Press.

Brock, Gillian. 1999. "Just Deserts and Needs." *Southern Journal of Philosophy* 37: 165–88.

Broome, John. 1991. *Weighing Goods*. Oxford: Blackwell.

Brown, S. C. (ed.) 1984. *Objectivity and Cultural Divergence*. Cambridge: Cambridge University Press.

Brown, Stephen. 2004. "Naturalized Virtue Ethics and the Epistemological Gap." *Journal of Moral Philosophy*: 197–209.

Budziszewski, Jay. 1986. *The Resurrection of Nature*. Ithaca NY: Cornell University Press.

Buss, Sarah. 1999. "Respect for Persons." *Canadian Journal of Philosophy* 29: 517–50.

2006. "Needs (Someone Else's), Projects (My Own) and Reasons." *Journal of Philosophy* 103: 373–402.

2008. "What Does the Structure of Intentional Action Tell Us About Our Reasons for Action?" *Mind* 117: 1–28.

Butler, Joseph. 1983. *Five Sermons Preached at Rolls Chapel.* Ed. by S. Darwall. Indianapolis: Hackett.

Calhoun, Cheshire. 1988. "Justice, Care, Gender Bias." *Journal of Philosophy* 85: 451–63.

Campbell, Joseph. 1956. *The Hero With a Thousand Faces.* Garden City NY: Anchor Books.

Card, Claudia (ed.) 1991. *Feminist Ethics.* Lawrence: University of Kansas Press.

——— 1999. *On Feminist Ethics and Politics.* Lawrence: University of Kansas Press.

Carlson, Erik. 1995. *Consequentialism Reconsidered.* Dordrecht: Kluwer.

Carson, Thomas. 2004. Review of Stratton-Lake (ed.) 2002. *Ethics* 116: 175–77.

Chang, Ruth (ed.). 1997. *Incommensurability, Incomparability and Practical Reason.* Cambridge MA: Harvard University Press.

Chappell, Timothy. 1995. *Understanding Human Goods.* Edinburgh: Edinburgh University Press.

Chatterlee, Deen K. (ed.) 2004. *The Ethics of Assistance: Morality and the Distant Needy.* Cambridge: Cambridge University Press.

Cicovacki, Pedrag. 2002. "The Illusory Fabric of Kant's True Morality." *The Journal of Value Inquiry* 36: 383–99.

Clement, Grace. 1996. *Care, Autonomy and Justice.* Boulder CO: Westview.

Coburn, Robert. 1982. "Morality, Truth and Relativism." *Ethics* 92: 661–69.

Conly, Sarah. 1983. "Utilitarianism and Integrity." *The Monist* 66: 298–311.

Cook, J. W. 1999. *Morality and Cultural Difference.* Oxford: Oxford University Press.

Cooper, David E. 1978. "Moral Relativism." *Midwest Studies in Philosophy* 3: 97–108.

Cooper, John M. 1975. *Reason and the Human Good in Aristotle.* Cambridge MA: Harvard University Press.

Copp, David. 1995. *Morality, Normativity and Society.* New York: Oxford University Press.

——— (ed.) 2006. *Oxford Handbook of Ethical Theory.* Oxford: Oxford University Press.

——— 2009. "Is Society-centered Moral Theory a Contemporary Version of Natural Law Theory?" *Dialogue* 48: 19–36.

Copp, David and David Sobel. 2004. "Morality and Virtue: An Assessment of Some Recent Work in Virtue Ethics." *Ethics* 114: 514–54.

Copp, David and David Zimmerman (eds.) 1985. *Morality, Reason and Truth.* Totowa NJ: Rowman and Allanheld.

Cottingham, John. 1983. "Ethics and Impartiality." *Philosophical Studies* 43: 83–99.

——— 1991. "The Ethics of Self Concern." *Ethics* 101: 798–817.

Cranor, C. F. 1982. "Limitations of Respect for Persons Theories." In *Respect for Persons*, O. H. Green (ed.) *Tulane Studies in Philosophy* 31. Tulane University Press.

Crary, Alice. 2007. *Beyond Moral Judgment*. Cambridge, MA: Harvard University Press.

Crisp, Roger (ed.) 1997. *Mill on Utilitarianism*. London: Routledge.

2006. *Reasons and the Good*. Oxford: Oxford University Press.

Crisp, Roger and Michael Slote (eds.) 1997. *Virtue Ethics*. Oxford: Oxford University Press.

Cullity, Garrett. 2004. *The Moral Demands of Affluence*. Oxford: Clarendon Press.

Cummiskey, David. 1996. *Kantian Consequentialism*. New York: Oxford University Press.

Cuneo, Terence. 2007. *The Normative Web: An Argument for Moral Realism*. New York: Oxford University Press.

Damasio, Antonio. 1994. *Descartes' Error*. New York: Quill.

Dancy, Jonathan. 2000. *Practical Reality*. Oxford: Oxford University Press.

2004. *Ethics Without Principles*. Oxford: Oxford University Press.

Danto, Arthur. 1981. *The Transfiguration of the Commonplace*. Cambridge MA: Harvard University Press.

D'Arms, Justin and Daniel Jacobson. 2006. "Sensibility Theory and Projectivism." In Copp (ed.): 163–85.

Darwall, Stephen. 1977. "Two Kinds of Respect." *Ethics* 88: 36–49.

2006. *The Second Person*. Cambridge MA: Harvard University Press.

Darwall, Stephen, Allan Gibbard and Peter Railton (eds.) 1992. "Toward Fin de Siecle Ethics: Some Trends." *Philosophical Review* 101: 115–89.

Dasgupta, Partha. 1993. *An Inquiry Into Well-being and Destitution*. Oxford: Clarendon Press.

Davidson, Donald. 1973–4. "On the Very Idea of a Conceptual Scheme." *Proceedings of the American Philosophical Association* 47: 5–20.

Dean, Richard. 2006. *The Value of Humanity in Kant's Moral Theory*. Oxford: Oxford University Press.

Deigh, John. 2002. "Promises Under Fire." *Ethics* 112: 483–507.

DePaul, Michael. 1993. *Balance and Refinement: Beyond Coherentism in Moral Inquiry*. London: Routledge.

De Tocqueville, Alexis. 1974. *Democracy in America*. 2 vols. New York: Schocken Books.

Deveaux, Monique. 2000. *Cultural Pluralism and Dilemmas of Justice*. Ithaca, NY: Cornell University Press.

Devlin, Patrick. 1965. *The Enforcement of Morals*. London: Oxford University Press.

Dickie, George and R. J. Sclafani (eds.) 1977. *Aesthetics: A Critical Anthology*. New York: St. Martin's Press.

Dillon, Robin S. 1992. "Respect and Care: Toward Moral Integration." *Canadian Journal of Philosophy* 22: 105–32.

2007. "Respect." *Stanford Encyclopedia of Philosophy*. http://plato.stanford.edu/entries/respect/

Donagan, Alan. 1977. *A Theory of Morality*. Chicago: University of Chicago Press.

Doris, John. 2002. *Lack of Character*. Cambridge: Cambridge University Press.

Double, Richard. 1999. "Morality, Impartiality and What We Can Ask of Persons." *American Philosophical Quarterly* 36: 153–63.

Dreier, James. 2006. "Moral Relativism and Moral Nihilism." In Copp (ed.): 240–64.

Driver, Julia. 2001. *Uneasy Virtue*. Cambridge: Cambridge University Press.

2004. Review of Vogler 2002. *Ethics* 114: 845–48.

Dworkin, Gerald. 2002. "Contractualism and the Normativity of Principles." *Ethics* 112: 471–82.

Dworkin, Ronald. 1978. *Taking Rights Seriously*. Cambridge MA: Harvard University Press.

1985. *A Matter of Principle*. Cambridge MA: Harvard University Press.

Eaton, Marcia M. 1988. *Basic Issues in Aesthetics*. Belmont CA: Wadsworth.

Etzioni, Amitai. 1995. *New Communitarian Thinking*. Charlottesville: University of Virginia Press.

Ewing, A. C. 1953. *Ethics*. London: English Universities Press.

Fairbanks, Sandra Jane. 2000. *Kant's Moral Theory and the Destruction of the Self*. Boulder CO: Westview Press.

Feinberg, Joel. 1982–88. *The Moral Limits of the Criminal Law*. 4 vols. Oxford: Oxford University Press.

Feldman, Fred. 1997. *Utilitarianism, Hedonism and Desert: Essays on Moral Philosophy*. Cambridge: Cambridge University Press.

2004. *Pleasure and the Good Life*. Oxford: Clarendon Press.

Finnis, John. 1980. *Natural Law and Natural Rights*. Oxford: Oxford University Press.

Foot, Philippa. 2001. *Natural Goodness*. Oxford: Oxford University Press.

Frankena, William. 1939. "The Naturalistic Fallacy." *Mind* 48: 464–77.

1973. *Ethics*. Englewood Cliffs NJ: Prentice Hall.

1986. "The Ethics of Respect for Persons." *Philosophical Topics* 14: 149–67.

Frey, R. G. 2000. "Act Utilitarianism." In LaFollette (ed.): 165–82.

Frey, R. G. and Christopher Morris (eds.) 1993. *Value, Welfare and Morality*. Cambridge: Cambridge University Press.

Friedman, Marilyn. 1989. "The Impracticality of Impartiality." *Journal of Philosophy* 86: 645–56.

1991. "The Practice of Partiality." *Ethics* 101: 818–35.

Galston, William. 2002. *Liberal Pluralism: The Implications of Value Pluralism for Political Theory*. New York: Cambridge University Press.

Gaut, Berys. 2002. "Justifying Moral Pluralism." In Stratton-Lake (ed.): 137–60.

Gauthier, David. 1986. *Morals By Agreement*. Oxford: Oxford University Press.

George, Robert P. 1993. *Making Men Moral: Civil Liberties and Public Morality*. Oxford: Clarendon Press.

Gert, Bernard. 1970. *The Moral Rules*. New York: Harper and Row.

1998. *Morality: A New Justification of the Moral Rules.* New York: Oxford University Press.

2004. *Common Morality: Deciding What to Do.* New York: Oxford University Press.

Gert, Joshua. 2006. Review of Audi 2004. *Mind* 141: 121–25.

Gewirth, Alan. 1977. *Reason and Morality.* Chicago: University of Chicago Press.

Gibbard, Allan. 1990. *Wise Choices, Apt Feelings.* Cambridge MA: Harvard University Press.

2008. *Reconciling Our Aims: In Search of the Basis of Ethics.* Oxford: Oxford University Press.

Gilbert, Jack. 1962. *Poems.* New Haven: Yale University Press.

Glover, Jonathan (ed.) 1990. *Utilitarianism and Its Critics.* London: MacMillan.

Goethe, J. W. 1960. *Faust.* Trans. by P. Wayne. Harmondsworth: Penguin Books.

Goodin, Robert. 1985. *Protecting the Vulnerable: A Reanalysis of Our Social Responsibilities.* Chicago: University of Chicago Press.

1995. *Utilitarianism As a Public Philosophy.* Cambridge: Cambridge University Press.

Goodin, Robert and Andrew Reeve (eds.) 1989. *Liberal Neutrality.* London: Routledge.

Gottlieb, Paula. 2009. *The Virtue of Aristotle's Ethics.* Cambridge: Cambridge University Press.

Gowans, Chris. 2008. "Moral Relativism." *Stanford Encyclopedia of Philosophy.* http://plato.stanford.edu/entries/moral-relativism/

Grenberg, Jeanine M. 2005. *Kant and the Ethics of Humility: A Story of Dependence, Corruption and Virtue.* Cambridge: Cambridge University Press.

Griffin, James. 1986. *Well Being: Its Meaning and Measurement.* Oxford: Oxford University Press.

Grisez, Germain and Russell Shaw. 1974. *Beyond the New Morality.* Notre Dame: University of Notre Dame Press.

Grunebaum, James O. 1993. "Friendship, Morality and Special Obligations." *American Philosophical Quarterly* 30: 51–61.

Gutmann, Amy. 1987. *Democratic Education.* Princeton: Princeton University Press.

Guyer, Paul (ed.) 1992. *The Cambridge Companion to Kant.* Cambridge: Cambridge University Press.

(ed.) 1998. *Kant's Groundwork of the Metaphysics of Morals: Critical Essays.* Lanham MD: Rowman and Littlefield.

2000. *Kant on Freedom, Law and Happiness.* Cambridge: Cambridge University Press.

Haksar, Vinit. 1977. *Equality, Liberty and Perfectionism.* Oxford: Oxford University Press.

Hampton, Jean. 2007. *The Intrinsic Worth of Persons: Contractarianism in Moral and Political Philosophy.* Cambridge: Cambridge University Press.

Hardin, Russell. 1995. *One for All: The Logic of Group Conflict*. Princeton: Princeton University Press.

Hare, R. M. 1979. "What is Wrong With Slavery?" *Philosophy and Public Affairs* 8: 103–21.

1981. *Moral Thinking*. Oxford: Oxford University Press.

Harman, Gilbert. 1977. *The Nature of Morality*. New York: Oxford University Press.

1999. "Moral Philosophy Meets Social Psychology." *Proceedings of the Aristotelian Society* 119: 315–31.

2000. "Moral Relativism Defended." In *Explaining Value and Other Essays in Moral Philosophy*. Oxford: Oxford University Press: 77–99.

Harman, Gilbert and Judith Jarvis Thomson. 1996. *Moral Relativism and Moral Objectivity*. Oxford: Blackwell.

Harré, Rom. 1980. *Social Being*. New York: Littlefield.

Harrington, Mona. 1999. *Care and Equality: Inventing a New Family Politics*. New York: Knopf.

Harris, George W. 1997. *Dignity and Vulnerability*. Berkeley: University of California Press.

1999. *Agent-centered Morality*. Berkeley: University of California Press.

Hart, H. L. A. 1965. *Law, Liberty and Morals*. Stanford: Stanford University Press.

Hauser, M. D. 2005. *Moral Minds: How Nature Designed Our Universal Sense of Right and Wrong*. New York: Harper-Collins.

Haybron, Daniel M. 2008. *The Pursuit of Unhappiness*. Oxford: Clarendon Press.

Held, Virginia (ed.) 1995. *Justice and Care: Essential Readings in Feminist Ethics*. Boulder CO: Westview Press.

2006. "The Ethics of Care." In Copp (ed.) 537–66.

Helm, Bennett. 2001. *Emotional Reason: Deliberation, Motivation and the Nature of Value*. Cambridge: Cambridge University Press.

Herman, Barbara. 1993. *The Practice of Moral Judgment*. Cambridge MA: Harvard University Press.

Heydt, Colin. 2006. *Rethinking Mill's Ethics: Character and Aesthetic Education*. New York: Continuum Books.

Hill, Thomas E., Jr. 1992. *Dignity and Practical Reason in Kant's Moral Theory*. Ithaca NY: Cornell University Press.

2006. "Kantian Normative Ethics." In Copp (ed.): 480–574.

Hittenger, Russell. 1987. *A Critique of the New Natural Law Theory*. Notre Dame: University of Notre Dame Press.

Hobbes, Thomas. 1958. *Leviathan*. Indianapolis: Bobbs-Merrill.

Honderich, Ted (ed.) 1985. *Morality and Objectivity*. London: Routledge & Kegan Paul.

Hooker, Brad. 2000. *Ideal Code, Real World: A Rule Consequentialist Theory of Morality*. Oxford: Clarendon Press.

2000a. "Reflective Equilibrium and Rule-consequentialism." In Hooker, Mason and Miller (eds.): 222–38.

2003. "Contractualism, Spare Wheel and Aggregation." In Matravers (ed.): 53–76.

Hooker, Brad, Elinor Mason and Dale E. Miller (eds.) 2000. *Morality, Rules and Consequences: A Critical Reader*. Lanham MD: Rowman and Littlefield.

Hooker, Brad and Margaret Little (eds.) 2000. *Moral Particularism*. Oxford: Oxford University Press.

Hopkins, Gerard Manley. 1953. *Poems and Prose of Gerard Manley Hopkins*. Ed. by W. H. Gardner. New York: Viking Penguin.

Horton, John and Susan Mendus (eds.) 1994. *After MacIntyre*. Cambridge: Polity Press.

Huang, C. (trans. and ed.) 1997. *The Analects of Confucius*. Oxford: Oxford University Press.

Hudson, S. D. 1980. "The Nature of Respect." *Social Theory and Practice* 6: 69–90.

Huemer, Michael. 2005. *Ethical Intuitionism*. New York: Palgrave MacMillan.

Hume, David. 1882. "Of the Standard of Taste." From *Essays, Moral, Political and Literary*. Ed. by T. H. Green. London: Lomans, Green and Company.

Hurka, Thomas. 1993. *Perfectionism*. Oxford: Oxford University Press.

2001. *Virtue, Vice, and Value*. New York: Oxford University Press.

Hurley, Paul. 2003. "Fairness and Beneficence." *Ethics* 113: 841–64.

Hursthouse, Rosalind. 1999. *On Virtue Ethics*. Oxford: Oxford University Press.

Illies, Christian. 2003. *The Grounds of Ethical Judgment: New Transcendental Arguments in Moral Philosophy*. Oxford: Oxford University Press.

Irwin, Terence. 2007. *The Development of Ethics: A Historical and Critical Study: Volume I: From Socrates to the Reformation*. New York: Oxford University Press.

Jaggar, Alison M. 1995. "Caring as a Feminist Practice of Moral Reason." In Held (ed.): 179–202.

Jeske, Diane. 2008. *Rationality and Moral Theory: How Intimacy Generates Reasons*. London: Routledge.

Joyce, Richard. 2006. *The Evolution of Morality*. Cambridge MA: MIT Press.

Kagan, Shelly. 1989. *The Limits of Morality*. Oxford: Oxford University Press.

1998. *Normative Ethics*. Boulder CO: Westview Press.

2000. "Evaluative Focal Points." In Hooker, Mason and D. Miller (eds.): 134–55.

Kamm, Frances. 1989. "Harming Some to Save Others." *Philosophical Studies* 57: 227–60.

1996. *Mortality, Mortality II*. New York: Oxford University Press.

2007. *Intricate Ethics: Rights, Responsibility and Permissible Harm*. Oxford: Oxford University Press.

Kane, Robert. 1985. *Free Will and Values*. Albany: State University of New York Press.

1988. "Prima Facie Good." *The Journal of Value Inquiry* 22: 279–97.

1993. "The Ends of Metaphysics." *International Philosophical Quarterly* 33: 413–28.

1994. *Through the Moral Maze*. Armonk NY: M. E. Sharpe Publishers.

1996. *The Significance of Free Will*. Oxford: Oxford University Press.

1997. "Four Dimensions of Value: From Experience to Worth." *Center: The Journal of American Architecture and Design* 10: 9–15.

1998. "Dimensions of Value and the Aims of Social Inquiry." *American Behavioral Scientist* 41: 578–97.

Kant, Immanuel. 1958. *The Critique of Pure Reason*. Trans. by N. K. Smith. London: MacMillan.

1959. *Foundations of the Metaphysics of Morals and What Is Enlightenment?* Trans. by L. W. Beck. Indianapolis: Bobbs-Merrill.

1964. *The Doctrine of Virtue*. Trans. Mary Gregor. New York: Harper and Row.

1976. "On the Supposed Right to Lie from Altruistic Motives." In *Immanuel Kant: Critique of Practical Reason and Other Writings*. Trans. by L. W. Beck. New York: Garland Press.

Kapur, Neera Badhwar. 1991. "Why It is Wrong to be Always Guided by the Best: Consequentialism and Friendship." *Ethics* 101: 483–500.

Kavka, Gregory. 1986. *Hobbesian Moral and Political Theory*. Princeton: Princeton University Press.

Kekes, John. 1989. *Moral Tradition and Individuality*. Princeton: Princeton University Press.

1993. *The Morality of Pluralism*. Princeton: Princeton University Press.

Kellenberger, James. 2001. *Moral Relativism, Moral Diversity and Human Relations*. Pennsylvania State University Press.

Kerstein, Samuel J. 2002. *Kant's Search for the Supreme Principle of Morality*. Cambridge: Cambridge University Press.

Kierkegaard, Soren. 1954. *Fear and Trembling and Sickness Unto Death*. Trans. W. Lowrie. New York: Anchor Books.

1959. *Either/Or*. Vols. 1 and 2. Trans. W. Lowrie. New York: Doubleday and Company.

Kirk, G. S. and J. E. Raven (eds.) 1960. *The Presocratic Philosophers*. Cambridge: Cambridge University Press.

Kitcher, Philip. 2006. "*Biology and Ethics*." In Copp (ed.): 163–85.

Kolakowski, L. 1989. *The Presence of Myth*. Chicago: University of Chicago Press.

Korsgaard, Christine. 1996. *Creating the Kingdom of Ends*. Cambridge: Cambridge University Press.

1998. "The Right to Lie: Kant on Dealing with Evil." In Rachels (ed.): 282–304.

Kraut, Richard. 1989. *Aristotle on the Human Good*. Princeton: Princeton University Press.

2007. *What is Good and Why: The Ethics of Well-Being*. Cambridge MA: Harvard University Press.

Kumar, Rahul. 2000. "Defending the Moral Moderate: Contractualism and Common Sense." *Philosophy and Public Affairs* 28: 275–309.

Kuper, Andrew. 2002. "Global Poverty Relief – More Than Charity." *Ethics and International Affairs* 16: 107–20.

Kupperman, J. J. 2007. *Ethics and Qualities of Life*. Oxford: Oxford University Press.

Kymlicka, Will. 1989. *Liberalism, Community and Culture*. Oxford: Oxford University Press.

2002. *Contemporary Political Philosophy: An Introduction*. Oxford: Oxford University Press.

LaFollette, Hugh (ed.) 2000. *The Blackwell Guide to Ethical Theory*. Oxford: Blackwell.

Larmore, Charles. 1987. *Patterns of Moral Complexity*. Cambridge: Cambridge University Press.

1996. *The Morals of Modernity*. Cambridge: Cambridge University Press.

Lear, Gabriel Richardson. 2004. *Happy Lives and the Highest Good: An Essay on Aristotle's Nichomachean Ethics*. Princeton: Princeton University Press.

Lem, Stanislaw. 1971. *Solaris*. New York: Berkeley Medallion Books.

Lemos, Noah. 1994. *Intrinsic Value: Concept and Warrant*. Cambridge: Cambridge University Press.

Lewis, C. S. 1962. *Perelandra*. New York: Collier Books.

Lincoln, Abraham. 1953. *The Collected Works of Abraham Lincoln*. Ed. by Roy Basler. New Brunswick NJ: Rutgers University Press.

Lisska, Anthony J. 1996. *Aquinas's Theory of Natural Law*. New York: Oxford University Press.

Lloyd-Thomas, D. A. 1988. *In Defense of Liberalism*. Oxford: Blackwell.

Lockhart, T. (ed.) 2000. *Moral Uncertainty and Its Consequences*. New York: Oxford University Press.

Louden, Robert B. 2000. *Kant's Impure Ethics: From Rational Beings to Human Beings*. New York: Oxford University Press.

Lovibond, Sabina. 2002. *Ethical Formation*. Cambridge MA: Harvard University Press.

Lyons, David. 1965. *Forms and Limits of Utilitiarianism*. Oxford: Clarendon Press.

1994. *Rights, Welfare and Mill's Moral Theory*. New York: Oxford University Press.

2000. "The Moral Opacity of Utilitarianism." In Hooker, Mason and Miller (eds.): 105–20.

Lyotard, Jean-Francois. 1987. *The Postmodern Condition*. Minneapolis: University of Minnesota Press.

Macedo, Stephen. 1990. *Liberal Virtues*. Oxford: Oxford University Press.

MacIntyre, Alasdair. 1981. *After Virtue*. Notre Dame: University of Notre Dame Press.

1988. *Whose Justice? Which Rationality?* Notre Dame: University of Notre Dame Press.

1990. *Three Rival Versions of Moral Enquiry*. Notre Dame: University of Notre Dame Press.

Mackie, J. L. 1977. *Ethics: Inventing Right and Wrong*. Harmondsworth: Penguin Books.

Malhotra, A. K. 1999. *Transcreation of the Bhagavad-Gita*. Upper Saddle River NJ: Prentice-Hall.

Matravers, Matt (ed.) 2003. *Scanlon and Contractualism*. London: Frank Cass Publishers.

Mayerfeld, Jamie. 1999. *Suffering and Moral Responsibility*. Oxford: Oxford University Press.

McCabe, David. 1995. "Liberal Education is Moral Education." *Social Theory and Practice* 21: 83–96.

McGinn, Colin. 1999. "Can We Ever Understand Consciousness?" *New York Review of Books* (June 10, 1999): 44–8.

1999a. "Reasons and Unreasons." *New Republic* (May 24, 1999): 35.

McMahan, Jeff. 2000. "Moral Intuition." In La Follette (ed.): 92–110.

McNaughton, David. 1996. "An Unconnected Heap of Duties?" *Philosophical Quarterly* 46: 433–47.

2000. "Intuitionism." In LaFollette (ed.): 268–87.

McNaughton, David and Piers Rawling. 2006. "Deontology." In Copp (ed.): 424–58.

McNaughton, David and Piers Rawling. 1998. "On Defending Deontology." *Ratio* 11: 37–54.

Mele, Alfred. 1992. *Springs of Action*. Oxford: Oxford University Press.

Mendola, Joseph. 2006. *Goodness and Justice: A Consequentialist Moral Theory*. Cambridge: Cambridge University Press.

Mendus, Susan. 2002. *Impartiality in Moral and Political Philosophy*. Oxford: Oxford University Press.

2003. "The Magic in the Pronoun 'My.'" In Matravers (ed.): 33–52.

Milgram, Elijah. 1997. *Practical Induction*. Cambridge MA: Harvard University Press.

Mill, John Stuart. 1956. *On Liberty*. Ed. by C. Shields. Indianapolis: Bobbs-Merrill.

Miller, Alexander. 2003. *An Introduction to Contemporary Metaethics*. Cambridge UK: Polity Press.

Miller, Dale E. 2000. "Hooker's Use and Abuse of Reflective Equilibrium." In Hooker, Mason and Miller (eds.): 156–78.

Miller, Harlan B. and William H. Williams (eds.) 1982. *The Limits of Utilitarianism*. Minneapolis: University of Minnesota Press.

Miller, Richard W. 1992 *Moral Differences: Truth, Justice and Conscience in a World of Conflict*. Princeton: Princeton University Press.

Montague, Phillip. 2000. "Why Rule-consequentialism is Not Superior to Rossian-style Pluralism." In Hooker, Mason and Miller (eds.): 203–11.

Moore, A. W. 2003. *Noble in Reason, Infinite in Faculty: Variations on Kant's Moral and Political Philosophy*. New York: Routledge.

Moore, G. E. 1903. *Principia Ethica*. Cambridge: Cambridge University Press.

Mulgan, Tim. 2000. "Ruling Out Rule-consequentialism." In Hooker, Mason and Miller (eds.): 212–21.

2001. *The Demands of Consequentialism*. Oxford: Clarendon Press.

Murphy, Liam B. 2000. *Moral Demands in Nonideal Theory*. New York: Oxford University Press.

Murphy, Mark. 2001. *Natural Law and Practical Rationality*. Cambridge: Cambridge University Press.

(ed.) 2003. *Alasdair MacIntyre*. Cambridge: Cambridge University Press.

Nagel, Thomas. 1986. *The View From Nowhere*. Oxford: Oxford University Press.

1991. *Equality and Partiality*. New York: Oxford University Press.

Nauta, W. and M. Feirtag. 1986. *Fundamental Neuroanatomy*. New York: Freeman.

Nelson, Mark. 1999. "Morally Serious Critics of Intuitionism." *Ratio* 12: 54–79.

Nichols, Shaun. 2004. *Sentimental Rules: On the Natural Foundations of Moral Judgment*. Oxford: Oxford University Press.

Nielsen, Kai. 1984. "Why Should I Be Moral Revisited?" *American Philosophical Quarterly* 21: 81–91.

Nietzsche, Friedrich. 1966. *The Will To Power*. Trans. by W. Kaufman and R. G. Hollingdale. New York: Random House.

Noddings, Nel. 2002. *Starting at Home: Caring and Social Policy*. Berkeley: University of California Press.

Norcross, Alastair. 1997. "Good and Bad Actions." *Philosophical Review* 106: 1–34.

Nowell-Smith, P. 1954. *Ethics*. London: Penguin Books.

Nozick, Robert. 1974. *Anarchy, State and Utopia*. New York: Basic Books.

1981. *Philosophical Explanations*. Cambridge MA: Harvard University Press.

Nussbaum, Martha. 1988. "Non-relative Virtues: An Aristotelian Approach." In P. French, T. Uehling, Jr. and H. Wettstein (eds.) *Realism and Anti-Realism*. Minneapolis: University of Minnesota Press: pp. 85–110.

2000. *Women and Human Development: The Capabilities Approach*. Cambridge: Cambridge University Press.

O'Connor, John. 1967. *Aquinas and Natural Law*. London: MacMillan.

Oddie, Graham. 2005. *Value, Reality and Desire*. Oxford: Clarendon Press.

Okin, Susan Moller. 1989. *Justice, Gender and Family*. New York: Basic Books.

O'Neill, Onora. 1989. *Constructions of Reason: Explorations of Kant's Practical Philosophy*. New York: Cambridge University Press.

Otsuka, Michael. 1997. Review of Kamm 1996. *Ethics* 108: 197–207.

Parfit, Derek. 1984. *Reasons and Persons*. Oxford: Oxford University Press.

2004. "Justifiability to Each Person." In Stratton-Lake (ed.): 67–89.

(unpublished manuscript) *Rediscovering Reasons*.

Paul, E., F. Miller Jr., and J. Paul (eds.) 1988. *The New Social Contract: Essays on Gauthier*. Oxford: Blackwell.

Pettit, Philip. 1991. "Consequentialism." In Singer (ed.): 230–40.

2000. "Two Construals of Scanlon's Contractualism." *Journal of Philosophy* 98: 148–64.

Pettit, Philip and Michael Smith. 2000. "Global Consequentialism." In Hooker, Mason and Miller (eds.): 121–33.

Piper, Adrian M. S. 1991. "Impartiality, Compassion and the Imagination." *Ethics* 101: 26–57.

Plato. 1987. *The Republic*. Harmondsworth: Penguin Books.

Pogge, Thomas W. 2002. *World Hunger and Human Rights: Cosmopolitan Responsibilities and Reforms*. Cambridge: Polity Press.

Popper, Karl. 1965. *Conjectures and Refutations*. New York: Harper Torchbooks.

Portmore, Douglas. 2001. "Can an Act-consequentialist Theory be Agent-relative?" *American Philosophical Quarterly* 38: 363–77.

Post, John. 1987. *The Faces of Existence*. Ithaca NY: Cornell University Press.

Prinz, Jesse. 2008. *The Emotional Construction of Morals*. Oxford: Oxford University Press.

Pritchard, H. A. 1912. "Does Moral Philosophy Rest Upon a Mistake?" *Mind* 21: 2–18. Reprinted in his *Moral Obligation* (Oxford: Clarendon Press, 1949: 3–20).

Pugh, George. 1977. *The Biological Origins of Human Values*. New York: Basic Books.

Putnam, Hilary. 1987. *The Many Faces of Realism*. Lasalle IL: Open Court.

Quinton, Anthony. 1989. *Utilitarian Ethics*. Lasalle IL: Open Court.

Rachels, James (ed.) 1998. *Ethical Theory II*. Oxford: Oxford University Press.

Railton, Peter. 1984. "Alienation, Consequentialism and the Demandingness of Morality." *Philosophy and Public Affairs* 13: 134–71.

2003. *Facts, Values and Norms: Essays Toward a Morality of Consequence*. Cambridge: Cambridge University Press.

(Unpublished) "Rationality in Belief, Desire and Action: A Unified Approach."

Rasmussen, David (ed.) 1990. *Universalism and Communitarianism*. Cambridge MA: MIT Press.

Rawls, John. 1971. *A Theory of Justice*. Cambridge MA: Harvard University Press.

1993. *Political Liberalism*. New York: Columbia University Press.

Raz, Joseph. 1986. *The Morality of Freedom*. Oxford: Clarendon Press.

2003. *The Practice of Value*. With C. Kosgaard, R. Pippin and B. Williams. Ed. by R. Jay Wallace. Oxford: Clarendon Press.

2004. "Numbers With or Without Contractualism." In Stratton-Lake (ed.): 46–66.

Reiman, Jeffrey. 1997. *Critical Moral Liberalism*. Lanham MD: Rowman and Littlefield.

Richardson, Henry. 1994. *Practical Reasoning About Final Ends*. Cambridge: Cambridge University Press.

Ridge, Michael. 2001. "Saving Scanlon: Contractualism and Agent-relativity." *Journal of Political Philosophy* 9: 472–81.

Riley, Jonathan. 1988. *Liberal Utilitarianism: Social Choice Theory and J. S. Mill's Philosophy*. Cambridge: Cambridge University Press.

Rilke, Rainer Maria. 1963. *Duino Elegies*. Trans. by J. B. Leishman and S. Spender. New York: W. W. Norton.

Rorty, Richard. 1989. *Contingency, Irony and Solidarity*. Cambridge: Cambridge University Press.

Rosati, Connie. 2002. "Agency and the Open Question Argument." *Ethics* 113: 490–527.

2006. "Moral Motivation." *Stanford Encyclopedia of Philosophy*. http://plato.stanford.edu/entries/moral-motivation/

Ross, W. D. 1930. *The Right and the Good*. Oxford: Clarendon Press.

Ruddick, Sara. 1989. *Maternal Thinking: Toward a Politics of Peace*. Boston: Beacon Press.

Ryan, Alan. 1970. *John Stuart Mill*. New York: Pantheon Press.

Ryan, Sharon. 1999. "What is Wisdom?" *Philosophical Studies* 93: 119–39.

2007. "Wisdom." *Stanford Encyclopedia of Philosophy* http://plato.stanford.edu/entries/wisdom

Sandel, Michael. 1983. *Liberalism and the Limits of Justice*. Cambridge: Cambridge University Press.

Sayre-McCord, Geoffrey (ed.) 1988. *Essays on Moral Realism*. Ithaca NY: Cornell University Press.

2000. "Contractarianism." In LaFollette (ed.): 247–67.

2005. "Moral Realism." *Stanford Encyclopedia of Philosophy*. http://plato.stanford.edu/entries/moral-realism/

Scanlon, T. M. 1982. "Contractualism and Utilitarianism." In Sen and Williams (eds.): 103–28.

1998. *What We Owe Each Other*. Cambridge MA: Harvard University Press.

2002. "Reasons, Responsibility and Reliance: Replies to Wallace, Dworkin and Deigh." *Ethics* 112: 507–28.

2004. "Replies." In Stratton-Lake (ed.): 123–38.

Scarre, Geoffrey. 1996. *Utilitarianism*. London: Routledge.

Scharfstein, Ben-Ami. 1980. *The Philosophers*. Oxford: Blackwell.

Scheffler, Samuel, (ed.) 1988. *Consequentialism and Its Critics*. Oxford: Oxford University Press.

1982. *The Rejection of Consequentialism*. Oxford: Oxford University Press.

1992. *Human Morality*. New York: Oxford University Press.

Schroeder, Mark. 2008. "Value Theory." *Stanford Encyclopedia of Philosophy* http://plato.stanford.edu/entries/value-theory/

Sen, Amartya. 1999. *Development as Freedom*. New York: Knopf and Co.

Sen, Amartya and Bernard Williams (eds.) 1982. *Utilitarianism and Beyond*. New York: Cambridge University Press.

Shafer-Landau, Russ. 2003. *Moral Realism: A Defence*. Oxford: Clarendon Press.

Shaw, William. 1999. *Contemporary Ethics: Taking Account of Utilitarianism*. Oxford: Blackwell.

Sher, George. 1987. *Desert*. Princeton: Princeton University Press.

1997. *Beyond Neutrality: Perfectionism and Politics*. Cambridge: Cambridge University Press.

Sherman, Nancy. 1989. *The Fabric of Character: Aristotle's Theory of Virtue*. New York: Oxford University Press.

Singer, Peter. 1972. "Famine, Affluence and Morality." *Philosophy and Public Affairs* 1: 229–43.

Singer, Peter (ed.) 1991. *A Companion to Ethics*. London: Blackwell.

Sinnott-Armstrong, Walter. 2006. *Moral Skepticisms*. New York: Oxford University Press.

    2008. *Moral Psychology Vol. 1: The Evolution of Morality: Adaptation and Innateness*. Cambridge MA: MIT Press.

    2008a. *Moral Psychology Vol. 2: The Cognitive Science of Morality*. Cambridge MA: MIT Press.

    2008b. *Moral Psychology Vol. 3: The Neuroscience of Morality: Emotion, Brain Disorders and Development*. Cambridge MA: MIT Press.

Sinnott-Armstrong, Walter and Mark Timmons (eds.) 1996. *Moral Knowledge: New Readings in Moral Epistemology*. Oxford: Oxford University Press.

Skyrms, Brian. 1996. *Evolution of the Social Contract*. Cambridge: Cambridge University Press.

Slote, Michael. 1983. *Goods and Virtues*. New York: Oxford University Press.

    2001. *Morals From Motives*. Oxford: Oxford University Press.

    2006. "Moral Sentimentalism and Moral Psychology." In Copp (ed.): 219–39.

    2007. *The Ethics of Care and Empathy*. New York: Routledge.

Smart, J. J. C. and Bernard Williams (eds.) 1973. *Utilitarianism: For and Against*. Cambridge: Cambridge University Press.

Smith, Maury. 1977. *A Practical Guide to Values Clarification*. La Jolla: University of California Associates, Inc.

Smith, Michael. 1994. *The Moral Problem*. Oxford: Blackwell.

Sober, Elliott. 1982. "Realism and Independence." *Nous* 16: 369–86.

Sober, Elliott and David Sloan Wilson. 1998. *Unto Others: The Evolution and Psychology of Unselfish Behavior*. Cambridge MA: Harvard University Press.

Solomon, David. 1988. "Internal Objections to Virtue Ethics." In Statmann (ed.): 107–21.

Somerville, John and Ronald Santoni (eds.) 1963. *Social and Political Philosophy*. Garden City: Anchor Books.

Sommers, Christina Hoff. 1986. "Filial Morality." *Journal of Philosophy* 83: 439–56.

Sosa, David. 1993. "Consequences of Consequentialism." *Mind* 102: 101–22.

    2004. "Critical Notice of T.M. Scanlon's *What We Owe to Each Other*." *Nous* 38: 359–77.

Sosa, Ernest. 1993. "Putnam's Pragmatic Realism." *Journal of Philosophy* 90: 605–26.

Spinoza, Baruch. 1996. *Ethics*. Trans. E. Curley. New York: Penguin Books.

Sreenivasan, Gopal. 2002. "Errors About Error: Virtue Theory and Trait Attribution." *Mind* 111: 47–68.

Statman, D. (ed.) 1997. *Virtue Ethics*. Edinburgh: University of Edinburgh Press.

Sterba, James. 1998. *Justice for Here and Now*. Cambridge: Cambridge University Press.

Stewart, Robert M. and Thomas Lynn. 1991. "Recent Work on Ethical Relativism." *American Philosophical Quarterly* (April): 85–100.

Stocker, Michael. 1990. *Plural and Conflicting Values*. Oxford: Oxford University Press.

Stratton-Lake, Philip. 1997. "Can Brad Hooker's Rule-consequentialist Principle Justify Ross's Prima Facie Duties?" *Mind* 106: 751–58.

2000. *Kant, Duty and Moral Worth*. London: Routledge.

ed. 2002. *Ethical Intuitionism: Reevaluations*. Oxford: Clarendon Press.

ed. 2004. *On What We Owe to Each Other: Scanlon's Contractualism*. Oxford: Blackwell.

Stroud, Sarah. 1998. "Moral Relativism and Quasi-absolutism." *Philosophy and Phenomenological Research* 58: 189–94.

2006. "Epistemic Partiality and Friendship." *Ethics* 116: 498–524.

Stuhr, Karen and Christopher Wellman. 2002. "Recent Work in Virtue Ethics." *American Philosophical Quarterly* 39: 49–72.

Sturgeon, Nicholas. 1985. "Moral Explanations." In Copp and Zimmerman (eds.): 49–78.

Sumner, L. W. 1996. *Welfare, Happiness and Ethics*. Oxford: Oxford University Press.

1998. Review of Feldman 1997. *Ethics* 108: 176–79.

Swanton, Christine. 2003. *Virtue Ethics: A Pluralistic View*. New York: Oxford University Press.

Taylor, Charles. 1982. "Responsibility for Self." In G. Watson (ed.) *Free Will*. Oxford: Oxford University Press: 111–26.

1989. *Sources of the Self*. Cambridge MA: Harvard University Press.

Taylor, Gabriele. 2006. *Deadly Vices*. Oxford: Clarendon Press.

Tersman, Folke. 2006. *Moral Disagreement*. Cambridge: Cambridge University Press.

Terzis, George N. 1994. "Human Flourishing: A Psychological Critique of Virtue Ethics." *American Philosophical Quarterly* 31: 333–42.

Thiele, Leslie Paul. 2006. *The Heart of Judgment: Practical Wisdom, Neuroscience and Narrative*. Cambridge: Cambridge University Press.

Thomas, Alan. 2000. "Consequentialism and the Subversion of Pluralism." In Hooker, Mason and Miller (eds.): 179–202.

Thomas, Laurence. 1989. *Living Morally: A Psychology of Moral Character*. Philadelphia: Temple University Press.

Tiberius, Valerie. 2008. *The Reflective Life: Living Wisely With our Limits*. Oxford: Oxford University Press.

Timmons, Mark. 1999. *Morality Without Foundations*. Oxford: Oxford University Press.

Timmons, Mark, John Greco and Alfred Mele (eds.) 2007. *Rationality and the Good: Critical Essays on the Ethics and Epistemology of Robert Audi*. Oxford: Oxford University Press.

Turner, Frederick. 1991. *Beauty: The Value of Values*. Charlottesville: University of Virginia Press.

Unger, Peter. 1996. *Living High and Letting Die*. New York: Oxford University Press.

Vallentyne, Peter (ed.) 1991. *Contractarianism and Rational Choice*. Cambridge: Cambridge University Press.

Velleman, David. 2006. *Self to Self: Selected Essays*. Cambridge: Cambridge University Press.

Vogler, Candace. 2001. *John Stuart Mill's Deliberative Landscape*. New York: Garland Publishing.

———. 2002. *Reasonably Vicious*. Cambridge MA: Harvard University Press.

Wall, John. 1998. *Liberalism, Perfectionism and Restraint*. New York: Cambridge University Press

Wallace, R. Jay. 2002. "Scanlon's Contractualism." *Ethics* 112: 429–70.

Warnock, G. J. 1967. *Contemporary Moral Philosophy*. New York: St. Martin's Press.

Wattles, Jeffrey. 1996. *The Golden Rule*. New York: Oxford University Press.

West, Henry. 2003. *An Introduction to Mill's Utilitarian Ethics*. Cambridge: Cambridge University Press.

White, Michael. 1997. *Partisan or Neutral? The Futility of Public Political Philosophy*. Lanham MD: Rowman and Littlefield.

Whitehead, Alfred North. 1955. *Adventures of Ideas*. New York: Mentor Books.

———. 1978. *Process and Reality*. Ed. by D. Griffin and D. Sherburne. New York: Free Press.

Williams, Bernard. 1972. *Morality: An Introduction to Ethics*. New York: Harper & Row.

———. 1973. "A Critique of Utilitarianism." In Smart and Williams (eds.): 77–155.

———. 1981. "Persons, Character and Morality." In Williams *Moral Luck*. Cambridge: Cambridge University Press: 1–19.

———. 1985. *Ethics and the Limits of Philosophy*. Cambridge MA: Harvard University Press.

Wilson, E. O. 1975. *Sociobiology: The New Synthesis*. Cambridge MA: Harvard University Press.

Wood, Allen W. 1999. *Kant's Ethical Thought*. Cambridge: Cambridge University Press.

Wong, David. 2006. *Natural Moralities: A Defense of Pluralistic Relativism*. Oxford: Oxford University Press.

Wright, Robert. 1994. *The Moral Animal*. New York: Vintage.

Zimmerman, Michael. 2001. *The Nature of Intrinsic Value*. Lanham MD: Rowman and Littlefield.

# Index

CPSIA information can be obtained at www.ICGtesting.com
Printed in the USA
BVOW03s0356190813

328835BV00006B/83/P